SOVIET STRATEGY AND ISLAM

Soviet Strategy and Islam

ALEXANDRE BENNIGSEN
Late Professor Emeritus
Ecole des Hautes Etudes en Science Sociales
CNRS, Paris

PAUL B. HENZE
Resident Consultant
RAND Corporation
Washington, DC

GEORGE K. TANHAM
Consultant
RAND Corporation
Washington, DC

and

S. ENDERS WIMBUSH
Associate Director
Radio Liberty

St. Martin's Press   New York

© Foreign Area Research Inc. 1989

All rights reserved. For information, write:
Scholarly and Reference Division,
St. Martin's Press, Inc., 175 Fifth Avenue, New York, NY 10010

First published in the United States of America in 1989

Printed in Hong Kong

ISBN 0-312-02481-9

LIBRARY OF CONGRESS

Library of Congress Cataloging-in-Publication Data

Soviet strategy and Islam/by Alexandre Bennigsen . . . [et al.].
p. cm.
Includes index.
ISBN 0-312-02481-9: $40.00 (est.)
1. Islamic countries – Foreign relations – Soviet Union. 2. Soviet
Union – Foreign relations – Islamic countries. 3. Soviet Union –
Foreign relations – 1917 – I. Bennigsen, Alexandre.
DS35.74.S65S68 1989
327.47017671 – dc 19

88-21702
CIP

Contents

List of Figures

Foreword

To the great regret of the rest of us, one of the co-authors of this book has not lived to see it in print. Professor Alexandre Bennigsen died in Paris in early June 1988. His loss is deeply felt not only by his colleagues and associates, but by the entire scholarly community concerned with issues relating to Islam in the Soviet Empire and Soviet policies toward the Muslim world. Fortunately during the final months of his extraordinarily productive life, Alexandre Bennigsen was able to follow the process of *perestroika* that had begun under Mikhail Gorbachev and to benefit from the policy of *glasnost'* which has resulted in remarkable revelations about the lives and attitudes of Soviet Muslims. Much of this information has substantiated and given further weight to some of the judgements Professor Bennigsen included in sections of this book that are primarily his work. He expressed the view before his death that while the Gorbachev era opens up new horizons for the rapidly increasing Muslim population of the Soviet Empire it also confronts the leadership in Moscow with new challenges. He concluded that there is little likelihood that the Soviets' revised Islamic strategy will differ in *its fundamental aims* from that they have followed for the past 70 years. We all share that view.

Paul B. Henze
George Tanham
S. Enders Wimbush
July 1988

Acknowledgement

This book had its origin in a study undertaken by the associates of Foreign Area Research, Inc. for the Office of Net Assessment of the US Department of Defense. The authors wish to express their deep appreciation to the director of that office, Mr Andrew Marshall, for his unfailing interest in seeing broad political problems examined in historical perspective and for his readiness to see work done in the first instance for the benefit of government analysts and policy-makers made available as soon as possible to the wider scholarly community.

Introduction

An Islamic strategy was not a matter of choice for the Bolshevik leaders who seized control of the Russian Revolution in November 1917 and set about transforming—and preserving—the Russian Empire by creating the Soviet Union to replace it. They *had* to have an Islamic strategy for two urgent reasons: (1) the Russian Empire had acquired a sizeable Muslim population. It was restive, as the revolt in 1916 in Central Asia had demonstrated. Tatars, Azeris and others had developed leaders who inspired movements that aimed at modernisation of their societies and rejuvenation of Islam. These peoples had to be won over to support the Bolshevik Revolution or they would attempt to become independent; (2) Muslims beyond the borders of the empire to the south and east represented both an opportunity and a danger. If they too could be inspired by the aims of the Bolshevik Revolution they could be turned into allies of the new Soviet state, topple traditional rulers or, as the case might be, overthrow their colonial masters, and speed the process of world revolution. On the other hand, if the Muslims of Turkey, Iran, India and the Arab World remained under the influence of 'reactionary' leaders and permitted themselves to be manipulated by the imperialist powers, they represented a deadly threat to the Soviet state. The threat was two-edged, for there was the danger of invasion by hostile Muslim forces manipulated by European powers and there was the problem of direct influence coming from abroad on the Muslims of Russia.

In its bare essentials, the problem has remained the same for the leaders of the Soviet Union ever since: how to ensure the loyalty of the country's own Muslims, how to keep them from developing a sense of common purpose with Muslims beyond the Soviet borders that could work contrary to Moscow's interests and how to keep Muslim countries beyond the southern borders of the Soviet Union from threatening it. During the first years following the Bolshevik seizure of power in 1917, proponents of an extremely active policy attempted to 'set the East ablaze', but this phase did not last long. Lenin gave priority to consolidation of Soviet power at home. Too much adventurism abroad undermined this aim. So the policy was shifted to a long-range and low-key approach. Only after World War II did Moscow fully embrace a more active programme. A major section of this book describes and analyses this shift and details the mechanisms which the Soviet Union has developed to deal with Islam, both at home and abroad.

Another major section of the book examines the manner in which the Soviet Union has dealt with key Islamic regions in the Near East and Africa, how it has attempted to manipulate political forces within them to gain leverage and long-term advantage for itself. Its performance has frequently been much less than skilful and the outcome of its efforts counterproductive to its own interests. Adverse results, however, have seldom discouraged the Soviets from trying again. Flexible opportunism in advancing the interests of the Soviet Empire remains the fundamental underlying principle. The three areas chosen for detailed treatment—Egypt, the Nile Valley and the Horn of Africa, and the Arabian Peninsula—are by no means the only focal points of Soviet Islamic strategy in recent decades. Detailed essays on techniques of application of the strategy could be extended to a dozen or more. The Maghreb, the Indian Subcontinent, Turkey, Iran, Indonesia and other countries of Southeast Asia all merit detailed examination and the authors hope to turn their attention to some of these countries and regions at some future time. Fortunately others have already been working on some of them. There is room— and a concrete need—for comprehensive case studies of Soviet Islamic strategy that consider, as the illustrative essays that form the second half of this book attempt to do, the full range of instruments and techniques which the Soviets use.

Part I
The Soviet Islamic Establishment as a Strategic Instrument: History, Evolution and Current Operations

Alexandre Bennigsen, Paul B. Henze, George K. Tanham and S. Enders Wimbush

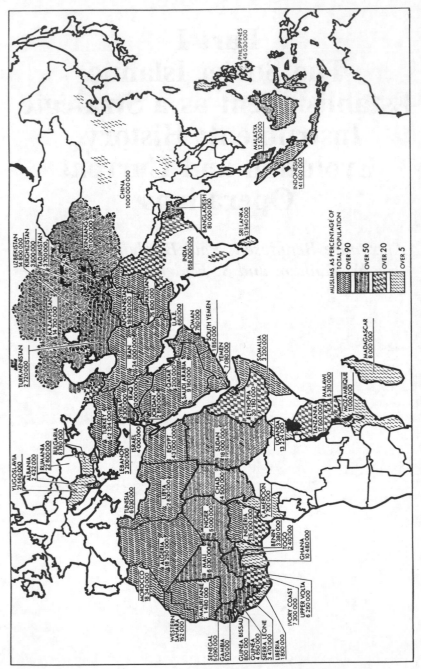

FIGURE 1 World Muslim Population by Country

1 The Forging of the Soviet Islamic Weapon

OBJECTIVES

This study examines the origins and evolution of the Soviet view of the Islamic World as a unique set of geo-strategic problems requiring special tactics; and Soviet efforts to design and put into operation these tactics in hopes of realising their short-and long-term political objectives. The study examines the origins, evolution and current operations of one—and probably the most effective—Soviet tactic for enhancing its prestige and authority in the Islamic states it seeks to influence: the Soviet use of its own substantial Islamic resources—its history as a major Muslim country, its important Islamic geography (cities and significant Islamic monuments), its own Muslim population, and, especially, its home-grown official Islamic establishment—in conjunction with other diplomatic initiatives and propaganda exercises in the Muslim world abroad. The study examines the evolution of the strategy, from Lenin's early caution to Stalin's wartime experiments to the unfolding of a systematic operational plan under Khrushchev and Brezhnev.

The study attempts to show that the Soviet Islamic strategy is now of a greater scale and is more successful at enhancing Soviet influence and prestige in the Muslim world than is generally recognised. Moreover, the Soviets are able to employ the Islamic element of their diplomacy successfully in situations where other, more routine diplomatic initiatives cannot be used.

Throughout the study, when we speak of the Soviet development of a political-propaganda weapon to penetrate and influence the Islamic world abroad we are referring to traditional, conservative Islamic states and not for the most part to radical leftist or fundamentalist states of the Libyan or Iranian variety. These societies are from time to time targets of the Soviet Islamic weapon—the official Soviet Islamic establishment—but they are not its main targets. Soviet tacticians have devised other approaches to the more radical Muslim states requiring more sophisticated and deceptive tools, such as the use of front organisations and similar conduits for Soviet influence, which deserve special examination and analysis. As will become clear, the main Soviet targets are among the 'main-line' Muslim states, that is the vast majority, such as Saudi Arabia, Jordan, Kuwait and Egypt, where radical political and/or religious trends have not yet become dominant.

We argue that the Soviets view their Islamic strategy and the tactics employed to make it successful in terms of *flexible opportunism*: the seizing of long-sought opportunities or temporary windfalls through the flexible use of any facet or combination of facets of Soviet diplomacy and/or propaganda. As will become clear, what we will call in this study 'the Islamic weapon' can encompass and exploit by itself a wide range of opportunities; it can also be used effectively in combination with other Soviet operational activities.

Soviet state priorities have changed very little over the nearly 70 years of existence of the reconstituted Russian Empire. The highest priority, of course, as with any state, is to maintain state power and authority throughout the territory of the state. In a system without a procedure for choosing and changing leadership that is independent of the power of the leadership itself, an equally high priority must be security of the leadership group. The nature of the Soviet system—its claim to being historically and scientifically sanctioned and to being predestined to world leadership—confronted it with special problems from the beginning. All other states were regarded as less legitimate than the Soviet state itself, for eventually they were destined to adopt—or to have imposed upon them—the Soviet system. As early expectations of worldwide revolution quickly faded, however, and as the Soviet state had to confront serious challenges to maintenance of control over its own territory, tactics had to be adjusted.

The adjustments which concern us in this series of studies are those which bear specifically upon Islamic issues and relationships, but in character they do not differ from the adjustments that had—and still have—to be made in dealing with other issues. Outside analysts have often misled themselves by inability to distinguish between what is rigid and what is flexible in Marxism-Leninism.[1] Several key features of the Soviet approach to both internal and external relations must be understood:

> the primacy of internal over external requirements for maintaining Soviet power and the development of strategy;
> the fact that while basic goals remain unaltered, the *manner* in which they are pursued and the *time-table* for pursuit of them are subject to almost infinite variation;

seemingly contradictory policies and objectives can be pursued simultaneously on different tracks.

The absence of an independent legislature or judiciary, the absence of independent media and other institutions which permit citizens to voice opinions and ask questions about government policies and actions permit a high degree of arbitrariness in decisions which Soviet leaders take. The pervasive secrecy in which the whoie system operates also shields leaders and subordinates from facing or even recognising the consequences of policies and actions which produce undesired results. The results of Soviet exertions toward groups and entire states, not surprisingly, can prove counterproductive.

Nowhere is this more apparent than in Soviet involvement with Islamic peoples and countries. For a totalitarian system whose leadership is self-perpetuating and whose governing class—the *Nomenklatura*—has, up until the Gorbachev era at least, steadily given higher priority to the maintenance of its own privileges—complications and failures in the execution of policies do not lead to adjustments and changes of the kind that would be inevitable in open, pluralistic social systems.

MARX AND LENIN ON THE MUSLIM WORLD

Marxism as such offers no prescription for dealing with the Muslim world. Marx knew little about Islam and was not interested in trying to understand it. He visited no Islamic countries until almost the end of his life, when he spent several weeks in Algiers in 1882. His letters from this journey reveal a totally European attitude toward Muslim culture and confirm, even at the end of his life, that Marx lived entirely within a European cultural context. For him, as for Engels, the Judeo-Christian-Classical tradition was an overriding fact of life and history. Marx's cultural myopia sharply limited his analytical horizons. Most of the rest of the world had no history in what Marx regarded as the proper sense of the term. He was especially scathing in his dismissal of India as merely the object of successive conquests, a society without any rationale or sense of purpose of its own.

A country not only divided between Mohammedan and Hindu, but between tribe and tribe, between caste and caste; a society whose framework was based on a sort of equilibrium resulting from a general repulsion and constitutional exclusiveness between all its members. Such a country and such a society, were they not the predestined prey of conquest? India, then, could not escape the fate of being conquered, and the whole of her past history, if it be anything, is the history of the successive conquests she has undergone . . . The question therefore is not whether the English had a right to conquer India, but whether we are to prefer India conquered by the Turk, by the Persian, by the Russian to India conquered by the Briton.[2]

This is curious for a prophet who advocated *world* revolution and who has been elevated by his Soviet disciples, as well as by Western and Third World intellectuals, as the God of Decolonialisation. That Marx was critical of colonialism there can be no doubt, but he also saw it as progressive, for it brought peoples with no history to the stage where they could adopt the civilisation of Europe and thus enter into the mainstream of human development.

There are profound contradictions in these attitudes and in Marx's 'scientific' analysis. When Marx was simply reporting and interpreting the unfolding of current history, as he did, often brilliantly, as a correspondent for the old *New York Daily Tribune* in the 1850s, he showed a good deal of sympathy for one of the most important Muslim-European confrontations of the period, the fight of the North Caucasian Mountaineers against Tsarist forces.[3] He also displayed consistent understanding for Turkey. The key to these attitudes was his intense hatred for Russian imperialism. 'The defeats of the Russians in European Turkey will lead directly to revolution in Russia . . .' he wrote optimistically to Engels in July 1877.[4] No nation drew more condemnation from Marx than Imperial Russia. His attitudes toward Russians seem often to contain a good deal of the primordial Germanic prejudice against them. Slavic nations, however, especially the Poles, attracted Marx's praise over and over again for the strong opposition they displayed toward Russian domination.

If we take Marx's reactions to some of the main political events of the 1850s and 1860s as a measure of what he might have to say today, we get exact parallels to prevailing Western attitudes toward the Soviet Union as the main bulwark of conservative, reactionary oppressive imperialism in the world. Marx was a strong champion of the Poles when they repeatedly rose against Russian domination, and he and Engels never doubted that Russia was an inherently expansionist power that must be stopped: '. . . is it probable that this gigantic and swollen power will pause in its career? Circumstances, if not her own will, forbid it', Marx wrote for the *New York Daily Tribune* in 1853.[5] He would undoubtedly be sympathetic to the Afghans today, just as he was to Shamil's fighters and to the Circassians who defied logic and fought the Russian invaders with ferocious tenacity. He was deeply concerned about the defence of Turkey in the 1850s and strongly supported the Crimean War. He would be equally concerned today with preservation of Pakistan's independence and efforts to prevent the Soviets from spilling over their southern borders, by force or guile, to gain permanent footholds in Iran, Turkey or the Arab world.

Lenin and the other leading Bolsheviks ignored Islamic issues before 1917. If anything, they may be said to have had a hostile indifference to the Muslim world, despite the Russian empire's long and strategically important association with the Muslim east and especially with Central Asia and the Caucasus.[6]

Where there were exceptions to this general rule, they are revealing. The main exception is the Russian revolutionaries' interest in Iran in 1908–11. But even here, Lenin and his Russian contemporaries were not demonstrating a unique interest. Indeed, nearly all socialist activists at this time—the French and Dutch for example, and Lenin personally—followed the progress of the revolution in Tabriz and the Constitutional Movement in Tehran with rapt attention. Their interest had little or nothing to do with the political dynamics of Islam in Iran, however, or for that matter even with the dynamics of revolution *per se*; rather, they saw in the Iranian turmoil opportunities to weaken British and Russian imperialism. They had no lasting interest in the Iranian socialist movement, and even less in the activity of the 'revolutionary' Muslim Shia religious hierarchy.

Somewhat later, in 1917–20, the Bolsheviks expressed an interest in the crumbling Ottoman Empire, which, they believed, could follow the pattern of the Russian revolution. The period is noteworthy for, among other things, Mustafa Kemal's (Ataturk) wrestling with the intellectual and practical task of reconciling Islam and Bolshevism.[7] Again, the Bolsheviks showed no marked interest in the question of the cohabitation of Islam and communism in a Muslim country.

Lenin was cautiously interested in using the political turmoil in peripheral Muslim countries to unseat the western powers. Inasmuch as Islamic issues were at the root or just a contributing cause of the turmoil which was threatening western domination, Lenin was prepared to consider how they might be exploited. Two episodes of the early Soviet empire, Lenin's dealings with the Muslims of India and with Amanullah of Afghanistan, illustrate this point and demonstrate how attitudes which are observable in the Soviet treatment of Islam as a foreign policy consideration today were forged at the beginning of the Soviet experience.

LENIN AND THE MUSLIMS OF INDIA

An episode in the revolutionary commotion of the first years after the Bolsheviks seized power in Russia, though it appears like comic opera, reveals in retrospect most of the opportunistic features that still characterise Soviet efforts to exploit Islam for purposes of extending Soviet power and influence. Key figures in the undertaking are Gregori Zinoviev, head of the communist International (Comintern); Lenin himself; the Turkish opportunist, Enver Pasha; Mikhail Markovich Gruzenberg—better know as Michael Borodin—later to become famous as Stalin's principal agent in China; and last but not least the ebullient Indian communist, Mabendra Nath Roy.

Roy, a Hindu newly converted to communism, had originally been an ardent Indian nationalist energised by hatred of the British. In 1914, when World War I began, he offered his services to Imperial Germany in the expectation that a German victory would bring freedom to India. His wartime adventures brought him to the United States in 1916, where he attended Stanford University for a few months and married an American girl. He also established contacts with Americans attracted to revolutionary ideology. He was so generously supplied with money by the Germans (with whom he was in direct contact in the US before the American declaration of war) that he was able to provide Borodin with much needed financial help when the two met in Mexico in 1917. His interest in Marxism had already been aroused by American radical intellectuals. In Mexico, in close contact with Borodin, the conversion process was completed: 'My lingering faith in the special genius of India faded as I learned from him the history of European culture.'[8]

Roy followed Borodin to Europe, where he still had funds to help cover expenses in Berlin, and then went to Moscow where revolutionaries from everywhere were gathering at the call of the Comintern. Borodin brought Roy to meet Lenin and from him he received encouragement for his contention that World Revolution—

which was already suffering serious setbacks in Europe—should concentrate on Asia. If Indian national aspirations were now too small an objective for Roy's boundless ambitions, exploiting the Muslims of India as a vehicle for arousing the entire Colonial East appeared to offer enormous promise. A *jihad* would be declared against Britain and an 'Army of God' would be formed to liberate Asia. Indian Muslims were unhappy at the outcome of the war and angered by what they considered the humiliation to which Turkey was being subjected, for which they blamed Britain—greatly over-simplifying the post-World War I Middle Eastern political scene. Turkey was actually experiencing a nationalist rebirth under Mustafa Kemal who, unlike the Muslims of India, cared little for the Sultan-Caliph whose secular government he was replacing and whose religious role he would abolish a few years later.

Mustafa Kemal's chief rival, Enver Pasha, had fled to Europe. He was invited to Moscow where he laid before Lenin a grand scheme for delivering India to the World Revolution by the roundabout route of seizing Chinese Turkestan, setting up an independent Islamic Republic there and organising a revolutionary army. This army would invade India as the first step in the liberation of the East. In return, Enver requested Russian help in gaining power in Turkey. The honesty of all parties to these schemes is open to serious question, for Lenin was already beginning a *rapprochement* with Mustafa Kemal. Enver himself was less interested in spreading Bolshevism than in opportunistically exploiting Bolshevik support to set up a Turkic-Islamic empire which would extend from Kashgar to the Balkans. Roy reacted negatively to Enver, suspecting him of wanting 'to carve out of the fallen Tsarist Empire a kingdom for himself and perhaps his descendants'.[9] Roy's suspicions were justified. Enver, we know from archives, had already declared to a fellow Turkish officer: 'I will set my son Çengiz on the throne of Turkistan!'[10] Lenin distrusted Enver and had him closely watched, but he admired his energy and drive and his ability to appeal to fellow Muslims, so he kept him in reserve for possible future use.

M. N. Roy was more successful in getting Soviet support for his Islamic *jihad*. While the rest of the Comintern assembled for the famous Baku Congress in September 1920, Roy went off to organise his great offensive of Indian Muslims. His scheme envisioned using Afghanistan as a base with the support of its radical moderniser King Amanullah. A group of Indian refugees had already set up a 'Provisional Government of Free India' in Kabul. Lenin's attitude toward Roy was typical of the approach Soviet leaders have taken toward useful radical enthusiasts ever since. They are judged on the basis of a low risk, 'what-is-there-to-lose?' standard. But he and Trotsky also asked Roy to assist in the more immediate task of securely establishing Soviet power in Central Asia. Roy and his entourage departed from Moscow in November 1920 in two trains and reached Tashkent by the middle of the month. While gathering recruits and preparing stocks of arms, Roy assisted in the dismantling of the Emir of Bukhara's court. This was a very unsettled time in the whole Central Asian region. Refugees, adventurers and intelligence agents were moving in all directions. The British were far from passive about the danger to India. Much of what Roy was trying to do was soon learned from reports of Indians working for British Intelligence and daring operators such as Col. F. M. Bailey and Col. P. T. Etherton were sending back directly reports from Soviet and Chinese Central Asia respectively.[11]

Lenin's larger strategy in embryo was to win concessions from the British Government by exerting pressure on India. Though in real terms little pressure was generated, exaggerated reports of networks of Indian agents under Bolshevik direction and plans for a liberation march by Indian Muslims to restore the Ottoman Empire must have had some impact. In March 1921 the Anglo-Soviet Trade Agreement was signed by Prime Minister Lloyd George over the objections of War Secretary Winston Churchill and Foreign Secretary Lord Curzon. A condition insisted upon by Curzon was that Moscow would commit itself to stop all harmful activities directed at British India. A note handed to the Soviets at the signing ceremony demanded that Roy's activities and all efforts to use Afghanistan for organising irregulars be halted. Lenin, desperately needing both British trade and what amounted to a form of recognition for the new Soviet state that had hitherto been regarded as an international outcast, had to accede. Compliance with the spirit of the concession was less than complete, for Russian agents continued to be dispatched into India. Roy, however, was transferred to Moscow.

The new University for the Toilers of the East had recently been established under the Eastern Department of the Comintern. Roy became head of the Eastern Department. Lenin sent him to discuss future strategy in Asia with Stalin. Stalin had no enthusiasm for Roy's Muslim armies or for conventional nationalism. Nationalists had first to be trained as revolutionaries, Stalin declared, and the University for the Toilers of the East had such training as its prime objective. Stalin went on to comment that it was naive to assume that nationalists would be allowed to take power after colonialists had departed. Moscow-trained revolutionaries would foment civil war and emerge victorious.[12]

The year 1921 was not a good one for the Soviets in Central Asia. Muslim opposition to Soviet rule had hardened and local opposition movements, the Basmachi, had gained support from the Muslim population who could readily see that the proletarian revolution in this colonial region was essentially a Russian-settler phenomenon. Enver Pasha had been whiling away his time in Moscow and had to give up hope for Soviet help to gain power in Turkey for, simultaneously with the signing of the Anglo-Soviet trade agreement, Moscow also signed an agreement with Ataturk's fledgling government. Enver secretly decided to betray his Bolshevik friends and his messianic vision grew. He would found a new Turkish empire in Central Asia. He played his cards very cleverly and by the end of summer 1921 Lenin had agreed to send him to Central Asia to help Bolsheviks win the local population away from Basmachi! No sooner had Enver arrived in Bukhara in early November than he made contact with local Basmachi leaders and soon he was leading them eastward to launch a *jihad* against the Bolsheviks. The deposed Emir of Bukhara from his refuge in Afghanistan designated Enver commander-in-chief of Bukharan forces resisting Russian invasion. Enver declared himself commander-in-chief of the 'Armies of Islam' and, capitalising on his wife's relationship to the Sultan, proclaimed himself 'Kinsman of the Caliph, Representative on Earth of the Prophet'. Enver's forces succeeded in capturing Dushanbe (later renamed Stalinabad) on 14 February 1922, and went on to threaten the recapture of Bukhara.

King Amanullah of Afghanistan, new to his throne and eager to expand Afghan influence in Central Asia as well as to protect his country against both Russian and British designs, was impressed by Enver Pasha's successes and offered encouragement as well as arms. Afghan nationalists—even those opposing Amanullah, who had come to power through severe intertribal rivalries—regarded Enver as 'the Champion of Islam' and the 'hope of the Muslim world's salvation'.[13] By the spring of 1922 Enver had 7000 troops under his command and was assisted by several Turkish officers; he had alarmed the Bolsheviks into action. First they sent a peace delegation to Bukhara to negotiate with him. He refused and vowed an unconditional fight for the freedom of Turkestan. Lenin was angered by

Enver's treachery and insolence and ordered an all-out offensive against him. By June, Enver was suffering major defeats by the Red Army, and his enthusiastic followers began to drift away. He was forced into 'eastern Bukhara'—Tajikistan—where threats of retaliation and clever Bolshevik tactics kept villagers neutral or drew them to their side. Increasingly beleaguered, Enver refused even to consider surrender and died in a fierce encounter with Bolshevik forces near the village of Abiderya, not far from the Afghan frontier, on 4 August 1922.

News of Enver's demise did not reach Europe until the end of the year 1922 and in Turkey itself, where Mustafa Kemal's forces were close to final victory in their war for the liberation of Anatolia, it meant little. Basmachi resistance continued in Soviet Central Asia into the1930s. That is another story.

M. N. Roy's great scheme for organising the 'Army of God' as well as Enver Pasha's abortive campaign to set up a Turkish-Islamic empire in Central Asia are only minor episodes in the colourful history of the period, but they reveal Soviet/Russian attitudes and operational principles that can be observed in much later Soviet activity directed toward the Islamic world and toward nations where Islam is an important aspect of the political and cultural heritage.

Islam as such was of little concern to Soviet leaders. Lenin's basic attitude toward it was supercilious hostility—but master tactician that he was, Lenin recognised the force of Islam, its supranational character and its usefulness as an emotional rallying cry. At home—within the borders of the Soviet/Russian empire itself—Islam was to be neutralised as quickly as possible. Abroad it was to be exploited opportunistically to give trouble to Russia's enemies. But there were few absolutes in this situation—except the preservation of Soviet/Russian power itself. All other considerations were secondary. World Revolution was a good slogan and if the east could be set ablaze under the guise of encouraging it, all the better. But the highest priority was the interests of the Soviet state from the viewpoint of its European orientation. Lenin saw Europe as the political centre of the world. M. N. Roy's adventures could be readily called to a halt when the opportunity arose for a deal with the British that opened up broad horizons for Moscow—trade, political recognition, legitimacy for the Soviets in Europe. But subversion in India was not stopped, it was simply scaled down. Likewise, a pragmatic deal with the new Turkey of Mustafa Kemal took precedence over Enver Pasha's dreams of empire. Lenin toyed with Enver Pasha for reasons of pure opportunism. It was poor judgement on Lenin's part to assume that Enver could be co-opted and used as an instrument for winning the Central Asian Muslims to Moscow's rule. Nevertheless, costly and embarrassing as the campaign to defeat Enver was, in the broader flow of history it was merely a minor setback from which the Bolsheviks emerged strong enough to force their rule on the Central Asians—and soon to gerrymander them into separate national republics which, at least until the late 20th century, has proved an effective method of stemming the evolution of a comprehensive, modernising Turkic/Muslim nationalism that could eventually challenge Moscow's hegemony.

We see another enduring feature of Soviet/Russian imperial policy in the entire Central Asian/South Asian region in this early period; the conviction that the best defence of Russian territories in Central Asia is a steady offensive—by whatever means are feasible at the moment—toward the lands beyond. The approach is always flexible: aggressive when low-risk opportunities for aggression arise; subversive when greater caution is in order.

Examination of Soviet-Afghan relations during the reign of king Amanullah will serve to demonstrate this process in operation.

THE SOVIET UNION AND AN ISLAMIC REFORMER— AMANULLAH OF AFGHANISTAN

> With the complete defeat of Turkey by a Christian power and the occupation by the victors of some of the Holy Places of Islam, fanaticism was aroused, together with bitter feelings that Afghanistan had failed Islam in the hour of need.[14]

It was in an atmosphere of intense nationalism closely bound up with religious enthusiasm that the ten-year reign of the Afghan reformer king, Amanullah Khan, began in 1919. His predecessor, Habibullah, had been assassinated because of his desire to maintain correct relations with Britain. Eager to claim total sovereignty for his country, Amanullah soon found himself at war with Britain. The so-called Third Afghan War was brief. The Afghans were defeated in the Khyber; they did not attract the support of the Pathan tribes along the Northwest Frontier. After the British Royal Air Force bombed Jalalabad and Kabul, the Afghans sued for an armistice at the end of May 1919 and in the subsequent Treaty of Rawalpindi, signed in August, Amanullah was forced to recognise the Durand Line. 'After some confusion and hesitation, Amanullah's foreign policy followed three distinct paths: he established diplomatic relations with Soviet Russia, gradually normalised . . . relations with Britain, and strove for solidarity within the Muslim World'.[15]

In a letter to Amanullah dated 27 November 1919, Lenin wrote that Afghanistan was 'the only independent Muslim state in the world, and fate sends the Afghan people the great historic task of uniting about itself all enslaved Mohammedan peoples and leading them on the road to freedom and independence'.[16] Afghanistan and the Soviets signed a friendship treaty in September 1920. The friendship was far from complete, for the ousted Emir of Bukhara had fled to Afghanistan and Amanullah became apprehensive that the Bolshevik advance in Central Asia might spill over into northern Afghanistan. As the strength of the Basmachi grew, and especially after the arrival of Enver Pasha resulted in a great outburst of Basmachi activity, Amanullah gave covert support to the Central Asian resistance to Bolshevism. During this same period he signed a treaty of friendship with Britain and expelled Indian revolutionaries who had found a haven in Kabul. With the defeat of Enver Pasha and the consolidation of Bolshevik power in Central Asia, Amanullah concentrated on internal Afghan problems, trying to maintain good relations with all major foreign powers as well as near Islamic neighbours, such as Persia and Turkey.

Although some Bolshevik leaders in Moscow had wanted to enlist Afghanistan as an active participant in the 'pacification' of Central Asia, it soon became clear to Lenin and Stalin that Soviet interests were going to be best served by a relatively stand-offish policy, avoiding confrontation with the British over Afghanistan, and avoiding provocative intervention in the internal affairs of the country. This policy served Soviet interests well during most of the 1920s. Taking Mustafa Kemal's (Ataturk's) reform programme in Turkey as a model, Amanullah embarked on a dramatic programme of domestic reforms. But Amanullah lacked Mustafa Kemal's patience and manipulative skills. Besides, Afghan society was far more backward than that of Turkey and much more rent by tribalism and regionalism. Trying to go too far too fast, Amanullah provoked strong resistance and internal rebellion. Ataturk had advised Amanullah to give highest priority to building a solid nationalist military establishment—the presence of which was a key to Ataturk's success in Turkey. Amanullah was too impatient. British sale of two World

War I aircraft which German mercenaries flew for the Afghans helped Amanullah subdue the most serious revolt, that of the tribes of the eastern mountainous province of Khost. The Soviet Union had sent Amanullah small planes, pilots and technicians as early as 1919 and during the 1920s had set up an air route from Kabul to Moscow via Tashkent, but the Russians appear to have avoided major efforts to manipulate the internal political situation in Afghanistan—a principle they might have been wise to have adhered to in the 1970s as well.

When Amanullah embarked on a grand tour of India, the Middle East and Europe in December 1927, he was confident that internal stability had been achieved. Travelling with a large official party under circumstances reminiscent of Ras Tafari's (Haile Selassie's) grand tour a few years before, he was hailed in India as 'King of Islam', called by King Faud in Egypt 'a champion of the Orient in its struggle with the West', welcomed by King Victor Emmanuel in Italy and given the Golden Spur by the Pope. His welcome in France was especially warm and in Berlin he was given an honorary doctorate by the University. In England he was decorated by King George and given another honorary degree at Oxford where the vice-chancellor called the King and his Queen 'a second sun and moon that have come from the East to illuminate this distant kingdom in the West'. In Moscow he was received by all the top Soviet leaders and then went on a tour of Leningrad, the Ukraine and the Crimea. On his way home Amanullah experienced the climax of his grand tour in warm visits with Ataturk in Turkey and Reza Shah in Iran. He returned to Afghanistan in July 1928 determined to follow in Ataturk's footsteps.

He proposed radical governmental changes to speed social and economic reforms, but he was out of touch with conditions in the country, where the religious establishment had grown increasingly hostile since the abolition of the Caliphate in Turkey in 1924. Religious leaders had encouraged tribal dissidents. Amanullah's loyalty to Islam was openly questioned. Rumours circulated that he had secretly converted to Roman Catholicism during his audience with the Pope. It was said he had eaten pork, drunk alcohol and danced in Europe and the Queen was severely criticised for travelling unveiled and being repeatedly photographed during the European tour. The crisis escalated rapidly. Amanullah's jailing of critics fuelled it. Tribes clashed and revolted and a Tajik bandit, Bacha-i-Saqao, attacked Kabul. Under heavy pressure, Amanullah agreed to cancel many of his reforms during the first days of 1929. When Bacha-i-Saqao's forces attacked Kabul again on 14 January 1929, Amanullah abdicated and fled to Kandahar, naming his brother Inayatullah, King. Three days later Inayatullah abdicated and the British arranged for the entire royal family to be evacuated to Peshawar. Bacha-i-Saqao took the title Amir Habibullah Ghazi and promised to re-establish the rule of Islamic law. At this point, Amanullah, still in Kandahar, rescinded his abdication and called on still loyal tribesmen to rally to his cause. The Afghan envoy to Moscow, Ghulam Nabi Charki, recruited an army in northern Afghanistan, reportedly with Moscow's blessing.[17]

This venture appears to have been an example of 'flexible opportunism' and the 'reinsurance syndrome' still characteristic of the Soviet approach to awkward situations such as these. Stalin, concentrating on internal problems, was not interested in adventurism in Central Asia on behalf of an Afghan leader whose own intemperance had brought him to disaster. But in case Amanullah should have been able to rally significant support, the army in the north could have joined the fight and gained certain advantages for the Russians. This did not happen. In late April Amanullah gave up his struggle and took asylum in India, going from there into exile in Italy.

Both at the time and ever since the Soviets have contributed to a great deal of mythology about Amanullah's fall. Disinformation techniques were already being practiced. Bacha-i-Saqao alleged to be a British agent. *Pravda* charged on 28 December 1928 that the Afghan uprising was being master-minded by T. E. Lawrence, who actually happend to be in India at the time. No evidence that he had anything to do with Afghanistan has ever been produced. But journalists are not to be deterred by lack of evidence. French and German newspapers embroidered British plot theories and journalists in Britain speculated upon them. A whole series of Soviet 'scholarly' works have expanded upon them in recent years.

The truth, as far as it can be ascertained, seems to be much simpler and more tragic. Amanullah's rash attempt to modernise his country in one brief decade not only failed; it ushered in a period of brutality and confusion which set back the whole cause of reform for a generation. Louis Duprée concluded in 1973:

> If [Mahmud] Tarzi, the thinker, and Amanullah, the activist, could have pooled their intellectual resources—backed by a loyal, Turk-

ish-trained army—Afghanistan might today be farther along the
road of modernisation, instead of just beginning.[18]

An astute Central Asian observer, the Uzbek exile political leader
Mustafa Chokaev, living in Paris, gave a similar evaluation in the
wake of Amanullah's fall:

> Amanullah chose to follow in the footsteps of Gazi Mustafa Kemal
> but forgot that the Turks had been for centuries in contact with
> the cultured world of Europe and that the governing class in
> Turkey had been long since Europeanised. Amanullah forgot also
> that Turkey knew not the tribal regime, and that she had a
> comparatively well-ordered centralised apparatus of power, such
> as did not . . . exist in Afghanistan. Mustafa Kemal had an army
> that was loyal and devoted to its leader. Nothing of the kind
> existed in Afghanistan . . . We have on one side the King-reformer
> considering the Afghan as a united, single political organism, as a
> unified nation-state; and on the other side the Afghan tribes, who
> looking at the state can comprehend it only from the point of view
> of their tribal interests, to the defense of which the principles of
> the 'sacred Shariat' are put forward.[19]

SOVIET DOMESTIC CONCERNS ABOUT ISLAM

When it became apparent that the East was not going to be easily
set ablaze in the early 1920s, Lenin—and then Stalin to an even
more decisive degree than Lenin—abandoned hope of being able to
exploit Islam for achieving world revolution or even for accomplish-
ment of high-priority Soviet foreign policy goals. The main preoccupation with Islam was to secure Soviet power in the territories of
the empire itself inhabited by Muslims. Internally, vigorous anti-
Islamic propaganda was carried out, independent Islamic institutions
were dissolved forcefully when they could not otherwise be eliminated. Many more subtle oppressive and pre-emptive measures were
also taken. These ranged from extensive territorial reorganisations
that divided Muslim peoples into ethnic units and stressed differences
in language and history—with the aim of discouraging the sense of
religious solidarity which is one of Islam's strongest characteristics—
to utilising schools and adult education facilities (which were greatly
expanded to inculcate the notion that Islam is incompatible with
economic development and a modern life style).[20]

When Islamic peoples rebelled, as they did in both Central Asia and the Caucasus, they were severely suppressed. Suppression took the form of mass population transfers to remote areas during World War II. These brutal relocations of whole nationalities[21] were dramatic evidence of the failure of Soviet nationalities policy during the first 30 years of the existence of the Soviet state. The situation had appeared more auspicious in the 1920s, when the Civil War ended. The Bolsheviks had shown themselves adept at appealing to Muslims by very effectively playing upon ethnic and tribal differences. They were greatly helped by the ignorance and shortsightedness of the anti-Bolshevik Russian forces—generally lumped together as 'Whites' who were often oblivious or scornful of the aspirations of the Muslim peoples. One important student of this period has summed up what happened:

> . . . during the first five difficult and tragic years 1918–1922, the Bolsheviks outsmarted their minority allies. Stalin was personally responsible for this remarkable success. With only a few unimportant exceptions, all Muslim nationalists—from the extreme pro-Bolshevik left to the moderate right wing, individuals and organised groups alike—terminated the civil war fighting side by side with the Reds. Their conservative religious elements included the well-organised Sufi brotherhoods. In the Chechen country, local Bolsheviks were able to partially neutralise the important Qadiri *tarikat*; the *sheikh* Ali Mitaev, head *murshid* of the Bammat Giray Haji branch, cooperated with the new regime and for a short time was a member of the Chechen *revkom*—until his arrest in 1924 and execution in 1925. Even in Dagestan the Bolsheviks managed for a short while to oppose one religious authority against another . . . It appears that the conservative Sufi 'fanatics', whose ideology went back to the Middle Ages and who were well versed in Arabic but totally ignorant of 20th century politics, understood the real essence of Bolshevism better than the sophisticated nationalist leaders educated in Russian and European Universities.[22]

Certainly one of the main reasons for this early lack of interest and concern on the Bolshevik's part either for the difficulties in reconciling Islam and Bolshevism or for the strategic and tactical opportunities such a reconciliation might offer to the new Soviet leaders sprang from their unconditional hostility to all religions, including Islam. The goal was to destroy religion within the Soviet state if circumstances permitted such drastic action. For most of the 1920s, however, such favourable circumstances did not exist inside the USSR, and the new regime found it necessary to reach at least a temporary accommodation with religion and attempt to exploit it.

In the case of Islam, the objectives of temporary accommodation were tactical and practical. In the first place, the Bolsheviks sought to keep a number of highly motivated and well-armed Muslim nationalist movements, some of which fought for avowedly pan-Islamic goals, from siding with the Whites in the Civil War. In this, Lenin was for the most part successful by forming a series of local alliances with disparate Muslim groups.[23] He would have nothing to do with Muslim clerics, however, and especially after 1920 he rejected out of hand proposals from one 'modernist' (*jadid*) theologian of the empire for co-operation against 'European Imperialism'.[24]

In the second place, the Russian Communist Party had become a home for a number of influential Muslim radical nationalists, who viewed co-operation with the Bolsheviks as the best way to achieve independence or autonomy from Russia in the post-revolutionary political order.[25] These Muslim national communists played an important role in ensuring the final Bolshevik victory; in exchange for their support, Lenin wisely agreed—at least for the short term—to treat them as partners. It was a marriage of convenience, and it was to be short-lived.

In the third place, most Bolshevik leaders, Russian and foreign, were convinced that world revolution was imminent, and that it would triumph in the industrial West. Most Bolsheviks looked on the colonial world as a marginal problem, albeit a useful one inasmuch as it offered a tempting entanglement for the European powers. But the new Soviet leaders showed no sustained interest in employing the USSR's own substantial Islamic capacity to export the revolution into the Islamic world on their empire's immediate periphery by using revolutionary Muslim cadres as vehicles for exportation; this despite Leon Trotsky's imprecation to the Central Committee in 1919, that 'the international situation is evidently shaping in such a way that the road to Paris and London lies via the towns of Afghanistan, the Punjab and Bengal'.[26] The Baku Congress of September 1920 was the venue of a good deal of militant talk about spreading revolution to the Muslim world, but in fact its practical consequence was to bind the revolutionary movement in Asia more tightly to the leadership of the European proletariat, that is, to put any 'Asian

Strategy' on the shelf. The Bolsheviks did undertake one unenthusiastic attempt to export revolution to Iran in 1920, but the Red Army division which landed in Ghilan to help local guerrilla fighters was an ethnically pure Russian unit which finally did not engage the Iranian army.[27] Those Muslim national communists who pointedly and frequently called for Lenin to employ Soviet Muslim cadres to carry the revolution into the Muslim world were systematically removed from positions of influence after 1921 and, after 1923, were dismissed, imprisoned and, finally, liquidated under Stalin.[28]

Moscow made it clear as early as 1921 that, for the most part, it preferred friendly and neutralist 'nationalist-bourgeois' regimes on its southern border, rather than political instability and chaos, and to this end was prepared to forego any immediate programmatic exploitation of the Islamic factor. The Soviet's early alliances with non-Marxist governments in Turkey (Kemal Ataturk), Iran (Reza Shah) and Afghanistan (Amanullah) underlined their concern about instability in the adjoining Muslim states. Even in their dealings with leaders of national-liberation movements in these countries, Moscow preferred to use Russians or other Soviet 'Europeans' as its spokesmen and organisers (Frunze and Aralov in Turkey, Rotstein in Iran, and so forth) rather than Soviet Muslims. For the most part, Soviet Muslims were not trusted to play these parts, probably because of the Soviet leadership's anxieties about uncontrollable Muslim activism of the kind exemplified by the Muslim national communists.[29]

Moscow did attempt during this period to export *communism* abroad by organising local communist parties in Turkey and Iran, but these were half-hearted attempts at best. The Soviets clearly distrusted the local communist movements, which operated independently of Moscow's control. Rather than take chances with unpredictable Muslim activists of the Muslim national communist stripe, the Soviet leadership chose to send to Turkey and Iran pre-fabricated communist groups from the USSR: the Iranian *Adalat* and the Turkish Communist Party (led by Mustafa Subhi).[30] Both attempts were badly prepared and ended in the massacre of the imported communists by their nationalist allies. Moscow issued no protest.

Moscow's anxiety about the possible implications for Soviet power of militant Islamic movements was heightened by Muslim revolts which broke out against the Bolsheviks in several parts of the empire. In Central Asia, the Basmachi rebellions took several years to bring under control and remained a running sore for at least a decade thereafter. The Basmachi were disparate groups fighting for a variety of reasons, but many of them fought the Bolsheviks as a Muslim holy war, or *jihad*. In the North Caucasus, a genuine *jihad* erupted under the leadership of the Naqshbandiya Sufi brotherhood. Eventually the Bolsheviks triumphed against both, but not before these struggles had left an indelible psychological and political heritage which remains alive even today.[31]

Soviet policy has since reflected the deep fear of conservative Islam at home as a dangerous adversary and, at least for the immediate post-revolutionary period, the untrustworthiness of Soviet Muslims abroad to faithfully represent Soviet interests. Although the Soviets have in the past demonstrated and continue to demonstrate considerable flexibility in their use of Islam as a strategic instrument, the enduring legacy of this earliest period of Soviet rule appears to be the proximity in Soviet official thinking of the domestic and foreign aspects of Islam for Soviet policy. Lenin's and Stalin's early policy on Islam, which was to crush Muslim rebellions at home and to encourage the consolidation of stable regimes, of whatever political colour, on the USSR's southern periphery, won the day over the more adventurous desires of the Muslim national communists to spread the revolution to the Muslim east, as well as of those European Bolsheviks, like Trotsky, who believed that the revolution could and should be made 'permanent', that it should continually expand beyond Russia's borders. However, this did not exclude from Bolshevik tactical thinking the necessity of cultivating patterns of destabilisation in Muslim states abroad or of engaging in political opportunism.

Bolshevik leaders were suspicious of all prominent Muslims under Soviet rule, regardless of whether they were those who led revolts against Soviet power, 'modernist' Muslim fellow-travellers or even members of the Bolshevik party, and eventually Stalin ordered the liquidation of most of them. They seem to have had a sound understanding that to use Russia's Islamic resources to promote Muslim national self-determination abroad, even if this would serve Soviet purposes by disrupting the empires of the major European powers, they necessarily would have to accept compromises on Muslim national self-determination at home. At this point in time, it would take little to imagine that the expulsion of the British or the French from one of their Muslim dominions could be understood by Turkestanis, Kazakhs or Tatars as an invitation to expel the Russians from the former's territories. With domestic Muslim revolts still simmering and armed Muslim units being an important military factor in the Bolshevik reconsolidation of the old empire from 1918 at least until the early 1920s, this particular Bolshevik fear was probably justified.

STALIN'S ERA (1923–53)

Under Stalin, the internationalist ideology of the new Soviet state— the USSR as 'the Fatherland of Communism'—was fused to the more parochial and nationalist notion of 'Mother-Russia'. Soviet communism rapidly acquired a Russian identity, and this had important implications for the Soviets' view of what Islamic politics meant and how they were to be used.

Beginning in 1923, Stalin launched a strong anti-nationalist offensive against the Muslim national communists, which, as noted above, led by the late 1930s to their virtual extinction. During this period Stalin liquidated nearly all of the nationalist Muslim intellectuals, as well as nearly all of the pre-revolutionary Muslim intelligentsia, regardless of whether they had opposed the Bolshevik regime or had favoured it. In 1928 he augmented the systematic elimination of the Muslim intellectual élite with a frontal assault on the USSR's Islamic infrastructure. Mosques were closed and destroyed by the thousands, clerics were arrested and liquidated as 'saboteurs' and, after 1935, as spies. By 1941, of the 25,000–30,000 mosques open in 1920, only about 1000 remained; all of the 14,500 Islamic religious schools were forcibly shutdown; and fewer than 2000 of the approximately 47,000 clerics survived.[32] By the outbreak of World War II the traditional Muslim religious establishment in Central Asia and the Caucasus had been destroyed.

This period of Stalin's calculated assault on Muslim élites and on the Islamic establishment at home coincided with important developments in the Muslim world abroad and in the shape of Soviet foreign policy. Of particular significance was the collapse of the USSR's and the Comintern's influence in the colonial world. Communist parties were outlawed in Turkey, Iran and Egypt, and in many other places simply disappeared from the scene. The pro-Soviet Afghan government of Amanullah was ousted, and in China attempts by the communist party to seize power in Shanghai and Canton ended in failure and massacres.

At the Sixth Congress of the Comintern in 1927, the delegates, under Soviet pressure, adopted a 'class versus class' strategy, which obliged local communist parties to undertake a two-pronged offensive simultaneously against 'Western imperialism' and local bourgeois socialist and progressive parties. A number of the colonial world's most influential communist leaders, such as the Indian M. N. Roy and the Indonesian Tan Malaka, declared this Soviet-inspired departure to be unworkable and inappropriate for the political conditions in their countries, and they broke with the Comintern. At the Seventh Congress in 1935, 'class versus class' was replaced by the no less inappropriate 'popular front' strategy, which was aimed primarily at shoring up the USSR's weak defences against the rising spectre of Nazi Germany rather than at directing a truly 'popular' appeal to the colonial, and in particular the Islamic, world.[33]

Throughout this period until World War II, which was a turning point for both the Soviet system and the strategies it would adopt in international relations, Stalin's policy toward the Muslim world abroad shows strong evidence of his belief either that the possibilities of revolution there were limited if not non-existent or that the Soviet Union was in no position to exploit whatever opportunities might exist to stimulate a wider revolutionary conflict among Muslims, or both. It is significant that with only one exception—that of Kerim Khakimov, a Tatar, who was the first Soviet Consul-General in Jeddah and representative at the court of the Imam Yahya in Yemen (1928)—Stalin avoided using Soviet Muslim diplomats abroad in visible positions and no Muslim 'clerics' from the official Soviet Islamic establishment served as diplomatic instruments. At home, Islam was vilified continuously by Soviet propaganda as the most reactionary of religions.

The memoirs of Ismail Akhmedov, a Soviet Muslim GRU agent who defected in Turkey during World War II, were published only in 1984,[34] They shed considerable light on Soviet thinking about the Islamic world during this period. A Bashkir, born in 1904 in Omsk, Akhmedov was selected for intelligence service in the mid–1920s after military training because he had already learned German and Turkish. He worked in the Caucasus until 1932 and had extensive knowledge of operations directed from there into Turkey and Iran, as well as of security problems in the Caucasus. His memoirs provide specific confirmation of much that was less authoritatively known or assumed about Soviet intelligence activities in Turkey during the 1930s and early wartime period, when he was assigned to work in Istanbul as press attaché of the Soviet consulate-general. The consul-general at that time, Akimov, was also a GRU officer, who knew both Turkish and Persian. Two 'Tass correspondents' were also intelligence officers and Akhmedov was responsible for maintaining contact with a large group of illegals, most of them third-country citizens or refugees. One of his main responsibilities was cultivating contacts and agents in the Turkish press, a Soviet intelligence function, it must be assumed, that has continued in Turkey to this day.

In the course of his overt duties, Akhmedov became familiar with a number of British and American newspapermen working in Turkey, which was a major crossroads for journalists as well as espionage agents during World War II. These newspapermen were eager to be friendly with him, but official Soviet policy was to maintain distance:

> On New Year's Day 1942 at a party at the consulate . . . I asked my 'comrades' if it were not time to drop old concepts and build real friendship with representatives of the western powers residing in Turkey, especially since we were fighting together. Naumov [NKVD security officer] . . . almost snarled back, 'To forget our old concepts? I really wonder if you understand the Party Line. To forget how American financial magnates helped to arm and build the German forces? To forget the close ties between Thyssen, Krupp and Wall Street? What you had better not forget is that the United States is the wealthiest, the strongest of all capitalist countries, it is a classic example of imperialism . . . and forever will be our enemy number one . . . You can wine and dine your Americans and British. Smile into their faces and show yourself a pleasant fellow. That is fine. But never forget that they are your enemies of tomorrow.'[35]

Religion—Islam at least—played no special role in Soviet operations in Turkey either before or immediately after World War II. Residually Russia's old 19th century role as protector of Orthodox Christians in the Ottoman Empire was of greater importance, for the Soviets took for granted their ability to manipulate the Armenian issue to their advantage and territorial demands which Stalin made upon Turkey at the end of World War II had their roots in the historic Georgian Orthodox legacy in northeastern Turkey. The severely oppressed Russian Orthodox Church experienced a modest renaissance during World War II because it was judged useful as a means of bolstering Russian (and Slavic) national spirit for resistance against the Nazi invasion. As the war neared its end, the Orthodox

Church was seen to have tactical usefulness abroad: in Eastern Europe, where Stalin was prepared to use every means available to lock Eastern Europeans into a tight Soviet relationship; and in the entire eastern Mediterranean area—from Greece and Turkey through Lebanon, Syria, Palestine and Egypt and as far afield as Ethiopia.

Old Orthodox church ties represented channels through which a reactivated Soviet/Russian Middle Eastern policy could hope to operate. Rivalry developed with the Ecumenical Patriarch of Constantinople after a *sobor* was held in Moscow in January-February 1945 and the energetic Metropolitan Alexei was elected Patriarch of Moscow. While the Orthodox churches of Eastern Europe were forcefully reoriented toward Moscow and the Ukrainian Uniate Church received even harsher treatment, Soviet-backed churchmen were unable to secure influence in the Constantinople Patriarchate and had to content themselves with developing a close relationship with the Patriarch of Antioch, resident in Lebanon, and through him to work for greater influence in Jerusalem, where Arab and Greek Christian communities have a long history of rivalry. With the election of a US citizen, Athenagoras, Patriarch of the Greek Orthodox Church of North and South America, to the patriarchal throne in Constantinople in 1949, the western orientation of this important Orthodox church seat was assured. Moscow, in effect, acknowledged defeat, branding Athenagoras as

> a man known for his pro-fascist sympathies and connections with the ruling circles of the USA, Greece, and Turkey [who was] elected Patriarch of Constantinople under pressure from the USA.[36]

But Moscow's efforts to use the ageing Patriarch of Antioch to further its political aims in the region continued and enjoyed some success. These efforts had very little impact on Soviet efforts to gain support of the Arabs, however, since only a very small minority of Arabs were Christian.

WARTIME DEVELOPMENTS AND FIRST OPENINGS TO THE MUSLIM WORLD

Three domestic developments, which had important implications for the eventual evolution of a Soviet Islamic strategy, mark the wartime period. First, during the war, nearly all Soviet Muslim nationalities reached by the invading German armies demonstrated strong anti-Russian and anti-Soviet tendencies.[37] Several units, 'East Legions', made up specifically of Muslims who had defected to the Germans or who had been captured during the fighting saw service with the German armies.[38] The numbers of Soviet Muslims in Soviet ranks was continually and significantly reduced throughout the war, reflecting the Soviet leadership's view of their questionable loyalty.[39] In the Muslim North Caucasus, Stalin's security forces gathered together a number of entire nationalities, who were charged with collaboration with the Germans, and deported them to isolated areas of Central Asia, genocide being the obvious objective.[40]

Second, in an attempt to reduce the flagrant anti-Soviet actions of a large part of the Soviet Muslim population during the war, in 1942 Moscow entered into a 'Concordat' with those Muslim clerics who had survived Soviet persecution during the 1930s, represented by the Mufti of Ufa, Abdurrahman Rasulaev. The Soviets agreed to reduce the intensity of their anti-Islamic propaganda and ceased the persecution of Muslim clerics willing to support them. Islam as an institution was granted legal status with the creation, in 1943–44, of an official Islamic administration, the four Muslim Spiritual Directorates, and of a Muslim higher school, and with the *madrasa* Mir-i Arab in Bukhara in 1945. The 'Concordat' with Islam marked the beginning of the creation of a new generation of younger Soviet Muslim clerics who would in the future act as loyal spokesmen for Soviet power. This evolution was to be a slow process, taking the better part of 40 years but, as we shall see below, it has begun to pay substantial dividends.

Third, Soviet foreign policy, which as noted above had conscientiously ignored or avoided opportunities and entanglements in the Muslim world until the war, was redirected in the early 1940s to include it. In 1943 the Soviets established diplomatic relations with Egypt, in 1944 with Syria, Lebanon and Iraq. At first, Moscow presented itself to its new diplomatic acquaintances behind its 'Mother Russia' face, symbolised by the tour of the Middle East in June 1945 by the Orthodox Patriarch Alexei, who was greeted in Cairo by the sheikh of Al-Azhar and in Jerusalem by the members of the Muslim Supreme Court. A second tour followed in 1946.

On the one hand, until 1949, contacts between the USSR and the Muslim world remained limited. Where they did occur for the most part they were conducted from the Soviet side by Russians. For example, the first 'Friendship Societies', which began to operate between the USSR and Lebanon in early 1947 were almost exclusively Russian affairs, as were the Societies for Cultural Relations— between the USSR and Syria, for example—which were controlled by the All-Union Society for Cultural Ties, or VOKS (*Vsesoiuznoe obshchestvo kul'turnykh sviazei*). On the other hand, this period did include the first tentative efforts to engage Soviet Muslims in the new diplomacy and to receive foreign Muslims in the Soviet Union. Regarding the latter, the first foreign Muslim delegation to the USSR, including a visit to Tashkent, arrived from Syria in 1945. This tiny opening was soon followed by similarly small but significant initiatives from the Soviet side:

1946: several Muslim (Shia) dignitaries from Azerbaijan visit the holy places of Qum and Mashhad in Iran;

1947 (summer): the first visit of a Soviet Muslim cleric abroad; Ziauddin Babakhanov (son of the Mufti of Tashkent) goes on the *hajj* to Mecca and stops in Cairo[41];

1947 (September): the Soviet government (through its Cairo embassy) requests Egypt to allow Soviet Muslims to study at the pre-eminent Islamic university, Al-Azhar. The sheikh of Al-Azhar accepts in principle. (In fact, the first Soviet students arrived much later.)[42];

1947 (October): TASS announces a large group of Soviet pilgrims to Mecca[43] but the *hajj* [pilgrimage] is later cancelled due to 'cholera in Egypt'.

Despite these limited openings to the Muslim world abroad, Soviet policy continued to isolate the Muslim regions of the USSR from these developments, even if Soviet authorities were prepared to make some concessions to their Muslims, such as the opening of approximately 500 new mosques between 1943 and 1954. In fact, anti-religious—and anti-nationalist—propaganda was resumed in 1945, although it was far less violent than it had been before the war. Still, in 1953 the official *Great Bolshevik Encyclopedia* continued to describe the regime's perception of Islam in familiar terms:

In the USSR, Islam is a vestige of the society of exploiters, and [abroad] it is a weapon in the hands of the local reactionaries and of foreign imperialism.[44]

Soviet media kept up the attack on 'reactionary Islamic rulers supported by US and British imperialism', and there appears to have been no let up in Soviet media denunciations of foreign Islam's 'reactionary character'.

In the years after the war until 1949, the Soviets' apparent caution in dealing with the Muslim world is in a sense paradoxical, reflecting, perhaps, the effects of Soviet war exhaustion and the weakness of the embryonic reed of official Islam in the USSR as a policy instrument. In 1945, for the colonial world and especially for the Arab Middle East, the USSR appeared as the one of the two powers (the other was the United States) in a position to help Arab and other Muslim countries liberate themselves from British and French imperialism. Soviet prestige was high, based in part on performance during the war and in part on the decolonialisation rhetoric which, with Roosevelt, Stalin adopted throughout. American prestige was quickly spent because of its strong support for Jewish claims on Palestine, however, and it appeared that, at least until 1949, Soviet prestige and the strategic opportunities inherent to it, might go the same way.

Even if Soviet planners were prepared to recognise possibilities for Soviet strategic gains in the Muslim world, they were hampered at this time by pressing technical problems. Stalin did not trust his recently created official Muslim establishment to support Soviet diplomatic objectives, undoubtedly with good reason, for most Soviet muftis in 1945 were left-overs from the old conservative pre-revolutionary clerical ranks. The younger cohort of Muslim clerics was of poor intellectual quality, possessing only weak theological training and bad Arabic; they could not be exhibited abroad. The 'equipment' for an Islamic weapon simply did not exist, certainly not to the extent that there existed the basic infrastructure for an 'Orthodox weapon'. The irony of the Soviet position was acute: Orthodox priests frequently represented the USSR in predominantly Muslim countries, such as Lebanon and Syria, as a way to drive home the point that the USSR was the direct heir to 'Eternal Russia' rather than a substantial Muslim power in its own right.

In 1949, however, Soviet policy took a turn which can be seen as a calculated decision to curry favour among Islamic countries and to set the stage for the development of an Islamic weapon: withdrawal of active support for Israel. Soviet support for the Jewish cause in Palestine had hitherto been considerable, and, consequently, its relations with the Arab part of the Islamic world experienced inherent limitations. After renouncing its support of Israel, Moscow rapidly set in motion a series of activities aimed at raising the USSR's

Islamic profile. Among the most conspicuous changes were the following:

1949 (April): the founding congress of the World Peace Movement. Many Muslim religious officials, both Soviet and foreign, participated in its activities. Soviet broadcasts in Arabic on religious themes begin at this time. Soviet muftis begin to posture as 'defenders of peace';

1950 (early): Soviet broadcasts to the Middle East begin to expound the themes of 'the happiness of Soviet Muslims', freedom of religion in the USSR, and the Soviet commitment to the restoration of religious monuments;

1950 (April): For the first time an Arab political leader, Maaruf al-Dawalibi, Syrian Economic Minister, calls for a *rapprochement* between Arabs and the USSR;[45]

1951 (November): At a Soviet peace conference, the mufti of Ufa, Abdurrahman Rasulaev, invites the Islamic world abroad to join the USSR in opposing imperialism, the first time a member of the Soviet Islamic establishment joins in anti-imperialist propaganda.

By the time of Stalin's death in 1953, the basic outlines of a tentative Soviet Islamic initiative were becoming clearer, although it might be overstating the case to call these cautious advances a weapon or even part of one. In that eventful year, however, Soviet media, especially Radio Moscow, began in earnest to elaborate the theme of the USSR as an 'Asian power'. Soviet *hajjis* arriving in Mecca that year were given media coverage to underline this new theme. They continued on to Baghdad, Cairo and Jeddah and were received at Al-Azhar where they granted a number of interviews to Iraqi and Egyptian newspapers. It is possible to speculate that at the time of his death, Stalin was seriously entertaining notions of Islam's practical uses in the service of Soviet diplomacy.

THE KHRUSHCHEV ERA (1953–64)

In the post-war years, Stalin agreed to an easing of persecution of Islam at home and the use of the Soviet Islamic establishment for tentative openings to the Muslim world abroad. Nikita Khrushchev reversed the first part of this formula and expanded the second. His tenure as Soviet leader as it concerns the development of an Islamic strategy is characterised by an uncompromisingly hostile attitude toward Islam—and all religions—in the USSR and by an expanded, but selectively targeted, use of the Soviet Islamic hierarchy for propaganda purposes abroad. Indeed, the legacy of the Khrushchev years, somewhat modified by his successors, is the notion that these two seemingly contradictory aspects can work well together.

Khrushchev's domestic policies are frequently interpreted as a return to pure Leninism. Regarding the condition of Islam in the USSR, his radical anti-clericalism indeed fits this description. Under Khrushchev, anti-Islamic propaganda was increased massively, with the new themes centring on the objective of destroying Islam in one generation. Soviet authorities again closed working mosques, the number dropping from about 1500 at the time of Stalin's death to about 500 in the early 1960s.

To the Muslim world abroad, Moscow continued to portray the USSR as a great Russian power of the classic type and as the centre of the world communist movement. Especially after the Bandung Conference of 1955, Soviet image-makers were successful in portraying the USSR as an important Asian power, though not yet as a Muslim power. Moscow's overriding interest in the Muslim world at this time was in countering the Baghdad Pact (1954). Due largely to Iraq's participation in the Baghdad Pact, Soviet propagandists regularly denounced the whole notion of Islamic solidarity as 'an American strategy',[46] and even as late as 1960 as 'a weapon in the hands of Western imperialists against the USSR'.[47] Soviet theorists writing in official party journals reflected this essentialy defensive position. They debated until the mid–1960s whether Islam was 'a factor of national solidarity', if it 'exercises any influence on the formation of views in Muslim society', and even if Islam's 'nature is as negative in foreign Muslim countries as it is in the USSR'.[48] But events like Bandung in 1955, the Suez crisis in 1956, and the fall of the Hashemite dynasty in Iraq in 1958 undoubtedly pushed Soviet thinking along regarding the political opportunities that might derive from a more active Islamic strategy.

By the mid–1950's, one can begin to see the first tentative outlines of a Soviet programme to employ its own Muslims in a more systematic way in contacts with specific foreign Muslim countries where the Soviets sought to promote their influence, particularly Egypt, Syria, Iraq (after the July 1958 revolution), and Lebanon. At this point, however, the Soviet approach was dichotomous: Muslim envoys sent abroad, with some exceptions, were 'secular' political figures from the Party, government or political front organisations whose message centred on the necessity of creating a common front between Soviet Asians and others to fight Western imperialism and, increasingly, Zionism; on the other hand, Muslim envoys to the USSR usually received well-planned exposure to official Soviet Muslim religious leaders and institutions. The implicit and frequently explicit message from the Soviets to their guests was that the USSR is an important Muslim country—'we can talk to one another as Muslims brothers'— and that Soviet Muslims enjoy extraordinary freedoms.

Regarding the first approach, the use of 'secular' Muslims abroad, the following examples are representative. Two newly-founded Soviet political front groups, the Soviet Afro-Asian Solidarity Committee (1956)—whose first Chairman was the Tajik Muslim writer Mirzo Tursun Zade—and the Peace Partisans prominently included Soviet Muslims in their activities. These included:

December 1957-January 1958: The first Afro-Asian Solidarity Conference is convened in Cairo, and is attended by a large Soviet delegation led by Saraf Rashidov, First Secretary of the Central Committee of the Communist Party of Uzbekistan;

1 April 1958: the Soviet Kazakh writer Muhtar Auezov, a member of the CP of Kazakhstan, is elected Vice-Chairman of the Afro-Asian Solidarity Council, whose seat is in Cairo;

April 1959: Several Muslims figure prominently in the important Soviet delegation (led by Mirzo Tursun Zade) to the Conference of Peace Partisans in Baghdad.

It is significant that no religious figures from the official Soviet Islamic establishment participated in the activities of these organisations. Throughout the 1950s, and indeed throughout much of the 1960s,[49] *religious* contacts abroad (but not at home) using Soviet muftis or other official Islamic representatives remained very limited. Religious contacts were confined for the most part to the *hajj*, which routinely included about 20–30 pilgrims divided evenly between aged men from Central Asian collective farms and young executives from the four Soviet Spiritual Directorates. The itinerary for the Soviet *hajis* seldom varied: stopovers in Cairo, Damascus, Lebanon, and Baghdad, where they were received by foreign Muslim dignitaries, such as the sheikh Al-Azhar, ministers of *waqfs* (pious foundations), the Mufti of Syria, and others. In each place, the *hajis* would be interviewed by local media, where they left mostly good impressions. But as one expert has noted, 'Not one of these manifestations can be used to demonstrate (official) Soviet encouragement of providing contact between Arabs and Soviet Muslims with any religious content'.[50]

There can be little doubt, however, that Soviet efforts to lure foreign Muslims to the USSR during this period played on the theme of the USSR as a brotherly Muslim country and, at least implicitly, that Muslim countries abroad shared a religious bond with the USSR. For example:

November 1953: Youth delegations invited by the Komsomol (Soviet youth organisation) arrive from Syria, Iraq and Lebanon. They visit Azerbaijan, and their visit is marked by Radio Moscow broadcasts, in Arabic, on the theme of religious freedom in the USSR;[51]

June 1954: Delegation of Algerian doctors visits the USSR, including Tashkent, where they are received by Mufti Ishan Babakhanov;

May 1955: Syrian Peace Partisans delegation visits Moscow where they are given a reception by the Imam-Khatib of the Moscow mosque;[52]

June 1955: Lebanese Trade Union delegation visits Moscow, where they are received by the same Imam-Khatib;[53]

July 1955: Syrian Parliamentary delegation visits Azerbaijan, where they tour the main Baku mosques;[54]

May 1958: Egyptian delegation visits Azerbaijan, where they are received by the government of the Azerbaijan SSR. The Sheikh ul-Islam of Baku is present and speaks of 'the prayers of Soviet Muslims at the time of criminal Israeli aggression against Egypt in 1956';[55]

April-May 1958: President Nasser of Egypt visits the USSR and is received in Tashkent by the Uzbek government. The muftis remain in the background, but Nasser takes part in a public prayer;

March 1959: An Iraqi Government delegation led by the Minister of Economy, Ibrahim Kubbo, visits Baku and Tashkent, where the Sheikh ul-Islam and the mufti are prominent in the background.

In June 1954 the Soviets convened the Muslim Conference of Ufa, and in March 1956 the Muslim Congress in Baku. Both conferences entertained a few foreign Muslims and both adopted the same political themes of 'world peace' and opposition to atomic weapons.[56] The first foreign Islamic *religious* delegation was admitted to the

USSR only in July-August 1958: a group of Syrian religious leaders
led by the Chief Mufti of Syria on the invitation of the Mufti of
Tashkent. In fact, between 1958 and 1962 Soviet strategists began
to shed whatever restrictions had existed on forging a specifically
Islamic context for diplomacy with friendly countries.

This particular meeting between Soviet and Syrian Muslim clerics
was a political watershed; it signalled important new directions for
Soviet Islamic politics and perhaps the beginnings of an attempt to
put into operation a comprehensive Islamic weapon. The meeting
was accompanied by a massive Soviet propaganda effort. Soviet
clerics laboured to develop the theme of Islamic solidarity, the first
articulation of this idea from Soviet clerics to foreign ones. Syrian
delegates concentrated on the perfect orthodoxy of Soviet Islam on
the one hand, and on the other offered an indication of the practical
ends to which this new solidarity could be applied: the desire of
Soviet Muslims to volunteer to defend Arabism and Islam against
Israeli imperialism.[57] For the next few years, similar meetings were
frequent:

> June 1960: Chief Mufti of Egypt, Hasan Ma'mun, visits Moscow
> and Tashkent. He is received by the Mufti of Tashkent;[58]
>
> February-March 1963: An Indian Muslim delegation led by
> Atiqurrahman Osmani, Grand Mufti of India, and Sayid Abdullah
> Bukhari, Imam-Khatib of the Shakhih-Jaghan mosque in Delhi,
> visits the USSR, including Tashkent, and gives an interview to
> *Radio Moscow*,[59]
>
> September 1963: A delegation from Togo led by Mohammed
> Husein, Minister of Religious Affairs, is invited by the Mufti of
> Tashkent to visit Tashkent, Dushanbe, Bukhara and Samarkand.

Other indications of the Soviets' more systematic planning for
using the Islamic element in their diplomacy appeared during the
same period (1958–63). For example, in 1959 the USSR initiated
Arabic broadcasts from Baku, and these broadcasts little by little
increasingly expounded the theme of Islamic solidarity. Although
Islamic religious themes had appeared infrequently in Soviet Arabic
broadcasts since 1956, the change of venue for these broadcasts to
Muslim Baku from non-Muslim Moscow and decidedly anti-Muslim
Erevan (Armenia) suggest more comprehensive political planning.
This move was followed in 1962 by the creation *in Moscow* of the
Department of International Relations of the four Muslim Spiritual
Directorates, which underlined the crucial international aspects of

the enterprise. The logical location for this department was Tashkent. By fixing it in Moscow, Soviet leaders were signalling their determination to keep a tight rein on the Islamic element in their policy and to integrate it with other facets of strategy.

The Soviet Islamic weapon began under Khrushchev. It developed cautiously, particularly in its use of Soviet clerics abroad, and as an adjunct to other political, economic and military changes in the Middle East. By 1964, Islam as a political instrument was still in its development stage, and it occasionally suffered setbacks.[60] Moscow still preferred to use 'regular' communists, even those from Muslim peoples, in its dealings with front organisations and political groups in the Muslim world abroad. This tactic, too, became ineffective and occasionally counterproductive: by 1968 it had nearly disappeared from the scene, as Soviet Muslim clerics began to assume ever expanding responsibilities for this aspect of Soviet foreign policy.

The most important theme developed by Soviet clerics at home during this period—and the one with the most far-reaching political implications—was that of Islamic solidarity: the notion that the USSR is in fact a Muslim state and that this fact transcends other political differences. Israel was, of course, a convenient bogey in this scenario, and Soviet propaganda made the most of it: 'Israel is our [that is, we Muslims'] common enemy'. Even Great Britain was threatened over its position in Suez by the legions of Soviet Muslims. In a statement which those directly in the sights of British guns must have found somewhat amusing, the Imam-Khatib of Moscow's mosque declared that 'the war in Suez is the fight of all Soviet Muslims'.[61] Still, as an expression of 'Islamic solidarity' the statement, like many others of its kind during this period, probably was not entirely wasted. It was part of the preparation of the Muslim world abroad for a more serious Soviet offensive which was soon to follow.

2 The Brezhnev Era Prior to the Soviet Invasion of Afghanistan, 1964–80

Under Brezhnev's direction, the Soviet leadership devised a flexible strategy to penetrate the Muslim world. This strategy may be divided into two periods: a preparatory period (1964–73), during which the USSR maintained a relatively low profile in the Middle East; and an offensive period (1973–80), during which the 'Islamic instrument' together with several other tactical applications, was successfully applied to contribute to the overall political and psychological objectives of Soviet strategy in the Muslim world.

THE PREPARATORY PERIOD (1964–73)

Khrushchev's fall in 1964 was followed in the Muslim territories of the USSR almost immediately by a dramatic reversal in Soviet official treatment of Islam. The deposed leader's strong anti-Islamic campaign was toned down substantially and the closing of mosques was stopped, the number remaining stable—about 500—until 1980. However, official Soviet Marxism-Leninism and the theoretical writings about religion, including Islam, inside the Soviet state for the most part remained uncompromisingly hostile. We can assume, therefore, that the Kremlin's decision to moderate its behaviour toward its own Muslims was not due to a new climate of political liberalism,, but was predicated instead on the leadership's realisation that Khrushchev's policies, which were designed to destroy all religions in one generation, were counterproductive.

During the 1960s, the Soviets made a major investment in analysis of Islam and the creation of related policy establishments. A new generation of young Soviet experts in Islam—most good sociologists and better trained than the *agitprop* specialists of the Stalin and Khrushchev eras—emerged from Soviet educational establishments and began to play an active role in the analysis of Islamic phenomena for policy development. Among other things, they discovered the existence of a 'parallel' Islam in the USSR, which their predecessors had missed.[1] The new group of Islamic specialists—which included the now well-known names of Saidbaev, Ashirov, Pivovarov, Demidov, Bazarbaev, Izimbetov, Makatov, Abdullaev and several others—quickly determined that the 'parallel', or underground Islamic trend among Soviet Muslims was far more aggressive and more militant that the largely quiescent official Islamic structure which Stalin had created to serve the political objectives of the Soviet state. At least in part because of this disparity, the Soviet regime engineered a *rapprochement* with its domesticated official Islamic hierarchy in the 1960s. The anti-clerical propaganda which characterised the Khrushchev period was mostly abandoned in favour of the propaganda of 'scientific atheism' and the denunciation of Islamic 'fanatics'—a term which encompassed Sufi adepts.

The emergence of the corps of new Islamic specialists coincided with Soviet efforts to produce reliable high-level Islamic religious cadres. To this end, Soviet authorities opened the Imam Ismail al-Bukhari theological school in Tashkent in 1971, which rapidly became an excellent training institution for the official Islamic establishment. This move was undoubtedly meant to improve actual operational opportunities within a more flexible political approach to Islam abroad.

This is not to say that the Soviets dropped their doctrinaire anti-Islamic line; indeed, the anti-Islamic campaign was never completely abandoned. Rather, the Soviet leadership realised that political flexibility was both necessary and possible on this issue, and they moved to develop a Janus-like strategy which stressed the dangers of unrestrained Islam at home while simultaneously, albeit cautiously, advancing the notion that Islam abroad could be a progressive, even a revolutionary factor.

The latter position is manifest in the marked theoretical reassessment of Islam's possibilities by members of the talented community of Soviet specialists on Islam. Contrary to the approach taken under Khrushchev, which emphasised the retrograde nature of Islam, Soviet experts now admitted that Islam in some cases could be 'a positive revolutionary factor'. A typical statement to this effect was that by G. M. Kerimov:

> Islamic socialism may be used by reactionary circles as a new ideological weapon against Marxism-Leninism; it may also become a new bourgeois illusion concerning socialism, but it may become

a revolutionary anti-capitalist reformist movement, for instance as was the case in Syria, Algeria or in the United Arab Republic.[2]

By the early 1970s, however, statements of this kind were uncommon, reflecting perhaps the Soviet establishment's ambiguity about how best to proceed. In fact, in 1973 the vaunted Soviet propaganda machine blundered severely when it released for publication two violently anti-Islamic pamphlets intended for foreign consumption: 'The Koran, Its Doctrine and Philosophy', in English and Arabic and signed by Nureddin Muhitdinov, the Soviet ambassador to Damascus and Nishanov, the Soviet ambassador in Sri Lanka; and 'Peut-on Croire au Coran' (Can one believe the Koran?), in French, signed by R. M. Rakhmatov, Soviet ambassador in Mauritania. All three of the signatories have Muslim names and probably were sent to their respective posts because of this. Thus we see the ambiguity of Soviet policy during this period in the apparently paradoxical situation of Soviet Muslim diplomats who are intended to trade on the cultural and social features of Islam while making anti-Islamic statements. The pamphlets were badly received in the Muslim world, and the Soviets rapidly attempted to disavow their blunder, hinting that the offensive material had in fact been produced by some Western (read US) intelligence agency to embarrass the USSR. The Head Mufti of Tashkent, Ziautdin Babakhanov, was pressed into service to deny the authenticity of the Muhitdinov pamphlet: 'I believe the real authors are those who slander the Holy Koran and falsify God's word shamelessly'.[3] A. P. Ivanov, probably a pseudonym for the Soviet collective leadership, denounced both pamphlets in *Izvestia* as typical 'ideological diversion . . . whose real authors are not known, but their aim is obviously to damage the relations between the USSR and the developing countries'.[4]

These are revealing complaints, and the entire episode may have had a formative influence on the evolution of Soviet thinking about dealing with Islam abroad. A watershed of sorts appears to have occurred in 1973, perhaps stimulated by the incident with the pamphlets but certainly accelerated by it in any case. For example, while the same three main channels for Soviet influence to the Muslim world remained in service as in Khrushchev's day, they underwent some significant restructuring. The activity in the 'official channel', represented by various government and Party contacts, youth organisations (Komsomol), trade unions (Profsoiuz), universities, academies of science and professional organisations, like the

Soviet Writers' Union, and their foreign counterparts in friendly countries or in those with whom the USSR had diplomatic or economic relations remained much as before. But whereas before 1973 Soviet delegations in this channel were composed mostly of Russians and other Soviet 'Europeans', after 1973—until 1980—they were headed almost entirely by Soviet Muslim communists. By contrast, the three main KGB front organisations targeted on the Muslim world—the Peace Partisans, the Friendship Societies and the Afro-Asian Solidarity Committees—were represented throughout this period, as before, almost exclusively by Soviet non-Muslims. This channel, whose aim was to create abroad a network of reliable and influential friends and agents of the Soviet Union, was exceptionally active during the period under review, noticeably more so than the official or Islamic channels.

Changes appeared after 1973 in the 'Islamic channel' as well. Prior to this, the propaganda messages conveyed through the three channels were roughly identical, stressing the general themes of Peace, Anti-imperialism, and Afro-Asian solidarity, with only slight difference in emphasis. For example, Soviet muftis would stress that the USSR is a *Muslim* country, while the propagandists for Afro-Asian solidarity usually presented the USSR as an *Asian* country. The same messages were scattered across a broad political and social spectrum: to the ruling élites, to the revolutionary and religious elements as well as to the political opposition. After 1973, when the Islamic channel became more active, a more productive—and seemingly ironic—balance was struck between the tasks of the Soviet muftis and the more straight-forward *agitpropshchiki* of the front organisations: the muftis began to speak more about politics, while the *agitpropshchiki* more and more frequently took up the subject of religion.

The Islamic channel was used during this period especially to enhance Soviet influence in those countries with which it had no official diplomatic relations and for which other points of Soviet entry were lacking. Particular emphasis was placed on relations with Saudi Arabia, Morocco, Jordan, Tunisia, the Gulf States and North Yemen. The Soviet Islamic channel was also used to assist in the restoration of Soviet prestige where it had suffered setbacks, for instance in Egypt after 1973.

If the period 1964–73 was one in which the Soviets began to sort out the ambiguities in thinking about the instruments to apply to their relations with the Muslim world and to give the bare-bones of their tenuous conceptual innovation some operational flesh, it was also a period in which Soviet prestige in the Muslim world suffered a series of serious political setbacks. In 1971 at the time of the India-Pakistan war, most Muslims viewed the USSR as siding with Hindu India. In 1972, Soviet advisors were ignominiously expelled from Egypt at great cost to Soviet prestige in the region. The Six Day War (1967) and the Yom-Kippur War (1973) further tarnished Moscow's image in the Muslim world by demonstrating its inability to save Soviet clients from defeat and the economic and technical weaknesses of the USSR compared to the strength with which the United States sustained Israel.

Following the last two setbacks to the images of 'the USSR as a Great Power' and 'Moscow—the Capital of World Communism', Soviet muftis reappeared on the scene more actively than ever before. Their goal was to recoup Soviet prestige by portraying the USSR as a brotherly Muslim country and a Muslim power. We begin to see here, for the first time, not only Soviet willingness to wield this particular instrument out of a sense of crying opportunity but out of considerable necessity and perhaps some desperation: very few other propaganda arrows capable of penetrating this target remained in the Soviet quiver.

In order to compensate for the political setback resulting from Arab humiliation in the 1967 Six Day War, Soviet propaganda in the Muslim world turned heavily to religious themes. In particular, the Soviets attempted what must be seen as a flagrant bluff by stressing the solidarity of Soviet Muslims with their Muslim brethren abroad. For example, Soviet propaganda claimed that Soviet Muslims had enrolled extensively as volunteers in Palestinian military units and as military instructors in Egypt and Syria. This bold lie was quickly picked up by progressive and leftist Arab media, as well as by the Israeli press. The Soviet press simultaneously published detailed information about 'spontaneous' protests in the North Caucasus and in Central Asia against Israeli imperialism. It was even hinted that pogroms directed against Soviet Daghestan's Mountain Jews had occurred.[5]

Soviet muftis took to the road, for the first time in any sustained and co-ordinated way. For example, in November 1968, Ziauddin Babakhanov led a Soviet delegation to the Islamic Conference in Rawalpindi, where he violently assailed US, Israeli and British imperialism.[6] In 1969 he visited Morocco for the first time; this visit was followed by another Soviet delegation in 1972 led by the Soviet sheikh I. Sattiev. In January-February 1971, Babakhanov led a Soviet Muslim pilgrimage to Mecca, with intermediate visits to Egypt, Syria and Jordan. En route home, he participated in an Islamic conference in Cairo.

While attempting to influence Muslim media abroad, this period also marks the initiation of two ambitious and effective Soviet journals aimed at the larger Muslim readership. The first, *Muslims of the Soviet East*, is a quarterly published by the Spiritual Directorate of the Muslims of the Soviet East, the co-ordinating body for official Soviet Muslim activities, in Tashkent. Printed originally in Arabic and Uzbek (transliterated in the Arabic script, which few Soviet Muslims can read), *Muslims of the Soviet East* introduced English and French editions (aimed primarily at North Africa) in 1974, a Persian (Farsi) edition in 1980 (obviously aimed at both Iran and Afghanistan), and a Dari (the Afghan form of Persian) edition in 1985.

The second medium established in this period was the Soviet journal, in Arabic, *Anba Musku* (1971). Among its usual fare are politically provocative speeches of touring Soviet muftis.[7] During 1971–72, *Anba Musku* dealt heavily in religious themes, including publishing photos of Soviet Muslim religious leaders and of Soviet mosques in Moscow and Leningrad, especially during important Islamic festivals, and reproducing sermons of Soviet Muslim preachers (imam-khatibs).[8]

Visits by foreign Muslims to Soviet Islamic sites had slowed between 1964 and 1968, but after this the tempo increased quickly. Of particular importance is the evident Soviet decision to underline the propaganda theme of Soviet Muslim solidarity with foreign Muslims by actually exposing foreign delegations from Islamic countries to highly selective and carefully orchestrated aspects of Muslim life in the USSR. When foreign Muslim visitors were religious leaders, for the most part their invitations originated from the Muslim Spiritual Board in Tashkent.[9] Most foreign delegations during this period were secular in nature, and their invitations usually originated from a counterpart Soviet Government or front organisation. However, with few exceptions, even the secular delegations were exposed to Soviet official Islamic institutions, usually in Tashkent, as part of their obligatory tour, and nearly all assisted publicly in Friday prayers at one of the seats of Soviet official Islam (Tashkent, Ufa, Buynaksk [later Makhach-Qala], or Baku). Most delegations were from the Arab world, as the sample from 1971, an especially active year, indicates:

January: Iraqi Minister of Education to Baku;
May:Egyptian Minister of Education and Culture to Tashkent;
June: Iraqi Deputy Minister of Information to Baku;
July: Lebanese Parliamentary delegation (including Rashid Karame and Kemal Jumblatt) to Tashkent;
September: Syrian Parliamentary delegation to Tashkent;
December: Syrian Baath delegation to Tashkent.

In yet another initiative to spread Soviet influence to the Islamic world via its own loyal Islamic establishment, on 6–8 October 1970, the Muslim Spiritual Board of Tashkent organised the first of many international symposia for Muslims. The theme of the first meeting is indicative of the symposium's political objectives: 'The Unity and Cooperation of Muslim Peoples in the Struggle for Peace'. The symposium was chaired by Head Mufti Babakhanov and attended by a hundred official Soviet Muslim teacher-elders (*ulema*) and by representatives from 24 Muslim countries. Establishing a custom which has come to characterise these meetings, Soviet and foreign representatives violently attacked US, Israeli and South African imperialism.[10]

By the end of 1973, it is possible to discern the crystalisation of a division of labour between Soviet communist party and front organisations and the Soviet Islamic establishment in their respective dealings with foreign Muslims. In the preceding decade the Soviet leadership successfully developed the infrastructure of both a strategy toward Islamic countries and the operational mechanisms to carry it out. Importantly, the Soviet official Islamic establishment rose from being an unknown, if strongly suspect quantity to become authentic partners in the process of spreading Soviet influence and prestige.

THE UNFOLDING OF BREZHNEV'S ISLAMIC STRATEGY (1973–79)

Following the Yom-Kippur War and the immense setback to Soviet prestige in the Arab world which resulted, Soviet leaders apparently concluded that an 'Islamic weapon', using the instrument that had been developed and sharpened over the last decade, was more necessary than ever. Within a short time, they brought its various parts into close co-ordination and the entire enterprise up to full speed. While some ambiguities continued to be evident, for the first time the pattern of Soviet involvement demonstrated conscientious targeting of some Islamic countries for special attention and a clearer set of political priorities.

Obvious targets during this critical period included the Arab Middle East, Afghanistan, and, to a lesser extent, Pakistan under Bhutto. Soviet leaders moved to establish contact with and spread influence through foreign Muslim religious and secular leaders in two principal ways. The first, through the instrument of the Soviet official Islamic establishment had three main thrusts: (1) out-reach activities by Soviet Muslim leaders; (2) hosting of foreign religious delegations in the USSR; and (3) convening of international conferences in the USSR organised by the Mufti of Tashkent. The second avenue for spreading Soviet influence among foreign Muslims focused on extensive exchanges with Muslim countries through front organisations.

Activities of the Soviet Official Islamic Establishment
I: Religious Delegations Abroad

On the international level, Soviet Muslim religious authorities were encouraged to cultivate relations with the ruling élites of the Muslim world abroad, especially in those of the conservative countries which had no (or poor) diplomatic relations with the USSR: Saudi Arabia, Jordan, Morocco, Tunisia, Kuwait, the Gulf emirates, Lebanon and Egypt. Soviet Muslim leaders emphasised several important themes in all of their work, logically on order of the Kremlin:

> the evils of US, Israeli, and Chinese imperialism. Occasionally South Africa or another state might be substituted or be added, but the broad outlines of an anti-American/anti-Israeli campaign remained constant;
> that the USSR is a substantial Muslim power and the best friend of Islam. As part of the world of Islam, the USSR joined with other Muslim countries to oppose continued domination and oppression at the hands of the hostile world of 'infidels', typified by the Americans;
> the religious tolerance of the Soviet Government, and especially the freedom, happiness and prosperity of the Soviet Muslim community.

Just the presence of Soviet Muslim representatives abroad, at least through 1980, carries with it several implicit messages. For progressive/radical Muslim countries, it was exciting and often unexpected news that here is a community of more than 50 million fellow believers who are part of a revolutionary process. In the absence of more complete knowledge of the condition of Islam in the USSR, many Muslims, especially those who subscribe to Soviet-style Marxist-Leninist political models, are inclined to view Soviet Muslims more in terms of their proximity to Soviet revolutionary claims and pretenses than as suffering co-religionists. Soviet muftis abroad encouraged this illusion by declaring everywhere how the Soviet Muslim community has benefited from Soviet life. At the very least, many otherwise discerning foreign Muslims were persuaded to reserve judgement.

For conservative foreign Muslims the implicit message is just the opposite but no less effective. For them, the discovery that Islam has survived a half-century of communist oppression proved that Soviet life is not as threatening to Islam as Western propaganda makes it out to be. Furthermore, the appearance of Soviet muftis, who obviously have led a successful resistance movement against communism, is proof of these muftis' authenticity (see below). Therefore, simply by putting their muftis in the field—at least in the absence of any conscientious efforts to compromise them and to tie them more closely to the oppression of Islam in the USSR rather than to its survival—the Kremlin could expect to win important propaganda victories.

Soviet Muslim authorities also acted frequently as middlemen in a broader sense for more routine Soviet diplomatic activity. This service was especially desirable among oriental audiences where Russian communists were handicapped by the double stigma of being both 'Europeans' and atheists.

Between 1973 and 1979 Soviet muftis leading official religious delegations visited 20 Muslim countries. They visited some countries more than once: Saudi Arabia—seven visits (usually for the annual pilgrimage); North Yemen and Algeria—two visits each; the Gulf states, Iraq, Egypt, Syria, Jordan, Tunisia, Libya, Turkey, India, Pakistan, Bangladesh, Mauritius, Mali, Senegal, Mauritania, Nigeria and Somalia—one visit each. Middle Eastern visits often coincided with the *hajj* to Mecca; the Soviet Muslim delegation characteristically would be composed of a token representation of aged, devout Muslims from the countryside and filled out with well-trained religious executives from the different Muslim religious boards.

Frequently the pilgrimage coincided with participation in an Islamic conference in Mecca.

These visits afforded the muftis an opportunity to engage in effective Soviet propaganda. In the first place, they usually faced little overt hostility from their hosts, and in most cases received considerable hospitality. They are, after all, authentic *ulema* who must be accorded the minimum respect due to any islamic scholar. In part, their reception is smoothed by a *Hadith* (teaching) of the Prophet: 'Thou must not doubt the faith of a believer'. In simple terms this means that Soviet Muslim leaders are generally given the benefit of any doubt surrounding their split loyalties; they are acknowledged to represent the atheistic Soviet state, but still they remain Muslims. Frequently one hears foreign Muslims who have had contact with Soviet Muslim authorities explaining that the latter admit in private that their road under Soviet authority is a hard one, but that the only way to preserve Islam in the USSR is to play the game. This may be true of some Soviet Muslim leaders and with others it may be pretentious; we are in no position to make the distinction. What is true, however, is that all Soviet Muslim leaders encourage this impression abroad, so that a foreign Muslim who denies the Soviet Muslim leader's authenticity must be prepared not only to ignore a teaching of the Prophet but to acquiesce in the possible destruction of one of the world's largest Muslim communites.

In the second place, Soviet muftis who travel abroad are nearly always received at the highest levels of the government and religious leadership—which often has a profound influence on the politics of their governments—in the host countries. Moreover, they usually are accorded substantial access to the media and public forums abroad. The following sample illustrates these points:

In 1974, Ziauddin Babakhanov, his deputy Abdulgani Abdul-laev and Azam Aliabarov, chairman of the Department of International Affairs of the Muslim Spiritual Directorate in Tashkent, led the *hajj* to Mecca. They visited Saudi Arabia, where they were received by King Faysal, by the Rector of the University, and by the Chairman of the Muslim World league. They travelled to North Yemen, where they were received at Parliament and where Babakhanov gave a well-publicised talk on 'The Common Struggle Against Imperialist Aggression'. The delegation continued on to Abu Dhabi, where they were received by the Sheikh Zayed B. Sultan al-Nahyan, Chairman of the Union of Gulf Emirates;

Babakhanov held a press conference and gave a talk on local television;[11]

In 1975:

—Z. Babakhanov led a pilgrimage to Mecca, where he attended the Conference on the Mission of the Mosques; he was received by King Khaled. In 1977, Babakhanov led the *hajj* and took part in a similar conference[12]

—Z. Babakhanov and his deputy, Yusufkhan Shakirov, and Azam Aliakbarov took part in the conference on The Mobilisation of All Efforts in the Struggle Against Zionism, Imperialism, and Their Lackeys in Baghdad (February). From there the delegation proceeded to Jordan, where they were received by King Husein, Abdullah Gasha, the Chief *qadi* of Jordan, and Dr Abdul Aziz Hayat, Minister of *Waqfs*. In Egypt, they were given a reception at the famous Al-Azhar University, and in Syria, they were received by Sheikh Abdul-Sattar, Minister of *Waqfs*;

—A smaller Soviet delegation travelled to Lucknow, India to participate in an International Symposium on Islamic Education at the invitation of Abdul-Hasan al-Husni al-Nadavy, Chairman of the Nadvat ul-Ulema Society of India;

In 1976 (February), Abdulgani Abdullaev and Azam Aliakbarov took part in the important Muslim-Christian dialogue organised in Tripoli. The Soviet *ulemas* were received by Colonel Qadhafi;

In 1977:

—(January-February) Abdulgani Abdullaev led a Soviet delegation to the International Conference on Islamic Thought in Wargla, Algeria;[14]

—(March) Abu Turab Yunus, Imam-khatib of the 'Tilla Sheikh' Mosque of Tashkent, led a delegation to the International Symposium of Muslim Preaching in Dacca, Bangladesh;[15]

—(October) Ziauddin Babakhanov led a Soviet Muslim delegation to the Conference of the Academy of Islamic Studies in Cairo, at the invitation of the Sheikh of Al-Azhar;

In 1978:

—Z. Babakhanov once again led the pilgrimage to Mecca and took part there in the session of the World Supreme Council of Mosques;

—(February) Yusufkhan Shakirov led a delegation to the Islamic Seminar in Kairouan, Tunisia;

—(Summer) A group of Soviet *ulema*, headed by Abdulgani

Abdullaev, visited Niger, where they were received by Omar Ismail, Chairman of the Islamic Association, Mali and Senegal;[16]
—(July) An important Soviet Muslim delegation, led by Z. Babakhanov, attended the International Conference on the Propagation of Islam in Karachi, where they were received by General Zia ul-Haq and held several press conferences;[17]
—(November) Z. Babakhanov led a Soviet delegation to the International Conference on the Hegira Calendar in Istanbul;[18]
—(December) A Soviet Muslim delegation attended the International Conference on Islamic Thought in Batna, Algeria.[19]

As these examples make clear, throughout the period under examination, Soviet muftis were both active and, on the basis of their levels and points of access, effective. This sample could be extended considerably to include visits by individual Soviet muftis to Muslim countries, where they probably act as unofficial diplomats where regular Soviet diplomats have no immediate access.

Activities of the Soviet Official Islamic Establishment
II: Foreign Muslim Delegations in the USSR

Throughout the period under examination, travels abroad by Soviet muftis to develop an effective public profile and, hence, influence in the larger Muslim world were more than matched by travels of foreign Muslims to the USSR at the invitation of the Soviet official Islamic establishment. These visits follow a characteristic pattern. Invitations are issued by the Mufti of Tashkent, who is also the Chairman of the Spiritual Directorate for Central Asia and Kazakhstan, in order of priority to (1) ministers and (2) directors of *Waqfs* (charitable foundations) and religious affairs of their respective countries: that is, to those individuals who have both religious and administrative responsibilities; next to leading religious personalities (head muftis and *qadis*); then to leaders of international Islamic organisations; and sometimes, though more seldom, to selected journalists. Occasionally foreign dignitaries who are known to be devout believers but are not directly involved in the administration of religious affairs in their countries are invited to visit the Mufti of Tashkent or the Shia Sheikh ul-Islam in Baku. Guests usually stay for two, seldom more than three weeks and are lavishly entertained, suggesting that the Muslim Spiritual Directorate has a substantial operating budget for such activities.

In Tashkent the delegations and dignitaries are welcomed by the Soviet Head Mufti; the foreigners attend Friday prayers in one of the few 'working' mosques in the city and pay a visit to the Imam Ismail al-Bukhari theological institute. If a delegation is politically important, it may also be received by the Government of the Uzbek Republic or by representatives of the Tashkent city government. Foreign delegates nearly always visit the ancient Islamic cities of Samarkand and Bukhara, where receptions are organised in their honour at the Muslim religious school (*madrasa*), Mir-i Arab. Some delegations also visit the Ferghana Valley (cities of Namangan, Andizhan, and Osh), Dushanbe (Tajikistan). Alma-Ata (the capital of Kazakhstan) and Frunze (the capital of Kirghizia), which are now mostly Russian cities, and Ashkhabad (the capital of Turkmenistan), in which all the mosques have been closed, are seldom visited. The 'Central Asian tour' also characteristically includes visits to collective farms and industries where the directors are, or are made to appear to be, native Muslims.

Following their tour of Central Asia, foreign delegations are usually received in Baku, Azerbaijan by the Shia Sheikh ul-Islam, Chairman of the Muslim Spiritual Board of Transcaucasia. There they attend Friday prayers in the 'Taze-Pir' cathedral mosque and are received by the Baku city government; in some exceptional cases, foreign delegates are received by the Government of Azerbaijan. Some delegations also visit Ufa, the capital of Bashkiria and seat of the Muslim Spiritual Board of European Russia and Siberia, and, more seldom, Kazan, the capital of the Tatar ASSR. The tour usually ends in Leningrad and Moscow with a visit to the 'working' mosques of those cities. In Moscow, the most important delegations are welcomed by Kuroedov, Chairman of the Council for Religious Affairs of the Council of Ministers of the USSR. Less important delegations are received by Abdullah Nuralaev (an Uzbek), Deputy-Chairman of the above council and Head of its Muslim Department.

Invitations of foreign Muslim leaders to visit the USSR and travels abroad of Soviet Muslim leaders are complementary aspects of the same strategy. While the latter, as noted earlier, aims to project abroad a favourable image of the USSR as a friend of Islam, the former has a more practical objective: to build in the Muslim world a network of influential friends (and eventually agents?) capable of influencing public opinion in their countries.

A great many of the foreign Muslim guests to the USSR seem to share a common general political profile. They are old-fashioned, moderate conservatives: neither too modernist and liberal nor too right-wing or fundamentalist. Many are strongly anti-revolutionary and even anti-communist in their own countries. The choice of such guests is certainly by design, for in order for foreign Muslim personalities to have credibility at home on issues concerning Islam in the USSR their own religious credentials must be unassailable. Soviet strategy, therefore, is not to transform them into convinced communist fellow-travellers, which, once they returned home and expressed demonstrably Soviet ideas, would be counterproductive to Soviet objectives. The Soviet aim is more modest and more pragmatic: to convince foreign Muslims with good religious credentials that Islam is alive in the USSR and that at some time in the future the Soviet Muslim lands could return to the larger Islamic community, the *Dar ul-Islam*. To accelerate this evolution, foreign Muslim leaders are encouraged to co-operate with the Soviet muftis and to help them win more concessions from Moscow.

For Moscow, these respected conservative foreign Muslims are not ideal allies, but they are by far the most reliable. For one thing, there is little danger that they will speak out publicly in the USSR about the discrepancies between the versions of Soviet Muslim reality put out by Tashkent and the Kremlin and that which they can see for themselves. Nor is there danger that radical foreign Muslims might use the opportunity to proselytize. To our knowledge, in the 1973–79 period, not a single radical fundamentalist foreign leader— of the Iranian or 'Muslim Brothers' type—visited the USSR on an official invitation.

Some foreign Muslim dignitaries are persuaded by the Soviet presentation, although it is impossible to know even approximately how many. On the other hand, we interviewed a number of foreign Muslim dignitaries who claim not to have been taken in by the 'Potemkin villages' they were offered while on official invitations from the Mufti of Tashkent; some even expressed strong hostility to the Soviets and published their findings (see below). Yet most, even the most critical of the Soviet treatment of Islam, expressed their admiration or respect for the Soviet muftis, whom they portrayed as labouring under difficult conditions and who were deserving of outside Muslim support. Thus this particular Soviet Islamic tactic, while imperfect, can be seen to be effective.

At the end of their visits, foreign Muslims are frequently asked for their impressions, which are then published in *Muslims of the Soviet East*. Their impressions, needless to say, are always positive, their visits being short enough and their contacts limited to prevent embarrassment to the Soviet hosts. For the most part they see Soviet Islam superficially, that is, full mosques for Friday prayers, free and happy believers, and so forth. Occasionally, however, a visitor will refuse to accept this rosy picture, returning home to publish a critical account of his journey. In these cases, Soviet religious authorities are mobilised to denounce the 'slanderer' vigorously. Since 1974, nearly every issue of *Muslims of the Soviet East* contains a section called 'For the Sake of Truth' signed by the Mufti of Tashkent himself or by one of his deputies. For example:

'Woe to the Falsehood Mongers', denouncing an American Muslim journalist, Thomas Abercrombie, for his 'slanderous' photos of Central Asia in the *National Geographic Magazine*[20];

'For Truth's Sake', by Abdulgani Abdullaev, denouncing a Moroccan journalist, Dr Ali al-Munasir, for his critical article in *Da'wat al-Hagg*;[21];

An article signed by Ziauddin Babakhanov attacking several Pakistani visitors, particularly Abdulhafiz, for his article in *Akhbar al-Alam-i Islami*, 'Communist Terror Against Islam'[22];

'A Biased Judgment', by Abdulgani Abdullaev, attacking other Pakistani visitors. During this period Pakistani visitors seem to have been among the most critical[23];

'The Truth about Soviet Reality', by Yusufkhan Shakirov, Deputy Chairman of the Muslim Spiritual Directorate in Tashkent, denouncing an Iranian visitor, Manuchehr Azum, who wrote in the journal *Views of Islam* (no. 35–6, Tehran) that 'in the USSR personal dictatorship has replaced the dictatorship of the proletariat'[24];

An article signed by Gulam Qadir Mirza Yakubov, denouncing the anti-Soviet character of *The Journal of the Institute of Muslim Minority Affairs* of King Abdul Aziz University, Jeddah.[25]

From 1973 to 1979 the Soviet media noted the presence of 24 foreign religious delegations from 20 Muslim countries in the Muslim republics of the USSR. They came from all parts of the Muslim world: from the Arab countries (Iraq, Egypt, Kuwait, Sudan, Jordan, North Yemen, South Yemen and Lebanon); from Africa (Mauritius, Somalia, Mauritania and Chad); from non-Arab Central Asia (Afghanistan, Iran, Turkey and Pakistan); from Asia (Singapore, Malaysia and Indonesia); and even from France (the imam-khatib of the Paris mosque). See *Appendix A* for a more comprehensive and detailed list of Muslim delegations visiting the USSR.

Activities of the Soviet Official Islamic Establishment
III: International Conferences Organised by the Mufti of Tashkent

Arguably the most successful channel for projecting a positive image of the USSR as a friend of the Islamic world during the 1973–79 period were the international conferences organised in Central Asia by Ziauddin Babakhanov. The conferences always had the facade of concern with religious topics, but in reality they almost always dealt with political-propaganda matters of concern to the Kremlin, such as projecting a positive image of Islam in the USSR and leaving the public impression of widespread support for Soviet-sponsored propaganda initiatives against various 'imperialisms', US militarism, Zionism, and so forth.

Most conferences were attended by delegates from the entire Muslim world, including countries that have no diplomatic relations with the USSR, such as Saudi Arabia. The following sample demonstrates these points:

—*13–14 November 1973.* Conference in Tashkent on the theme 'Soviet Muslims support the just Struggle of the Arab People against Israeli imperialist aggression'. Ziauddin Babakhanov chaired the debates. All four Soviet muftis were present. Delegates attended from Egypt, Iraq, Libya, North Yemen, Kuwait and Lebanon. Babakhanov expressed pride "that in the hard times for the Arab countries, the Soviet Union without hesitation offered its hand of friendship to our brethren'. The conference was also addressed by the Grand Mufti of Lebanon; by Nafi Kasim, Chairman of the Department of *Waqfs* of Iraq; and by sheikh Izzeddin al-Ghiriany (al-Jirayni) of the Department of Religious Affairs and of Justice of Libya. The conference's final appeal called on 'all Muslims and all people of good will to support the Arab struggle against Israeli aggression'.[26]

—*August 1974.* An important conference organised in Samarkand to commemorate the 1200th anniversary of Imam Ismail al-Bukhari. This conference was attended by high-ranking personalities from 27 Muslim countries, including Sheikh Mohammed Safat al-Sakkah al-Amini, Deputy Director of the Muslim World League; Sheikh Mohammed Abdurrahman Bisar, Pro-Rector of Al-Azhar University; Hasan Khalid, the Grand Mufti of Lebanon; Abdullah Gosha,

Chief *Qadi* of Jordan; Dr Awn al-Sharif Kasim, Minister of *Waqfs* of Sudan; Dr Nafih Kasim, Minister of *Waqfs* of Iraq; Dr Ibrahim Tewfik al-Takhawi, Secretary-General of the Union of Muslim Youth (whose seat is in Cairo); Mohammed Sayed Afghani, member of the Afghanistan Supreme Council for Muslim Affairs; also delegates from Bangladesh, Indonesia, Malaysia, Somalia, Pakistan, Saudi Arabia, Kuwait, Sri Lanka, North Yemen, Senegal and Bulgaria.[27]

—*October 1976.* International Congress in Tashkent to celebrate the 30th anniversary of the creation of the Muslim Spiritual Directorate of Central Asia and Kazakhstan. The Congress was attended by distinguished representatives from Syria, North Yemen, Morocco, Jordan, Tunisia, India, Pakistan and Lebanon; for example, Mohammed al-Fassi, Chairman of the Association of Islamic Universities (Morocco); Abu Bakr Hamza, Rector of the Islamic Institute of Paris; Ahmed Quftaru, Grand Mufti of Syria; Abdul Aziz Hayat, Minister of *Waqfs* of Jordan; Sheikh Ahmed Zabara, Grand Mufti of North Yemen. The final resolution of the Congress, 'an appeal to all men of good will', was a violent attack on Israel and the US.[28]

—*6–10 June 1977.* World Inter-Religious Conference for Long-Lasting Peace, Disarmament and Equitable Relations Among Nations. This conference, held in Moscow, was attended by 650 delegates from 107 countries. Ninety-eight delegates attended from 40 Muslim countries. Among the distinguished guests are several who were hailed by the Soviet media as good friends of the USSR: Dr Abdul Aziz Hayat (Jordan); Ahmed Zabara (North Yemen); Dr Imanullah Khan (Pakistan), Dr Kemal al-Sharif (Jordan); and Ahmed Quftaru (Syria).

—*3 July 1979.* International Jubilee meeting in Tashkent to celebrate the 10th anniversary of the journal *Muslims of the Soviet East.* The meeting was chaired by Ziauddin Babakhanov and attended by high-ranking delegates—some now very familiar—from several countries: Sheikh Abdul Hamid al-Saikh and Dr Abdul Aziz Hayat (now Dean of the Shariat Faculty of Amman University); Abdullah Nasir al-Shaikhli, Chief Editor of the journal *Al-Risala al-Islamiya*, Baghdad; Dr Ziya ul-Hasan al-Faruqi from India; Hamid Mardin, Deputy Chairman of the Department of Religious Affairs of Turkey; Dr Al-Tahami Nagra, Professor of Koranic Research of the Theological College and Chief Editor of the journal *Al-Hidayat*, Tunis; Mufti Hasan Khalid of Lebanon; Dr Abubakr Marimoto, Chairman of the Japanese Islamic Cultural Society; Grand Mufti Mohammed Topchiev of Bulgaria; and representatives from

Pakistan, Kuwait, Iran and Ethiopia. The final Declaration, signed by all delegates, including those from pro-Western countries, contained strong attacks on Israel, China, the US and South Africa.[29] —*September 1979*. International symposium in Dushanbe on the theme: 'The contribution of the Muslims of Central Asia, the Volga and of the Caucasus to the development of Islamic thought, to the cause of peace and social progress'. The symposium was attended by delegates from 30 countries: Sheikh Minatullah al-Rahmani, Secretary-General of Muslim Affairs, Bihar, India; Dr Shamsuddawla, chief editor of the journal *Islam and the Contemporary World*, Dacca, Bangladesh; Inamullah Khan, Secretary-General of the Muslim World League, Pakistan; Ahmed Mohammed al-Khulail, Director of the Department of Religious Affairs, Jordan; Abdul-Wahhab Hamudi, from the Ministry of Religious Affairs, Algeria; Ahmed Zabara, North Yemen; Sheikh Mustafa Kemal al-Tarzi, chief editor of the journal *Al-Hidayat*, Tunisia; Dr Mehmet Talgat Karacazmali, Ministry of Religious Affairs, Turkey; Zeinullah Minali, Afghanistan Ministry of Justice; Ali Guizade-Gafur, member of the Committee for the Preparation of the New Constitution, Iran; Dr Ibrahim Abdullah Rupeyda, Professor at Fatih University, Libya; Ahmed Abdal-Latif al-Usfur, Director of the Holy Koran Organisation, Kuwait; Zakariya Hasan, Secretary-General of the *Fetwa* Committee, Chad; Tadi Drami, Secretary-General of the Department of Religious Affairs and the Ministry of Youth and Sports, Mali; Ahmed Ould Abdallah, Ministry of Religious Affairs, Mauritania; Mufti Amin Ibrahim, Bulgaria; Aziz Pasha, Secretary-General of the Union of Muslim Organisations, Great Britain; Dr Ismail Balic, National Library of Vienna, Austria; and representatives from Saudi Arabia, South Yemen, Lebanon, Guinea, the Maldives and France. The symposium strongly denounced Israeli, American and South African imperialism.[30]

The Dushanbe conference was a great success according to the Soviet media, but it was intended as preparation for a major event: the conference of September 1980 in Tashkent to commemorate the beginning of the 15th century of the Islamic calendar, which was advertised by Soviet media as the most important postwar political meeting of the Muslim world. The latter event, however, foundered over the Soviet invasion of Afghanistan (see below).

Activities of Soviet Front, Party and Government Organisations

Existing parallel to the activities of the Soviet official Islamic establishment during the 1973–79 period were the activities of a number
of Soviet front organisations (described earlier) which, although
nominally secular, gradually assumed more prominent 'Muslim'
profiles. The three most important of these organisations were the
Afro-Asian Solidarity organisation, the Friendship Societies, and the
Peace Partisans. Also of importance were exchanges to and from the
USSR organised by the women's and youth organisations, by the
Communist Party, the Soviet Government and by the Supreme
Soviet.

As a rule, the front organisations focused more specifically on
those Muslim countries with which the Soviet had already established
relations. Soviet Muslims were usually included in the delegations
sent abroad by the front organisations, but it was not until 1978 that
Muslims actually began to lead the delegations. Foreign delegations
from Muslim countries invited by the front organisations to the
USSR usually visited Moscow and Leningrad: the visit to Tashkent or
another Muslim capital, obligatory for foreign religious delegations,
appears to have been considered unnecessary by Soviet authorities.

On the other hand, Communist Party (CP), Soviet Government
(SG) and Supreme Soviet (SS) delegations abroad were frequently
headed by Communist Party personalities of Muslim background
(see Chart 1).

Front organisation exchanges (both ways) favoured the following
countries in 1973–79: Algeria (10); Syria (8); Iraq (6); Afghanistan
(5); Libya, Palestinians, Lebanon (4 each); Ethiopia, Turkey,
Somalia, Bangladesh, South Yemen, Morocco (3 each); Niger,
Sierra-Leone, Jordan, Oman, Pakistan and Iran (2 each).

Governmental, Party and Parliamentary exchanges of delegations
focused mainly on the following countries: Iraq and Iran (9 each);
Turkey (8); Jordan (7); Algeria and Syria (6 each); Pakistan, Afghanistan, South Yemen (4 each), Egypt, Bangladesh, Guinea (3 each).

If we count all three channels—Government, front and religious—
the following 15 countries are most prominent targets (Chart 2,
p. 54).

54   *The Soviet Islamic Establishment*

CHART 1   *Soviet Delegations Abroad*

Year	Delegation	Destination	Leader
1973	CP	Iraq	Rashidov (Uzbek)
——	CP	Congo	T. Kulatov (Kazakh)
——	CP	Egypt	G. Aliev (Azeri)
——	CP	Bangladesh	K. Kamalov (Karakalpak)
——	SS	N. and S. Yemen	Tabiev (Tatar)
1974	CP	Iraq	Ponomarev (Russian) and Khalilov (Azeri)
——	CP	Bangladesh	Gafurov (Tajik)
1975	CP	India	Rashidov (Uzbek)
——	SS	India	Niyazbekov (Uzbek)
——	SS	Iran	Shitikov (Russian)
——	SS	Jordan	Machanov (Uzbek)
——	SS	Sudan	Niyazbekov (Uzbek)
1976	Trade Union	Iran	Yagizbaev (Kazakh)
1977	CP	Guinea-Bissau	Usubaliev (Kirghiz)
1978	SS	Liberia	Niyazbekov (Uzbek)
——	CP	India	G. Aliev (Azeri)
——	CP	Mozambique	Vlasov (Russian, but Chairman of Chechen-Ingush Obkom)

CHART 2   *Chief Targets of Soviet Concern*

Country	Total	Front	Government	Religious
Algeria	17	10	6	1
Iraq	16	6	9	1
Syria	16	9	6	1
Turkey	13	3	8	2
Jordan	12	2	7	3
Iran	12	2	9	1
Egypt	8	2	3	3
South Yemen	8	3	4	1
Pakistan	8	2	4	2
Libya	7	4	2	1
Saudi Arabia	7	0	0	7
Bangladesh	7	3	3	1
Somalia	6	3	2	1
Morocco	5	3	2	0
North Yemen	4	1	1	2

CONCLUSIONS

The three aspects of activity of the Soviet official Islamic establishment—travel abroad, hosting delegations from foreign Muslim countries in the USSR, and convening international conferences—plus the enhanced 'Muslimness' of front, Party and Government profiles in their dealings with Muslim states, demonstrate beyond doubt that in the 1973–79 period, a coherent and powerful Islamic strategy came into existence under Brezhnev's guidance.[31] The range and intensity of the activity leads to several conclusions. First, the Soviet official Islamic establishment through its simultaneous sending-receiving mechanism was able by 1979 to reach every corner of the Muslim world, from the most radical progressive left-wing Muslim states, such as Libya and Syria, to the most conservative-fundamentalist and anti-communist ones, such as Saudi Arabia and Iran. Moreover, through its Islamic arm the USSR was able to reconcile parties where Soviet politics would seem to be in conflict, for example Sudan and Ethiopia, and carry them along in a seeming anti-American, anti-Israeli concensus of Muslim countries.

Second, judging from the frequency with which specific representatives of different Muslim countries appear in the USSR or as hosts of Soviet muftis abroad, the Soviet Islamic strategy by 1979 was becoming increasingly successful at creating a network of 'friends', perhaps even agents of influence, in many of the Muslim countries they were courting.

Third, the activities of the Soviet official Islamic establishment received wide media coverage during this period, both in the Soviet media, which advertised important developments and news to all parts of the Muslim world in local languages by radio and printed media, and by local media in places Soviet representatives visited. While foreign media coverage was not always favourable, most appears to have been; moreover, Soviet Islamic figures themselves were directed to dispute negative reports from abroad, especially those about the conditions under which Muslims in the USSR live, suggesting that Soviet planners believe that the kind of bold mendacity typical of other Soviet propaganda exercises is not inappropriate to defend the credibility of Soviet muftis.

Fourth, and following from the above, the propaganda themes chosen by the Soviets for attention by the official Islamic establishment indicate that by 1979, the Soviet 'Islamic weapon' had been well-integrated into the larger spectrum of Soviet propaganda and disinformation efforts. As such, the activities of the Soviet muftis and of the Muslim-oriented front organisations supported to a large extent other Soviet propaganda efforts, such as the more general 'peace' campaigns and condemnation of American involvement in South Africa.

One important measure of the success of the activities of the Soviet official Islamic establishment during this period is the number of agreements—approximately 50—and in particular cultural exchange agreements, that were signed between the Islamic countries being courted by Soviet muftis and the USSR.[32] Of course, it is not clear to what extent the Soviet official Islamic establishment was responsible for the fruition of these agreements, but it is reasonable to assume that the influence of the Soviet muftis was important in most cases, critical in some. If nothing else, their activities neutralised many foreign Muslims with influence in their own political processes, convincing them to suspend judgement on the Soviet treatment of their own Muslims and on the religious *bona fides* and mixed loyalties and responsibilities of the Soviet Muslim clergy.

3 The Soviet Islamic Strategy After the Invasion of Afghanistan, 1980–86

THE TASHKENT CONFERENCE (SEPTEMBER 1980) AND ITS AFTERMATH

The Soviet invasion of Afghanistan in December 1979 caused a significant setback to the gains of the Soviet Islamic strategy of the previous decade. It is difficult to see how this could have been avoided in light of the substantial publicity that attended the invasion and the flagrantly anti-Islamic flavour the occupying authority quickly assumed. At two Islamic conferences held in Islamabad in January and May 1980, all Muslim countries, with the exception of Syria, Libya, South Yemen (and the PLO, with Algeria expressing strong reservations), condemned the Soviet act, and Ayatollah Khomeini publicly elevated the USSR to demonic supremacy over the United States, calling the Soviets 'the greatest Satan' (*Shaytan-i bozorgterin*) for the benefit of the listeners of Radio Tehran.[1]

Compounding the damage the invasion caused to the notion of the USSR as a friend of Islam, Soviet muftis were pressed into service to defend the act in terms that were at once pleading and ingenuous. Their plea was for the Muslims of the world, and particularly the Arabs, to remember the debt they owed to the USSR's Muslims for standing by them in 1967 and 1973.[2] The plea is noteworthy because it was made directly on behalf of Soviet Muslims, and not on behalf of the USSR and its political leaders, and it assumed a perception of Soviet support which was closer to reality: the Soviets had not stood firmly by the Arabs in either conflict. Even at this late date, Soviet leaders presumably believed that their investment in an Islamic strategy could be salvaged by divorcing it from both Russian power politics and the notion of advancing communism.

Moreover, the muftis' slavish repetition of Soviet propaganda about the invasion—that 'foreign imperial powers' were interfering in Afghan affairs—was demonstrably false, and most foreign Muslims knew it.[3] We may assume that the Soviet leadership also understood this and took a calculated risk to harness the Soviet official Islamic establishment and the credibility it had acquired directly to a political issue in which the USSR had an immediate stake: that is, to allow them to leap from an abstract condemnation of 'foreign imperialism' to the concrete complaint that 'foreign imperialists' were killing Soviet soldiers. Most Muslims knew that the only people killing Soviet soldiers were fellow Muslims, and so the muftis' credibility suffered. The muftis had stepped over the fine line between political involvement and partisan political advocacy; their image of being 'more Muslim than Soviet' suffered accordingly.

The muftis' denunciation of 'foreign imperialist intervention' and their defence of Soviet policy abroad was linked to the preparation of the Tashkent conference celebrating the beginning of the 15th century of the Hejira. As noted earlier, this meeting was intended to be 'the most important post-war meeting of the Muslim world'. Many preliminary announcements indicated that the conference was intended to be the focal point of a massive anti-imperialist campaign, whose aim undoubtedly was to deflect attention from Soviet involvement in Afghanistan by pointing the finger at others. For example, when the four Soviet muftis met in Moscow in late January 1980 to discuss the conference they issued a common declaration against 'US imperialists, Israeli Zionists, the traitor Sadat and Chinese hegemonists' meddling in Afghan affairs.[4]

Two other lines were developed simultaneously. The first extolled the contribution of Soviet Muslims to the Islamic heritage.[5] A permanent exhibition of 'Islam in the USSR' was announced, as was the publication of a new book, *The Life of Soviet Muslims*.[6] The second line was advanced in parallel with the efforts of the official Islamic establishment. This was a clever attempt to interpret events in Afghanistan and Soviet involvement in them as the logical joining of revolutionary-democratic forces and Islamic ones into a workable alliance. Revolutions in Algeria, Syria, South Yemen and Afghanistan were cited as good examples of this political-religious synthesis.[7]

This three-track propaganda effort was intended to show the Muslim world abroad that, as a Muslim country itself, the USSR could not be an imperialist aggressor. The spectacular failure of the Tashkent Conference in September 1980, however, demonstrated that the Muslim world would not accept Soviet propaganda at face value, even if it came from respected Soviet Muslim personalities.

All Muslim countries were invited to send delegations to Tashkent; invitations were sent to more than 500 important Muslim dignitaries, but only 76 attended the conference.[8] Twenty-five Muslim countries, among them the most important, refused to attend in protest against the invasion of Afghanistan: Saudi Arabia, Iran, the Gulf States, Egypt, Indonesia, India, Tunisia, Morocco, Mauritania, Iraq, Bahrain, Oman, Cameroon, Djibouti, Gabon, Gambia, Guinea-Bissau, Malaysia, Upper Volta, Chad, Qatar, the Maldives, Nigeria, Somalia and Comoros. Of the 33 counries represented in Tashkent, seven were non-Muslim. Austria, DDR, Mongolia, Finland, France, Japan and Switzerland. Five communist countries with Muslim minorities did not attend: China, Yugoslavia, Albania, Roumania and Poland.

Pakistan, Guinea, Bangladesh, Benin, Tanzania, Lebanon and Algeria were represented only by journalists. Only 14 Muslim or partly Muslim countries were represented by officials of ministerial or religious rank: Ghana, Jordan, North Yemen, Cyprus, Kuwait, Libya, Mauritius, Mali, Senegal, Syria, Sudan, Togo, Turkey, Uganda and Sri Lanka. It cannot be ignored that most of these countries were conspicuous targets of the Soviet Islamic strategy for the previous decade.

Some delegations, particularly the Sudanese,[9] adopted markedly anti-Soviet attitudes throughout the proceedings. The Soviet muftis attempted to force a final declaration on the assembly but it was not accepted, and no final communiqué was published. Most foreign Muslims were requested to leave the USSR without delay. The regular Soviet press gave no explanation of these events, and *Muslims of the Soviet East* offered only restrained comments, including a few favourable reports from delegates: again those who had been the objects of considerable attention by the Soviet Islamic establishment for some years earlier.[10] Thus even in a moment of disaster, the Soviet Islamic strategy paid a few dividends.

RE-TUNING THE ISLAMIC STRATEGY: NEW FACES, OLD TARGETS

The spectacular failure of the Tashkent conference marked a turning point for Moscow's Islamic strategy. For nearly two years the Soviets, including Soviet muftis, were forced to adopt a low profile in the Muslim world abroad. The Soviets resumed a more vigorous Islamic strategy in late 1982. In the meantime, Soviet authorities re-evaluated their Islamic weapon in light of Soviet involvement in Afghanistan and made a number of significant changes.

First, they ordered a complete change in the upper levels of the Islamic hierarchy. Either just before the Tashkent conference or immediately after it, a new generation of head muftis was put in place and the old cadre retired. The new Muslim clerics are better trained than their predecessors, albeit having been raised within the confines of Soviet Islamic politics; hence, there is every reason to suspect that they are more loyal to Soviet political objectives than had been the case with the earlier generation. They are all good *apparatchiki* and belong to the Soviet *nomenklatura*.

The new muftis are Talgat Tajeddin (Taziev), a Tatar, who replaced Abdul Bari Isaev as Mufti of Ufa in July 1980; Mahmud Gekkiev, a Balkar, who replaced Abdul Hafiz Omarov as Mufti of Makhach-Qala in November 1978; the Shia Sheikh ul-Islam Allah Shukur Pasha Zade, an Azeri, who replaced Mir Kazanfar Akbaroglu in Baku in July 1980; and Shamsuddin Babakhanov, an Uzbek, who replaced his father, Ziauddin Babakhanov, in the pre-eminent post of Mufti of Tashkent in October 1982. The average age of the four new muftis at the time of their inception was 35, nearly 30 years younger than the average age of their predecessors, which demonstrates a conscientious decision by the Soviet authorities to opt for youth. All four had received advanced religious training abroad (Cairo, Libya, Morocco, Syria and Jordan) and secular training in the USSR's universities. They know the Muslim world well and they are capable in many foreign languages. Thus, despite their stronger ties to Soviet political aims, they are probably better accepted by foreign Muslims because of their more classical training and broader Muslim world perspectives.

Second, after the fiasco in Tashkent the Soviet authorities significantly reduced the amount of public exposure of their own Muslim population to foreign Muslim scrutiny. In part, this tactical retreat was the result of the escalating war in Afghanistan and the negative impact of the involvement on Soviet Muslims themselves; in short, when they became an unreliable strategic asset, Soviet Muslims ceased to be an attractive public relations commodity. Between 1980 and 1986 no international Islamic conferences were organised in the USSR. Invitations to foreign Muslims were extended only rarely and selectively. Instead, the new young Soviet muftis were used extensively abroad, more frequently and more systematically.

Third, after 1980, the Soviet authorities moved to create a kind of symbiosis between the Islamic establishment and the political front organisations. This symbiosis is symbolised by the selection of Ziauddin Babakhanov to become one of the leading personalities in the Uzbek Society of Friendship and Cultural Relations with Foreign Countries in March 1981.[11] Two of his deputies, A. Abdullaev and Y. Shakirov, were elected members of the Society's Uzbek-Arab branch at the same time. This change significantly enhanced the possibilities for more frequent access by the muftis to the world abroad. The Uzbek Society maintains contacts with 120 countries.

From 1982, Soviet Muslim leaders could be found participating, often as leading figures, at most international and domestic meetings of the various political front organisations, especially Afro-Asian Solidarity, the Peace Partisans, and the Friendship Societies. Thus, for example, we find several members of the Tashkent Spiritual Directorate participating actively at the Seventh Conference of Asian and African Writers in Tashkent, which ended with foreign delegates joining Mufti Shamsuddin Babakhanov in a public prayer at the Tilla Sheikh mosque[12]; and the election, in January 1985, of Shamsuddin Babakhanov to the Presidium of the Peace Partisans of Uzbekistan.[13] Examples of this kind of Islamic/political-front-organisation symbiosis are numerous.[14]

One should not minimise the importance of this development in as much as it is the muftis' presence which gives the front organisations authentic Islamic rspectability and, therefore, makes them acceptable to foreign Muslims. After 1982 it becomes more difficult to distinguish the purely religious activities of either type of group from the purely secular ones; indeed, they begin to overlap almost to the point of changing roles: the muftis increasingly talk about revolution and the anti-imperialist struggle, while the front organisations—that is, the operating arms of the KGB—talk religion.

SOVIET MUFTIS ON THE ROAD AGAIN

Soviet muftis did in fact continue to participate in purely religious activities, but at a much reduced level from the 1973–79 period. Several things are noticeable about these appearances. First, at least in the immediate post-invasion period, Soviet muftis participated in meetings that for the most part were broadly religious instead of specifically Islamic, such as the Congress of the World Council of Churches in Vancouver (July-August, 1983).[15] Second, Tashkent was avoided as the venue for major Islamic gatherings until after 1982. Thus we find a conference of religious leaders of all creeds 'For the Defense of Peace', attended by 600 delegates from 90 countries, for which in pre-invasion days Tashkent would have been a natural location for the entire, or at least sub-gatherings of the conference. Instead, the entire affair was held in Moscow.[16]

Until late 1981 the muftis were restrained in their attacks on the various imperialisms,[17] which had been their daily fare until late 1979, probably in anticipation of a much stronger reaction from abroad to the invasion of Afghanistan. In 1980, Soviet religious delegations abroad were relatively few, and Soviet muftis received distinctly cool receptions in a number of cases, especially in the conservative Gulf states.[18] On the other hand, they continued to be well received in states which had been their special targets before the invasion of Afghanistan, for example Jordan, North Yemen and, less surprisingly, Syria.[19] In 1981, if we exclude the frequent visits of Soviet *ulema* to Afghanistan, we can find only one Soviet delegation visiting abroad: 13–16 November, a small group of Soviet *ulema* headed by Mahmud Gekkiev, the Mufti of Makhach-Qala, to Benin.[20]

This hesitant behaviour ended abruptly in 1982. Having expected a strong reaction to the Soviet invasion of Afghanistan and then realising that the reaction—both from the Western or Islamic worlds—was not sustained, Soviet leaders probably decided that the time was opportune to put their muftis back on the road. The scale and the nature of the muftis' travels after 1982, and especially in the 1983–84 period, suggest that Soviet authorities never believed that the wound inflicted on their Islamic strategy by the debacle of the Tashkent conference was terminal or even debilitating for more than a short period. Clearly a good deal of planning had gone on during the period of inactivity. For example, we can identify a number of innovations and revisions to earlier practices.

First, after 1981, Soviet muftis began to figure regularly in Soviet delegations to all important religious or political meetings, for example to Vancouver and Prague in 1983, and even to commercial exhibitions (Casablanca).

Second, after 1981, all four Soviet muftis and their deputies began to assume active roles in exporting the Soviet message abroad. Prior to this the pre-eminent role had been played by the Mufti of Tashkent and his deputies. The new and younger muftis representing the other Muslim regions of the USSR undoubtedly had been chosen with a view toward expanding the propaganda outreach of the Soviet's Islamic arm.

Third, since 1981, the Soviet muftis have included more non-Muslim or partly Muslim countries on their itineraries. Their intent seems to be to sell the USSR as a 'friend of the Third World', rather than their concern with exclusively Islamic matters. Thus, for example, we find Soviet muftis in the United States (1982), Bulgaria (1982), Ethiopia (1983), Mozambique (1983), Finland (1983), as well as in Spain, France and other non-or less specifically Muslim states.

Fourth, there seems to have been a good deal of attention paid to the qualitative aspects of Soviet mufti outreach: the importance of the delegation, the character of their reception abroad, and so forth. Four countries became special targets: Jordan, Kuwait, North Yemen and Saudi Arabia. These countries, which had been special targets of the Soviet muftis before the invasion of Afghanistan, quickly drew back from estrangement from the Soviets because of the invasion, and by mid–1982 it is possible to discern in each country the resurgence of a network of Soviet 'friends' who smoothed the Soviet. muftis' post–1982 reappearance. These countries, especially the first three, have no organised fundamentalist radical groups hostile to the Soviets, as in Egypt, Algeria or Syria, or left wing political parties or groups, as in Morocco, which the Soviets could approach through other channels, such as the various front organisations. Therefore, it is not difficult to understand the importance to the Soviets of the Islamic channel as a penetration instrument for these societies, or the strong emphasis Soviet authorities put on good Islamic relations between them and the Soviet muftis.

From 1982 to 1985 21 Muslim countries were visited by 35 Soviet Muslim delegations. The main effort was aimed at the conservative, pro-Western countries of the Arab Middle East (13 visits): Saudi Arabia (4); Jordan (3); North Yemen (2); Kuwait (2); Egypt (1); Syria (1). North Africa—five visits—was a secondary target: Tunisia (2); Morocco (2); Algeria (1); followed by Black Africa: Ghana (2); Benin, Mali and Upper Volta (1 each).[21]

FOREIGN MUSLIM DELEGATIONS TO THE USSR IN THE POST-INVASION PERIOD

In the immediate post-invasion period (1980–81), the pattern of invitations to foreign Muslim delegations followed closely the pattern of Soviet muftis' visits abroad. Those Muslims invited were chosen largely from friendly countries: Libya, Afghanistan, South Yemen and Syria. Some especially 'close friends' of the Soviet muftis, such as Ahmad Zabara, the Grand Mufti of North Yemen, also received invitations.[22]

During these two years, religious relations with Afghanistan became especially intense. *Muslims of the Soviet East* and Soviet broadcasts gave the maximum coverage to the innumerable delegations of Afghan mullahs touring Soviet Central Asia. These visits did little to enhance the credibility of the Afghan clerics in their own country; in fact, a number of them were later assassinated by the Afghan mujahideen. Nor is it likely that visits by Soviet muftis to Afghanistan enhanced the credibility of the Babrak Karmal regime. Many Afghans, and most resistance figures, looked on them simply as another kind of KGB agent.

One important exception to this general pattern of activity was the Soviet attempt to use its official Islamic establishment to initiate relations with the new regime in Iran. In 1981 two Iranian delegations visited the USSR. The first, in February, were representatives of the Iranian Revolutionary Organisation, headed by Jelaleddin Farsi, a member of the Supreme Council of the Cultural Revolution Organisation. The delegation visited Moscow, where it was given red-carpet treatment and received by Kuznetsov, Deputy-Chairman of the Supreme Soviet, and by the Soviet-Afro-Asian Solidarity Committee. The delegation also visited Tashkent, where they were received by the mufti, participated in public prayers and had an audience with Osman Khojaev, Chairman of the Supreme Soviet of the Uzbek SSR. During talks with Uzbek leaders, J. Farsi strongly attacked the Soviets for invading Afghanistan.[23] He was answered by E. Ivanov, Vice-Chairman of the Soviet Friendship Societies.[24] A second Iranian visit occurred in June, when a group of Iranian religious personalities, led by Ayatollah Khalkhali Sadegh, visited Moscow, Leningrad, Baku, Tashkent and Samarkand at the invitation of the Sheikh ul-Islam (Shia) of Baku. To our knowledge, this is the first time an invitation had been extended by the Baku organisation.[25]

In 1982, unlike the accelerated campaign to send Soviet muftis abroad, only three Muslim countries—not counting Afghanistan—sent delegations to the USSR: Tunisia, Benin and Nigeria. In 1983, this pattern continued, with only a handful of Muslim countries sending delegations (again, Afghanistan excepted). In 1984–85, however, the number of delegations to the USSR increased dramatically; moreover, all four branches of the Soviet Islamic establishment (Tashkent, Ufa, Makhach-Qala, and Baku) became active hosts.

As was the case somewhat earlier of the Soviet muftis travelling abroad, the role of the official Islamic establishment as host changed in the direction of greater overlap between its religious and political tasks. Thus, for example, we find many more non-Muslim delegations—including one from the Vatican—being entertained by the four Soviet Muslim centres than previously had been the case. There can be little doubt now that part of the therapy administered by the Soviet leadership to its Islamic establishment to cure it of the malaise caused by the invasion of Afghanistan was to redefine and refine its profile as a more integral part of Soviet political machinery. The Soviet muftis and their deputies have come to appear more as fully-fledged, trusted and efficient partners of the Soviet secular authorities and of many of the secular organisations, such as the various front organisations targetted on the Muslim world.[26] They play with great skill the role of middlemen between the USSR and the world of Islam—a task which the secular fronts would find very difficult or impossible.

4 Conclusions

This study has attempted to demonstrate four things. First, the Soviets have the capability to use their Islamic establishment in different contexts and in combination with other Soviet political-propaganda organisations to influence the policies of many states of the Islamic world and to create a psychological climate which is at best favourable to Soviet strategic objectives or, less immediate but no less important, neutral in respect to the expansion of Soviet power and influence.

Second, the scale of this Soviet effort—of the 'Islamic weapon'—is far greater than is generally known or acknowledged. The activities of the Soviet Islamic establishment are more intensive and extensive than is assumed. A network of Muslim 'friends' of the USSR—usually respected individuals in their own countries—now covers the entire Muslim world, including the pro-Western countries (Morocco, Kuwait, Jordan, Saudi Arabia, North Yemen), as well as the pro-Soviet ones (Syria, Libya, Algeria, South Yemen).

Third, since the beginning of the Brezhnev era the Soviet Islamic channel has steadily acquired sophistication in planning and operation. While Soviet efforts in this regard suffer occasional setbacks, as they did as a result of their invasion of Afghanistan, since the late 1960s the net result of the extensive labours of the corps of Soviet muftis and their staffs has been highly beneficial to Soviet objectives.

Fourth, although Soviet spokesmen might argue that it is perfectly natural for the USSR to have good relations with Muslim states and to employ Soviet Muslims to consolidate them, in light of the evidence it is hard to explain this Soviet preoccupation as other than a critical strategic concern. As we noted earlier, the scale of involvement of the muftis and their staffs in all of their different capacities—as travelling salesmen, gracious hosts, conference organisers and high-visibility personalities in non-religious organisations—proves that the Soviet leadership has identified their activities as a high political priority and allocates significant funds to it.

Soviet hostility to Islam in the USSR testifies to the paradoxical nature of this interest and underlines its political basis. The targeting of Soviet muftis on Muslim regions which Soviet authorities clearly view as contestable and/or penetrable and in which they see US interests as vulnerable, again, demonstrates the political intent behind the Islamic strategy. There is nothing even-handed in Soviet overtures toward different Muslim countries which might be explained as a general interest in and concern for the larger community of Muslim believers. Why, for example, has the Soviet leadership focused the attention of its Islamic establishment on the vital Middle Eastern, Persian Gulf and African Arab states and virtually ignored Indonesia, the most populous Muslim country in the world? The answer, we would argue, has to do with strategic priorities.

The Soviet Islamic strategy has a number of objectives. The main one is to portray the USSR as a Muslim country which is prepared to act in concert on vital issues—especially Arab-Israeli issues—with the Muslim world. Logically, the ultimate objective of this approach is to penetrate Saudi Arabia. If Soviet muftis can gain in Mecca the same privileged position they already enjoy in Syria, Jordan, North Yemen, Algeria or Kuwait, they will have moved far in the direction of being able to influence the thinking and politics of the Muslim world from its very centre. At the very least, Western influence would be severely curtailed, if not eliminated, in this scenario.

Other objectives are more flexible and short-term. They include recreating a favourable image of the USSR in the Muslim world following Soviet diplomatic blunders or political setbacks; to give a religious colouring to the activities of various front organisations in which Soviet Muslims participate; and to cultivate a large network of reliable 'friends'—a kind of 'Muslim lobby'—in the Muslim world abroad, in contrast to a 'Russian' or 'communist' lobby. In some Muslim countries, Soviet muftis operate with an historic advantage. Many Arabs, particularly Syrians, Lebanese and Palestinians, have a long tradition of good relations with Russia. Unlike the Turks or Iranians, they have never experienced Russian invasion or felt threatened by Russian/Soviet imperialism.

In the last objective the Soviet muftis have clearly been successful, as their rapid recovery from the embarrassment of the invasion of Afghanistan demonstrates. These foreign 'friends' of the Soviet muftis, who may be implacably hostile to communism, have usually visited the USSR several times and have hosted the Soviet muftis in their own countries. It would be wrong to conclude that all have been brain-washed by the Soviets or that they are on the KGB's payroll. Their motives are certainly complex and in many cases even honourable. We have spoken to a number who clearly believe that by abstaining from criticism of the Soviet record on Islam in the

Soviet Russian Empire or of the Soviet killing of Afghan Muslims they are protecting the future of Islam in the USSR. Still, a common characteristic is the 'friends,' willingness to identify the future of Soviet Islam with the power of the Soviet state and the success of the Soviet Government. They may have exaggerated notions of the Soviet Islamic establishment's independence *vis-à-vis* Moscow and a badly distorted view of the freedoms and rights of Soviet Muslims generally. We would note, however, that one of the objectives of the Soviet muftis' activities as hosts at home and salesmen abroad is to create exactly this impression.

Soviet Muslim leaders, especially the new generation, are eager to co-operate sincerely with Soviet authorities. All were born under the Soviet regime—they are in this sense 'Soviet men'—and loyal citizens, even if they are not necessarily enthusiastic Soviet patriots. Their decision to co-operate with the Soviet regime does not represent treason against Islam, although it is probable that some representatives of the Soviet Islamic establishment are *bona fide* KGB agents who profess a commitment to Islam in order to use it for Soviet political objectives. The infiltration by Soviet intelligence organisations of their own religious establishments, whether orthodox or Islamic, is a well-established practice.

Most Soviet muftis and their subordinates, however, probably seek to establish a working relationship with the Soviet regime for the benefit of Islam; indeed, this kind of co-operation is an old tradition among Muslim leaders in the Russian empire. Pre-Soviet Russian governments rejected co-operative arrangements with the Muslims of the empire, an offer that Brezhnev eventually accepted, however cautiously. Soviet Muslim leaders probably seek such an agreement, among other reasons, to give themselves a certain measure of protection against Soviet offensives against Islam in the USSR.

In the short term, the Soviet Islamic strategy and use of the official Soviet Islamic establishment as a principal operational tool can founder over acts of aggression that the larger Muslim world finds it impossible to ignore. The Soviet invasion of Afghanistan was one such act. It must be noted, however, that Soviet Islamic strategy was not side-tracked for long. In the absence of any concerted and sustained opposition to Soviet political-military activities in the Muslim world from Muslims themselves, we can expect the Soviet Islamic strategy to adjust rapidly and to resume its operations in every direction possible.

Few things could demonstrate better both the lack of cohesiveness among Muslim states when one of their members is faced with Soviet aggression *and* the Soviet Islamic strategy's ability to recover rapidly from setbacks, such as the Tashkent conference in 1980, than apparently successful recent Soviet efforts to reassert the USSR's position as a Muslim power. In April 1986, for example, the Soviet Muslim establishment hosted a 14-day visit of a delegation from the World Muslim League. Then, in October of the same year, with very litle advance publicity, the Soviets hosted a three-day international Islamic conference in Baku with the title of 'Muslims in the Fight for Peace', the first such Islamic conference since the disaster of Tashkent in 1980. This conference marks the nearly complete reversal of the Soviet Union's highly unfavourable position among Muslim states after Tashkent in 1980. According to one source, possibly a participant, the conference included '850 delegates from 60 Asian, African, European and American countries', and 'focused on the theme of peace and Islam'. Muslim delegates were urged to 'strive to stop nuclear war', heip 'stop the arms race', and support 'a moratorium on nuclear testing'. 'The conference also called for an end to the Iran-Iraq war and expressed solidarity with Muslim countries in struggles against imperialism, Zionism, racism and apartheid . . . The delegates passed a verdict saying that the Soviet Union is a natural ally of the Muslim people in their struggle for emancipation from feudalism, capitalism, poverty and ignorance. They also urged the Muslim people to follow the Soviet model to eradicate all social and political evils.' Significantly, no one raised a protest against the Soviet occupation of Afghanistan. 'On the contrary they were told by Russian hosts that the present Afghanistan regime was committed to Islam and that Russian troops were there to help Muslims to preserve their Islamic identity. Most delegates took the Russian words for granted as they were there by Russian invitation and at the Soviet government's expense.' The observer noted that the delegates had one thing in common: 'They were all either ex-Marxists or sympathisers with communist parties or socialists. Those without any political allegiances were active in organisations that act as front organisations for either the communist parties or Soviet embassies.'[1] Soviet media insisted that the participants were a sober group of 'religious dignitaries, statesmen and theologians . . . and representatives of many international and Muslim organisations.' They included 'twelve supreme muftis, fourteen ministers of waqfs . . . and thirteen judges of sharia courts'. Major Islamic States, such as Bangladesh, Egypt, India, Iran,

Pakistan and Saudi Arabia were represented.[2] Thus it would seem that the damage wrought at Tashkent in 1980 is repaired, that the Soviet network of Muslim friends is stronger than ever, and that the Soviet Islamic strategy is geared up for new and more extensive activities. The choice of Baku for this conference is in itself revealing. It demonstrates, as we noted earlier, the importance the Soviets now attach to engaging all of their Islamic assets and venues in the struggle for short- and long-term objectives in the Islamic world.

In the longer term, the Soviet authorities in charge of the conduct of the Islamic strategy must seek to minimise public awareness of the huge gap which separates Soviet professions of support for the concerns of the Muslim world abroad from Soviet treatment of its own Muslims at home. This is a potential minefield for Soviet objectives among Islamic states. If the Muslim world became fully aware of the extent of Soviet oppression of Soviet Muslims, Soviet leaders, and particularly Soviet muftis, would find it considerably more difficult to sell their pro-Soviet progaganda lines and to create a network of reliable 'friends' abroad. In our estimate, many parts of the Muslim world remain largely totally ignorant of the real state of Soviet Islam, although in recent years, especially since the 'full flowering of *glasnost*' under Mikhail Gorbachev, more has been known.

Finally, the Soviet Islamic strategy succeeds in large measure because US interests in the Muslim world are, in the view of many Muslims, inextricably bound to support for Israel. Unquestionably there has been some moderation in recent years of the rigid anti-Americanism of some Muslim leaders, particularly Arabs. But the problem persists, and there is little evidence—indeed, the evidence could be interpreted to buttress the opposite conclusion—to suggest that this moderation has anywhere infected the Muslim masses. Soviet Islamic tacticians have a great stake in undermining any change in this situation.

American policy would undoubtedly benefit from treating the Muslim world in its broader outlines, rather than approaching the subject as a patchwork of separate political-military problems. There are both regional issues and Muslim issues. As the Soviets continue to demonstrate, policies and instruments intended to deal with each do not have to be in conflict: they can frequently work in concert. Moreover, the Soviets have learned that where policy conflict does exist, thoughtful treatment of Islamic issues can still produce positive results.

Those American policies which stress the positive commitment of the US to the welfare of millions of Muslims have not been well advertised. This is probably the result of American policy-makers' preoccupation with Arab-Israeli issues and their failure to see the opportunities for a broader and more responsive policy toward the rest of the Muslim world. The most elementary facts about the world of Islam bear repeating in this regard: most Muslims live far from the Arab Middle East, and many have only a passing interest in the Arab-Israeli conflict, despite their occasional ritual condemnations of US involvement. An objective of American policy, therefore, should be to develop its own Islamic strategy based on an appreciation of the larger Islamic world and the opportunities that positive engagement could create. In addition to putting US policy toward the Muslim world on a more productive footing, few things would do more to render the efforts of the Soviet Islamic strategy less effective.

Part II
Flexible Opportunism

Three Essays Examining Soviet Strategy in
Egypt, the Nile Valley, the Horn of Africa and
the Arabian Peninsula

5 Introduction

The purpose of the three essays which follow is not merely to recapitulate the history of relations between the USSR and the countries under examination. These essays are intended to serve broader purposes:

> to examine the evolution of Soviet strategy and tactics as they have been applied to important Islamic countries over time;
> to see how the Soviet approach has been adjusted in response to both unanticipated problems and unexpected opportunities;
> to demonstrate the kinds of response Soviet initiatives have generated in target countries and groups.

Naturally, a primary concern has been the religious factor. Another major interest has been feedback, both on the Soviet side and in the countries which have been the object of Soviet attention. Interactions between countries and the regional impact of Soviet activities have also been stressed.

There is a sizable body of academic research and reflective journalism on Soviet policy toward, and operations in, some of these countries, especially Egypt. In respect to others, comprehensive studies are absent. Memoirs, such as those of Mohammad Heikal, are unusally valuable for the insights they provide into both sides' views of each other, but they are rare. We have tried to take much of the available specialised literature into account, as footnotes demonstrate, but these essays are not intended to be surveys of scholarly literature. They attempt, in fact, to go beyond much of the scholarly production by considering facets of the Soviet approach which are often neglected. These include the relationships between the various levels at which Soviet policy operates: the diplomatic, the propagandistic and the clandestine.

This last area is often neglected by scholars because there is so little hard information that meets conventional scholarly criteria. I have drawn on defector memoirs, among other sources, to try to give a total impression of the Soviet presence and impact on a country or region. In writing about American strategy and operations in key regions of the world, scholars and journalists often concentrate on differences in perception and aims of various components of government as well as private interests of various kinds and frequently overstress the clandestine aspect. In respect to the USSR, all too often they do the opposite. There are no private interests as such in the Soviet Union, but there are certainly differences among the various elements of the official power structure. The Soviet press does not report on them and Soviet scholars to not probe into them. As a result, too many Western researchers take lack of evidence as proof of absence of rivalry and controversy or, to put it more simply, absence of differences in perspective and perception of interests. Common sense dictates that such must exist. I have tried to allow for these factors in some of my analysis.

I have included Libya in the Nile Valley/Horn of Africa essay because the full impact of Soviet activities in this region and the interactions between the countries composing it are less understandable if Libya is not taken into acount. Likewise I have had to include Ethiopia as an integral—in fact, crucial—part of the Nile Valley/Horn survey though it is not primarily an Islamic country. In this region, however, we see another important principle of Soviet strategy being applied: the regional approach. Ethiopia and Egypt are the two most important countries in the Nile Valley/Horn area. Although the Russians sometimes neglect specific lessons of history, including their own, their overall strategic approach is almost always based on a much more comprehensive and conscious historical assessment than American policy has been. They take a long view of both their strategic interests and opportunities available to them for causing history to flow in the direction they desire. Among other things, this means that they are much less constrained by existing boundaries than American policy-makers and American scholars usually are.

Boundaries throughout the entire region dealt with in these essays are recent and fluid. This is true even of the oldest states of the area, Egypt and Ethiopia. Arab leaders' aspirations have almost always extended beyond the boundaries of the particular states where they happen to exercise political power. Quarrels over coveted regions, whatever they appear to be on the surface, often encompass far more than issues of territory. The Soviet conception of strategy includes an almost automatic awareness of the transcendence of current boundaries and the importance of other elements in determining the aspirations of leaders eager for power. American policy-makers, on the other hand, have a tendency to ignore history and deal with each existing state as a discrete and immutable unit. While it is true that recent boundary changes even in this region of great historical fluidity have been few and far between, the interplay of political forces that transcend boundaries has been great and is likely to remain so.

This factor has been important for an aspect of Soviet strategy and tactics which I have already stressed: covert and clandestine operations of many kinds. The subversive end of the Soviet operational spectrum is too often downgraded—or neglected entirely— because it is inherently less easy to deal with than routine diplomacy, overt propaganda operations, military and economic aid and cultural exchange activities. Excessive American concern in recent years with drawing sharp, bright lines around covert operations and treating them as a separate aspect of policy has contributed to forgetfulness about the fact that the Russians have never acknowledged or observed such distinctions and never accept imposition of them in practice. All their activities form part of a continuum that often reflects both short- and long-range objectives. Furthermore, the total absence of legislative review and of media and other forms of public scrutiny in the USSR means that in Soviet policy contradictory initiatives can be pursued simultaneously. Two, three or more opposition groups may be supported so that whoever wins out, the Russians will have entrée, and their beneficiaries obligations to them. Strategies which are in conflict on a short-term basis may each get a certain measure of support to ensure long-term advantage.

I have underscored several instances of this kind of flexible opportunism in these essays. Where the West too often permits itself to be confronted with 'either/or' choices (both of which may be unpalatable), the natural Soviet inclination is toward 'both/and'. This does not mean that the Soviets expend resources wisely, of course. On the strategic level, they can probably be shown to have spent much more, and gained much less, than the West.

The memoirs of Soviet intelligence defectors from the earliest period of the existence of the USSR—Agabekov's account of activities in the Middle East in the 1920s, for example—demonstrate the principle of regionally diversified covert operations which has remained important and has been greatly refined in recent years. Operatives of OGPU (the Special State Political Administration, later renamed the CHEKA, predecessor of the KGB) in the 1920s knew that countries would be much less sensitive about operations carried out from their territory against other countries than they would about operations with direct, domestic impact. Thus the Yemens and Kuwait have served Soviet purposes well in this respect.

Libya still and Egypt in the heyday of the Soviet relationship have also served Soviet interests in many ways that had little to do with specific Soviet objectives in the countries themselves. Soviet policies pursued abroad may also be in direct contradiction to Soviet domestic policies. This has almost always been the case in respect to religion. Over and over again the Soviets have worked to impress officials of Islamic countries with the alleged freedom Islam enjoys in the USSR and to propagandise people about the material and social advantages which the Soviet Muslim peoples enjoy. The results have been mixed, but the Soviets have persisted nevertheless, making increasing use of Soviet Muslims to deliver the message.

The purpose of these three essays is less to seek definitive judgements than to encourage more detailed study and informed debate about Soviet activities directed at Islamic countries, to establish criteria for judging their future course of development and ways in which the basic interests of the Islamic countries themselves as well as constructive Western relations with the Muslim world can be protected in face of them.

6 The Russians in Egypt: Key to the Arab World

Turkey, Iran, Afghanistan and India, the USSR's direct southern neighbours, were major areas of concern from the early days of the Bolshevik revolution. The Arab world was distant and of only marginal interest. When the Soviets began developing an active Arab policy at the end of World War II, it was motivated by a determination to leap over the *cordon sanitaire* that the states immediately south of their border formed, for crude Soviet interference in both Turkey and Iran left both counties firmly on the side of the West in the wake of World War II, and the partition of India brought the bulk of Indian Muslims into Pakistan, a state based on religion. It was initially judged negatively by Moscow and dismissed as a neo-colonial creation of the Western alliance.

What scanty evidence there is of awareness on Lenin's part of the Arabs has had to be embroidered elaborately to make a case for Leninist roots of Soviet Arab policy.[1] The Comintern was active in the Arab World in the 1920s but had difficulty finding Arab recruits. Jews, Greeks, Copts, Lebanese Christians, Armenians—all ethnic and religious minorities—were prominent in the small communist parties that were organised in Arab areas. The Chairman of the illegal Communist Party of Palestine, Haim Auerbach, complained in 1927:

> We were the only Communist front in the Arab orient and in the absence of anybody else we had to attend to every question. All the duties in relation to the revolution fell on our shoulders. We had to look into matters relating to Syria, Egypt and Islamic congresses in Cairo, Mecca and elsewhere.[2]

The Egyptian Communist Party was founded in Alexandria in 1921 with a central committee composed of a Jew, a Lebanese and an Egyptian Arab intellectual. It was accepted into the Comintern the following year. Egypt was granted substantial internal political autonomy by Britain at this time. The communists supported the nationalist movement led by Sa'ad Zaghlul with Stalin's blessing. Stalin wrote in 1924:

The struggle of the Egyptian merchants and bourgeois intelligentsia for the independence of Egypt is an objectively *revolutionary* struggle in spite of the bourgeois origin and bourgeois status of the leaders of the Egyptian national movement, in spite of the fact that they are against socialism.[3]

Zaghlul as prime minister had already cracked down on the party following a workers' strike and imprisoned its central committee. Thereafter Egyptian communists had little political influence. They were regarded as foreign and outside the nationalist mainstream. Leftist political activity in Egypt continued to be monitored closely by the British. In their own small world, Egyptian and other Middle Eastern communists quarrelled over Trotskyist deviations and other doctrinal problems.[4]

In the late 1930s a young, wealthy Jewish member of a predominantly Coptic Trotskyist faction in Cairo, Henry Curiel, opened a Marxist library which during World War II became for all practical purposes the headquarters of the communist movement in Egypt. Moscow had accorded little importance to quarrelsome Middle Eastern communists since the mid–1920s, but they were now encouraged to become more active and develop a broader base in their societies in anticipation of the varied purposes they might serve for the Soviets in a time of increasing international tension. Foreign members of the Egyptian communist movement were instructed to recruit native-born Egyptians. Nevertheless, the first three such recruits were all Jews—but they 'decided it would be tactically better for them to become Muslims and accordingly effected the change'.[5]

The Nazi-Soviet Pact caused a good deal of confusion—as it did among communists everywhere—but the German invasion of Russia cleared the air. The British occupation authorities in Egypt relaxed their vigilance over left-wing groups. They even enlisted some communist groups to help spread anti-Nazi propaganda. Allied troops stationed in Egypt included pro-Marxist elements. Henry Curiel set up an organisation called the Egyptian Movement for National Liberty which was more nationalistic than most of the other leftist groups, and more grass roots-oriented. It concentrated on Nubians and Sudanese students instead of urban intellectuals. Can we see in this the outlines of a sophisticated long-range Soviet strategy for gaining influence in a country now recognised as the keystone of the Arab World? It is difficult to be sure. The best hypothesis to explain Curiel's long and mysterious career as a servant

of a multitude of communist causes is that he was a long-term
Moscow agent who was left free to avoid some of the tactical twists
and turns which often hampered Soviet efforts to influence the
political evolution of the Arab World, but much about him remains
unclear. He was imprisoned after World War II, fled abroad in 1948,
returned again in 1952 but was again expelled by Nasser and spent
much of the rest of his life in Paris, where he was murdered in 1978.[6]

If Curiel was indeed functioning as a Soviet agent in Cairo in the
years 1939–45, the Soviets were not relying only on his activities.
Their approach was already multifaceted, as it has remained in Egypt
ever since.[7] The Soviets opened diplomatic relations with Egypt in
1943. King Farouk, sending off his ambassador to Moscow, whom
he chose from one of Egypt's prominent conservative families, told
him that relations had been established only because of British
pressure. The ambassador's job in Moscow was not to stimulate good
relations, the king cautioned him, but to block them.[8]

The Russians sent a Tatar Arabist, Abdurrahman Sultanov, to
take charge of their embassy. His first act upon arrival was to pay a
call upon the sheikh of Al-Azhar University. He showed a strong
interest in students. By 1946 curiosity about communism was growing
among students of most major political orientations: nationalists
(those oriented toward the Wafd Party), 'Young Egypt' pro-fascist
elements and even some Muslim Brethren. 'There is evidence that
the Soviets played an active role in supporting, financing and sometimes even attempting to arm student organisations.'[9] At least eight
different Egyptian university student groups appear at one time or
another to have benefited to some degree from Sultanov's largesse.
Among them was a faction organised by Henry Curiel, 'the
Omdurman Group'. It combined communist propaganda with advocacy of the unity of the Nile Valley, a popular Egyptian nationalist
concept.

But how effective was all this investment? A British graduate
student who spent the academic year 1950–51 at the University of
Cairo was impressed by the shallowness of student attitudes:

> A large proportion [of Egyptian students] say that they are commu-
> nist but very few of these know even the first thing about that
> creed. One self-confessed communist, in his third year at the
> University, could not say who was the author of *Das Kapital*.
> Nevertheless, the communists seem to be an organised body
> among the students and, after a meeting during one of the strikes,

I saw, lying about the paths and gardens of the University, scores of leaflets which bore the name of the (illegal) Communist Party of Egypt. There is no doubt that many of the young men have identified communism, on the one hand, with anti-Westernism: Russia is communist, so they too, will be communist. On the other hand communism has gathered in the bitter feeling against the great landlords of Egypt. Here some of the clearer-sighted students see the drawbacks; they accept them nevertheless. 'We know', they say, 'that to acquire economic freedom through communism means sacrificing our political freedom; but it is we, the educated, who have political freedom to lose, and we are ready to lose it for the peasants' sake.' It is particularly difficult to find out from the students what the policies of their various parties are . . . The members of the Muslim Brotherhood were particularly bad in this respect. They would not come down to brass tacks at all, but talked vaguely and without details of economic reform and a return to the principles of Islam. Only on the virtues of political assassination were they precise.[10]

The success of investments in encouraging student activism cannot be judged, however, by how accurate the understanding of the students may be for the ideas they espouse. From the viewpoint of the flexible opportunistic approach which the Soviets take to such groups, the most important consideration may be essentially disruptive and negative. The commitment to activism—the capacity to act as emotional pressure groups or to push a polarised political situation toward violence when violence is seen to serve Soviet purposes—may alone justify the modest investment student operations cost. If only a few future political organisers, propagandists, agitators or even political leaders are years later recruited from student circles energised and infected with communist ideology, the return may be worth it to Moscow. A few martyrs—victims of 'police brutality'—may also be valuable as propaganda symbols. In the Egyptian case, however, it is difficult to see how Moscow has yet reaped a return from Egyptian student investments comparable to what was gained from similar expenditures on Ethiopian student activities a generation later.[11]

On issues where more immediate and specific political pay-off could have been expected, the Soviets gained very little in Egypt and in the Middle East in general as a result of the expanded efforts during and immediately after World War II. The astute observer and participant in the Egyptian-Soviet relationship over many years, Mohamed Heikal, comments:

. . . the greatest mistake made by Arab communists was their failure to understand what was happening in Palestine. This was not just because of the long involvement of Jews in Arab communist parties and their ambivalent feelings toward Zionism; most of the blame must rest with the Soviet Union, which made a totally erroneous analysis of the situation. Stalin seems to have believed that the creation of a Jewish state might help to solve the Jewish problem in Russia and might also inject into the backward area of the Middle East a new progressive element. This thinking was probably influenced by a superficial knowledge of the kibbutz movement, by the number of Zionist leaders who came from Russia, and by the prominent positions held by Jews in the new communist regimes then establishing themselves in Eastern Europe. Moscow saw everything in terms of the struggle between communism and western imperialism . . . Theorising in Moscow bore no relation to the realities of the situation. When, only . . . hours after Israel had been born, Russia became the second country to recognise the new state, the Egyptian communists obediently issued a statement that the war which was then erupting between Israel and the Arab armies was one imposed by British imperialism on behalf of the Arab bourgeoisie with the aim of suppressing the growing proletarian forces in Palestine . . . [12]

Considering the closeness of the relationship that developed in the mid-1950s, it is astonishing to recall how negative Moscow was about the seizure of power by Nasser's Free Officers. They were denounced as a 'regime of reactionaries linked to the USA' and accused of 'savage repression of the workers' for having moved swiftly against the seizure of an Alexandria textile factory shortly after they came to power in the summer of 1952 by a group of workers possibly motivated by communists. This was the end of the Stalin era. It took Khrushchev very little time to begin experimenting with a more positive approach. The Soviets encouraged Egyptian toughness in negotiations with Britain over the Suez Canal during 1953 and 1954 and a trade agreement was concluded in March 1954. Inauguration of the Baghdad Pact in early 1955 gave Moscow motivation for quick action. The famous Czech arms deal was announced in September 1955 and a Soviet cultural centre was opened in Cairo. A nuclear co-operation agreement followed in January 1956 and a permanent Russian trade mission was set up in Cairo in July 1956. The Suez crisis of October-November capped the process, giving the Soviets an unexpected opportunity to cast themselves in the role of defender of Egyptian and Pan-Arab interests against European colonial powers and Israel. Negotiations for the Aswan Dam got under way, leading to an agreement for a $175 million loan in October 1958, signed on behalf of the USSR by Uzbek party secretary Mukhitdinov. Additional arms were supplied to cover losses in the Suez War, and Nasser visited Moscow twice during 1958. Khrushchev was enormously buoyed by these successes and Soviet propaganda exploited them through the Arab World.

The Soviet-Egyptian marriage lasted a decade and a half. The Russians, much more than the Egyptians, had hoped to make it permanent and to develop Egypt as a vehicle for drawing the entire Arab World into the communist camp. They made great ideological compromises to pursue this goal, accepting Nasser's ban on the Egyptian Communist Party, tolerating a major role for religion and providing not only military, but substantial economic aid. Compared to the grudgingly small commitments of economic aid the Soviets were later prepared to make to client regimes in Somalia and Ethiopia, Egypt benefited from remarkable generosity, comparable only to aid to Cuba. Mohamed Heikal calculates that during the years 1955–67, Soviet non-military aid to Egypt on a per capita basis was 15 times as much as India received and 20 times greater than that given to China.[13] Military aid, of course, was even more generously supplied, as it always is by Moscow. Exact statistics are difficult to obtain even today and dollar figures do not always supply an accurate measure of quantities. Conservative estimates are that close to $5 billion in military aid was provided to Egypt through the year following the 1973 war.[14]

The Russians always hoped that Nasser's Arab Socialist Union (ASU) could eventually be replaced by or evolve into a Marxist-Leninist Vanguard Party (though this term was not yet used). After a coup in Iraq in the summer of 1958 jolted the Baghdad Pact (turning it into the Central Treaty Organisation—CENTO, based in Ankara) and brought the pro-Soviet Qassem government to power, the first period of serious Soviet-Egyptian strain ensued, for Khrushchev was tempted to favour a radicalised Iraq, where 'a more advanced system is being established than in neighboring countries of the Arab East',[15] as more likely to be able to further Soviet objectives. There were sharp polemics—the honeymoon in Egyptian Soviet relations was over. But relations warmed again in 1960—both Nasser and Khrushchev needed each other too much. Nasser had made great progress toward establishing Cairo as the focal point of the Third World. In 1962 Moscow found Egypt a convenient proxy for a new phase of forward movement into South Arabia—where the overthrow of the Imamate in North Yemen provided opportunities for gains. In 1963 the Qassem regime was overthrown in Iraq and communists replaced by Baathists and nationalists. Krushchev's and Nasser's aspirations to play a larger role among the newly independent countries of Africa complemented each other. R. A. Ulianovsky, a deputy of Boris Ponomarev, head of the International Department of the Central Committee of the CPSU, came to Cairo at this time to lecture the Egyptians on the need for adopting a programme that would make the road toward 'non-capitalist' social and economic development irreversible. Communists should merge with nationalists to combat religious, tribal and family influences everywhere in the developing world, Ulianovsky urged.[16]

Conservative ideologues in the Soviet hierarchy were becoming increasingly doubtful about Khrushchev's infatuation with Egypt during the very period when the Egyptians became eager for a warmer Soviet embrace. The completion of the first phase of the work on the Aswan Dam provided an opportunity for Khrushchev to move directly onto the Egyptian scene and attempt to reconcile differences both with the Egyptians and within his own CPSU leadership. On 6 May 1964 Khrushchev boarded the *Armenia* at Yalta for a four-day voyage to Alexandria. His party included Nasser's confidant (and later Minister of Information), Mohamed Heikal (returning from a May Day visit to Moscow), who has provided a revealing account of Khrushchev's attitudes and concerns as expressed in conversations during the course of the voyage. These indirectly reveal many of the constraints the Politburo had placed upon Khrushchev. He bristled on hearing that Nasser planned to ask for a new loan for industrial development:

We've given you enough . . . The High Dam—first and second phases, and a big loan for industrialisation. Too much, in fact. One hundred million rubles is quite enough. The next day . . . Khrushchev and I had a long discussion . . . about Arab unity. He insisted that the only real unity was the unity of the working

classes throughout the world. Then I made the mistake of bringing
up the forbidden subject. 'Mr Chairman,' I said, 'working class
unity isn't enough. Look at you and China. The proletariat is
ruling in both countries, yet you are quarelling, and I think that
a part of the quarrel is because of feelings of nationalism.' 'Ach,'
said Khrushchev, 'It's much more complicated than that.'

. . . Then Khrushchev began to ask why we had been arresting
communists and how he should bring the matter up with Nasser.
'All communists are out of prison now,' I told him. He went on
to ask me questions about a great variety of subjects—Islam; the
role of the mullahs; the size and population of Cairo; of Egypt
and of other Arab countries; did we all speak the same language;
what did the Arab League do; what had gone wrong with Qasim?
The reception when we landed was quite indescribable. Many
elements combined to make it a unique occasion—Nasser's prestige was at its height, and Khrushchev had become a legendary
figure, not just in Egypt . . . I asked him [after we arrived in
Cairo], 'What do you think of it?' I saw there were tears in his eyes.
Never anywhere had he been received as the Egyptian crowds had
received him that day.[17]

The visit was an unbroken triumph for both Nasser and Khrushchev. They jointly pressed the button that shifted the Nile from its
course in the presence of Algerian and Iraqi Presidents Ben Bella
and Arif. The day before Khrushchev's departure (25 May 1964)
Nasser announced that Egypt would receive a new long-term Soviet
industrial development credit of 250 million roubles. Khrushchev
requested a Central Committee decree to award Nasser the title of
Hero of the Soviet Union and conferred the same honour on Vice-
President Amer. The Egyptian leadership was elated to be officiallly
back in the number one position with Moscow again, but for Khrushchev it was the beginning of the end. According to Khrushchev's
biographer Roy Medvedev:

The awards were a mistake . . . In Egypt the Communist party
was obliged to work underground, and many communists had
been imprisoned and cruelly tortured. In Moscow Khrushchev's
misguided generosity was to have serious repercussions.[18]

Many rancorous issues, most of them domestic, contributed to
Khrushchev's removal, which took place in October 1964 and
surprised him, so dizzy with his own success had he become and so

preoccupied with foreign political ventures.[19] In the field of foreign policy, his conduct of relations with Egypt and the Arab world had raised much disquiet in the CPSU:

> There was a fundamental split over policy in the Kremlin, and the Middle East played a big part in it; some of Khrushchev's critics, notably Suslov, were making use of the same arguments that local Arab communist parties had been using. By concentrating all their efforts on supporting Nasser, the argument went, local communists were putting themselves in an equivocal position: the stronger Nasser became, the weaker they became, and if he tried to achieve unity they would find themselves dissolved.[20]

Moscow's new leaders went to considerable lengths to assess the Egyptian situation:

> They wanted to know . . . how much backing Nasser had from the army and from the people, how strong the [Arab] Socialist Union was, how able it was to defend itself and Egypt's social revolution, how far rightist or religious elements had infiltrated the army, and whether there was any political organisation inside the army, what was the strength of the reactionary forces inside the country, etc.[21]

Moscow broadened its relations with other Arab states during this period, but in the end, much as the more conventional and cautious Brezhnev might have preferred a more pliant Egypt, there was no convenient substitute for Nasser as the centrepiece of Soviet efforts in the Arab World. Many of the features of a more crass and systematic Soviet approach to the Third World nevertheless became apparent at this time, according to Heikal:

> . . . a considerable increase in KGB activities in the Arab world became noticeable. Before . . . there had been little need for the Soviets to make special efforts to acquire information—the arms traffic they had with Egypt and other countries provided more or less all the opportunities they needed for acquiring it. But now they felt there were many puzzling questions to which they required an answer, particularly in regard to Egypt's relations with America, of which they were perennially suspicious . . . Two attachés at the Egyptian Embassy in Moscow, who had been caught trying to smuggle in a hundred gold coins, were arrested and told that they would be released if they agreed to work for the KGB.[22]

The observation seems naive, for it is hard to believe that the KGB had not long been taking advantage of opportunities to recruit agents in Egypt and elsewhere in the Arab World. (We have the testimony of several defectors to this effect, for example, Vladimir Sakharov in *High Treason*, cited below.) There was certainly an intensification of both KGB information-collection and of influence operations and a willingness to take greater risks for furthering Soviet objectives. There was also more emphasis, both in clandestine and overt Soviet activities, on communism as a doctrine for gaining, maintaining and manipulating power:

> Egyptian army officers on courses in the Soviet Union were aston-ished to find one day that the Russian textbook assigned for their sociology studies was called *Scientific Fundamentals of Communism*. They also found communist literature deposited in their bedrooms. As there was a written agreement with the Soviets that Egyptian officers studying with them should not be subjected to any political indoctrination, Amer wrote Gretchko to complain.[23]

It was during this same period that the Soviets developed a high degree of interest in the Palestinians. Nasser, in effect, had founded the Palestine Liberation Organisation (PLO) in 1964 by persuading the Arab League to pass a resolution bringing it into existence.[24] He intended to use it not to fight Israel but to undermine Jordan. The Russians were at first not much interested in it and were uneasy about its religious links and Yasser Arafat's oratory about Jerusalem as a holy city. George Habash's Popular Front for the Liberation of Palestine (PFLP) was Marxist, but he favoured China over the Soviet Union. The Soviets preferred an organisation over which they could exercise more direct control and use for operations they considered specifically advantageous to them, so they encouraged a Syrian army officer, Ahmad Jibril, to organise the Popular Liberation Front (PLF). It benefited from Bulgarian and East German support as well as KGB assistance, and carried out over 90 raids on Israel before the Six Day War of 1967.[25]

A combination of general and specific Soviet moves brought on the Six-Day War which Nasser would have preferred to avoid, for he had long been bogged down in an unwinnable struggle in Yemen and was reluctant to take on Israel, even with the help of Syria and Jordan. Syria had been generously armed by the Soviets. Palestinian raids, Syrian air attacks, artillery shelling in the border region and

Soviet reports to the Syrians of alleged Israeli preparations for attack produced a crisis to which Nasser had to respond to preserve his own pride by moving troops into the Sinai and ordering UN troops to be withdrawn. He closed the Gulf of Aqaba and in quick succession announced defence pacts with Jordan and Iraq. Israel rose to the challenge by destroying the Egyptian air force and driving Arab forces out of the Sinai, the West Bank and the Golan Heights. It was the most humiliating defeat Nasser could have imagined. All Arab states were discouraged by the Soviets from considering Israel's offer to negotiate the return of captured terrorists for peace.

The Soviet response to the Six Day War was to intensify a policy for which the groundwork had already been laid: do everything possible to exacerbate Arab alienation and anger with the West; to become an active supporter of the Palestinians, using them as a vehicle for furthering Soviet purposes throughout the Middle East and Africa; and to embark on vast expansion of subversion and terrorist operations worldwide, with special emphasis on medium-term programmes for destabilising Western-oriented governments through clandestine techniques. The increasing and frustrating involvement of the US in Vietnam encouraged the Soviet appetite for intensified exploration of opportunities for expansion every-where. Egypt was quickly rearmed and Soviet programmes for military support of other Arab countries were expanded. But Nasser's health had been adversely affected by his defeat. He remained intensely active during the following three years and visited Moscow in the summer of 1970. In September 1970, in the wake of the civil war in Jordan between Palestine guerrilla forces and King Hussein's army, he died.

The Russians, who had almost 20000 'advisers' in Egypt by this time, had become increasingly unpopular. Both the Egyptians and the Russians knew it and the subject was discussed, though in gingerly fashion, during Nasser's final Moscow visit. Nasser's successor, Anwar Sadat, came into power knowing that the Russian relationship was deteriorating and resolved to shift Egypt's orientation toward the West. But 'paradoxically, Sadat's first major foreign policy act was to sign a treaty of friendship with the Soviet Union (27 May 1971)'.[26] It was the beginning of a complex process of disengagement and shift of orientation which culminated in the Camp David Agreements of March 1979. Sadat expelled the bulk of Soviet military personnel from Egypt in July 1972. This did not, however, terminate the Soviet-Egyptian marriage. The Soviets, in fact, responded by pouring vast quantities of military equipment into Egypt in 1973. 'It looks as if they want to push me into a battle', Sadat observed, and Heikal concludes:

> I think they probably did. Certainly I believe that the military, backed by Brezhnev, wanted to make it possible for Egypt to embark on a limited war. By the beginning of 1973 the Soviets realised that, having lost the political battle, they might be able to recoup their losses in the military field. They were not instructing the Arabs to fight, but they were providing them with sufficient arms to make the idea of fighting extremely tempting, particularly since all advance in the political and diplomatic fields seemed to be blocked.[27]

Thus, in perhaps an even more profound manner than in 1967, the Soviets were instrumental in instigating the 1973 Yom-Kippur War. Before the war led, in effect, to an acceleration of the Middle East process and Camp David, it provoked the worldwide Arab oil embargo and all its consequences, from which the West has only recently begun to recover. Without this war and its aftermath, it is doubtful whether the revolution that occurred the following year in Ethiopia would have taken the course it did, or even have occurred at all, for it was precipitated by severe economic crisis caused by the oil price hike. It is doubtful, too, whether events in Portugal and its colonial empire would have developed as they did in 1974–75, apparently so favourable to Soviet interests. The Shah of Iran might not have fallen if his vastly increased oil income had not led to lavish spending and the contradictory political and economic policies he adopted after 1973. And the Soviet invasion of Afghanistan would probably not have occurred if Iran had not fallen victim to revolution the year before. Mohamed Heikal is justified in observing 'Few limited wars in recent years have had such far-reaching repercussions as the October War of 1973'.[28] If the Soviets profited widely and indirectly from this war, they gained nothing concrete in Egypt or in the Arab World where, by and large (with the exception of countries such as South Yemen and Syria and through the destructive use of the PLO) they lost influence and respect. 'By 1975 the great Soviet offensive, which had begun in 1955, was a spent force.'[29]

A student of Soviet Russian history on a much broader plane, the late Hugh Seton-Watson, evaluated the Soviet approach to the Arab World in the late 1970s in strategic terms:

Though the Soviet leaders still had very little prospect of getting a Middle East political-social system that was firmly based on their principles or interests, it is arguable that this was not in fact the aim of their policy. Rather, they seemed to be aiming at the preservation and intensification of a state of chaos that could dangerously weaken their American enemies . . . Disruption of Western oil supplies may be expedited no less by the actions of 'reactionary' sheiks than by those of 'progressive' democrats . . . Mass production of intelligentsia and mass production of skilled workers doomed to work in frustrating circumstances amounted to mass production of future revolutionaries. As for the already existing revolutionaries, who were mainly Palestinians, though the great majority were certainly not communists, it did not follow from this that they were not accessible to material assistance, or manipulation, by the secular arm of the Soviet regime, the KGB.[30]

Looking back over the Soviet-Egyptian marriage, it is difficult to avoid the conclusion that the weightiest divisive factor was *creed*, that is, *religion*. The conflict was between Islam and the secular religion of the Soviets, communism. The Russians asumed that Egyptian leaders, thirsty for power and impatient both to modernise their own country and lead the entire Arab World, could be won to communism as the best modern formula for exercising power in the name of the people without taking the risk of consulting the people. Each party was using the other for secular political ends which conflicted with the priorities of the other. The Egyptians were more deeply attached to Islam than Russian communists were able to appreciate.[31] The concept of Arab unity was bound up with Islam. Islam was an essential part of it. Neither Egyptians nor other Arabs saw any need to abandon Islam to achieve Arab unity and were unwilling to accept abandonment of Islam as a condition for cooperation with the Soviets. The Soviets could not afford to set such a requirement. Neither were the Egyptian leaders convinced that they needed to operate a completely totalitarian state on the Soviet model—they knew the complexity of their own society, and of the Arab World itself. They knew that to try to force all aspects of life into a rigid socialist mould, would be self-defeating. Finally they had all been too deeply influenced by the West to take seriously the Soviet pretension that communism would create a class-free, problem-free society.[32]

There was a head-on clash on the issue of Islam early in the

development of the relationship—in 1961—and the man involved
was Anwar Sadat, whose Islamic roots and Islamic sensitivities ran
deeper than Nasser's. In May 1961 Khrushchev held a reception for
a visiting delegation, which Sadat headed, and gave a speech:

> In the course of his speech Khrushchev turned to . . . nationalism
> and communism and forecast that some members of the Egyptian
> delegation would . . . eventually become communists. He went on
> to say that while Egypt and all states would turn to communism
> of their own free will, for 'people cannot be driven to paradise
> with a stick,' it was inevitable that this should happen since 'Arab
> nationalism is not the zenith of happiness.'[33]

Sadat was angered. *Pravda*'s 'Observer' reminded the Egyptians
that it was unwise to 'cut the tree that provides the shade'. Radio
Cairo reminded the Soviets of the practical view the Egyptians held
of their relationship:

> In its campaign against us, *Pravda* quoted an old Arab saying . . .
> that one should not cut the tree which shades us . . . We treat
> Russia as a bank. The bank which grants me a loan has no right
> to interfere in my own affairs.

Sadat sent a letter to Khrushchev in June 1961 in which he declared:

> We do not believe that the historical development of man runs
> along the blind alley of which capitalism is the beginning and
> communism is the imperative end . . . We refuse capitalism . . .
> But this refusal does not mean that communism will succeed in
> our country.

Later in the 1970s it became clear that Sadat was expressing the
conviction of many Muslims and most Arabs that communism and
Islam are incompatible while capitalism and Islam are not.

Every channel of the Soviet propaganda apparatus was brought to
bear on Egypt. By the late 1950s Soviet broadcasting in Arabic had
begun to expand dramatically and the expansion continued to the
mid–1970s when more than 80 hours weekly were broadcast. Egyptian book stores were flooded with cheap Soviet periodicals and
books and Soviet films were supplied at favourable prices. They were
never very popular among Egyptians. As early as 1957 the Soviet
film version of Gorky's *Mother* was ordered suspended by Nasser
because it featured a woman rejecting religion in favour of atheism

and communism. Combined American and British film imports always vastly exceeded those of Soviet films.

During his first visit to the Soviet Union (1958) Nasser was taken to Muslim areas to impress him with their material progress and also to try to convince him that there was religious freedom.[34] There was a great deal of propaganda in Egypt as time went on, about the good life of Soviet Muslims and numbers of Soviet Muslims were assigned to Soviet missions in Egypt. Since they were neither encouraged, nor in many instances even permitted, to have any closer contact with the Egyptian population than any other Soviet citizens, their impact was limited. Saudi Prince Amir Fahd al-Faysal was publicised in 1962 as having declared on departing from a visit to the Soviet Union:

> We have offered prayers with thousands of Soviet Muslims in the mosques of Moscow, Leningrad and Baku. We are convinced that there is complete religious freedom in the Soviet Union.[35]

Such obviously self-serving declarations had little impact compared to the practical experience of students, technicians and military men who went to the USSR for various kinds of training. What is remarkable about these programmes, on which the Soviets placed great stress, providing generous scholarships, is that when the statistics for the period of the warmest relationship are examined, they show that invariably far larger numbers of Egyptian students kept going to the United States and the United Kingdom to study than to the USSR. In all, only a very small proportion of the comparatively large Egyptian university student population went abroad at all.[36] Student and cultural programmes were suspended completely in 1977.

The clandestine side of Soviet activities in Egypt has not been widely publicised. Egyptians were at first rather naive about this aspect of the Soviet relationship, as the quotation from Mohamed Heikal above demonstrates. By the end of the 1960s, the Egyptians had become more concerned about Soviet efforts to subvert Egyptian officials, but both sides had a vested interest in not publicly acknowledging differences over such activities when they were exposed. During the entire period of the Soviet-Egyptian marriage no Soviet official was publicly implicated directly in internal disorders or declared *persona non grata*[37] The totality of what became known to the US and other Western governments about Soviet clandestine activities in Egypt has not yet become public.[38] We are fortunate, however, in having the testimony of a highly intelligent Soviet KGB co-optee who served in the Soviet consulate in Alexandria from 1968 to 1970 and who was drawn into a wide range of activities in Cairo as well because of his fluent Arabic: Viktor Nikolayevich Sakharov. His information was first publicised by John Barron[39], who talked to Sakharov shortly after he arrived in the US after defecting in Kuwait, where he was also involved in extensive KGB activities directed at the entire Arabian Peninsula. Sakharov, by the time he was assigned to Egypt, had already been recruited by the CIA, with whose agents he was in regular contact. The US was thus informed of Soviet clandestine activities in Egypt in which Sakharov took part or of which he had knowledge. We may also assume that pro-Western Egyptian officials were also informed. Sakharov describes his recruitment and contacts with the CIA in his book *High Treason*, published in 1981.[40]

By 1968 there were 50-odd KGB and GRU officers in Soviet missions in Egypt plus a small élite embassy unit that reported directly to the Information Department of the Central Committee. Among themselves the Russians jokingly referred to Egypt as 'The Soviet Egyptian Republic', so pleased were they with the degree of penetration they had achieved of Nasser's government and the influence they excercised. But they were also not resting on their laurels. Barron sums it up:

> Nasser, however, commanded the allegiance of the Egyptian populace and thus retained at least an option of independent action. The Russians also worried about a quiescent minority of Western-oriented Egyptians who opposed subserviency to the Soviet Union . . . Therefore, the KGB endeavored to build a hidden foundation for an enduring Soviet dominance. It recruited agents in the Egyptian military, the security services, the press, the universities, the . . . Arab Socialist Union and even among Nasser's personal advisers. Shortly before Sakharov arrived, it also started to penetrate those groups sympathetic to the West. The Russians relied on all of these agents to reinforce covertly their influence over the existing Egyptian regime. And they counted on them to form the nucleus of an Egyptian New Class wholly beholden to the Soviet Union. [41]

The talented journalist Mohamed Heikal, whose later writings have provided so much insight into the Soviet-Egyptian relationship and the internal affairs of the Nasser era, was regarded as too moderate by the Soviets, but they felt they were countering his influence on Nasser through Sami Sharaf, chief of the Presidential Secretariat, who began to be cultivated by the KGB in 1955 when he visited Moscow with one of the first Egyptian military missions. Sharaf's close ties with the Soviets are confirmed not only by Sakharov, but by Heikal.⁴² He was closely associated with the group led by Ali Sabry, General Secretary of the Arab Socialist Union, whom Moscow hoped to see emerge as Nasser's successor. On the morning of 22 May 1971 Vladimir Sakharov, already in Kuwait for several months, stepped into the office of the KGB *rezident* there, a man named Lobanov (an expert on Turkey), and was greeted with the anguished question: 'Have you heard the news from Cairo?' Sakharov had not. 'They have wiped us out—Sadat arrested all our people: Sabry, Gomaa, Fawzi, everybody!' 'Was there a man named Sharaf?' 'Yes, him too.'⁴³

Sakharov's retrospective analysis of the Soviets' exploitation of the Sabry group points toward what may well have been the lessons Moscow drew from this setback:

By 1970 the Soviets reached one of their goals—putting the Arab Socialist Union under the control of the Central Committee of the CPSU . . . Sabry became a natural successor to Nasser . . . Soviet political support for Sabry brought him exposure in the press, radio and TV second only to Nasser, while Sadat was considered by the Soviets as not strong and popular enough among the Arab leaders to effectively implement the policy of Soviet-sponsored Arab socialism. Such over-confidence and insensitivity to Egyptian nationalism and Pan-Islamism was to give them a costly lesson . . . The Soviets failed to understand that the ASU was no substitute for Islamic and Egyptian nationalism.⁴⁴

The Soviets did not lose everything with the imprisonment of the Sabry group for the Soviet clandestine services operate in depth and allocate a great deal of effort to 'investment' for the future, as Sakharov demonstrates in his description of the basic Soviet programme in Egypt when he arrived:

At the covert level, orders from Moscow were to penetrate and subvert the country at every stratum . . . The goal was . . . to encourage the Egyptians to pattern their newly reorganised armed forces and Nasser's ruling ASU party on the Soviet model . . . To complete the process of Sovietisation, the massive Soviet military-diplomatic-political-intelligence community was in the midst of a well-organised effort to recruit and develop likely Soviet agents in every military, political and government organisation in Egypt. Our specific orders . . . were to look for promising recruits among those who either held power or had the potential to do so. This means officers and officer trainees in the armed forces, customs officers, bureaucrats, ASU officials, national and local police, technicians, labor leaders and managers, journalists, students and businessmen. One group pointedly excluded were local Egyptian communists. They were regarded by the KGB as untrustworthy idealists who would compromise the all-important marriage with Nasser's party and government.[45]

The techniques were the classic ones:

Sbirunov [the KGB *rezident*] and his colleagues . . . [used] me as a recruitment front-man. Since my consular duties put me in constant contact with Egyptian officials, I was to scout each of them for qualities that would make them candidates for recruitment—sympathies with the Soviet Union, overwhelming ambition, job dissatisfaction, and exploitable weaknesses for drugs, alcohol, or women. I was to cultivate these persons as friends, soften them up, and convince them to go to Moscow for training or finesse them into doing the Soviets some favor that might turn out to be embarrassing later. When the candidate was sufficiently wooed, I was supposed to turn him over to Sbirunov, who would direct other operatives to complete the job.[46]

Sakharov provides insight into an often unsuspected target of KGB operations in Egypt: religion. The gregarious priest who served the Russian Orthodox Church in Alexandria, Father Anatoly Kaznovetsky, was a KGB agent. He maintained contact with a wide range of Christian and Muslim religious leaders, not only in Egypt but in nearby Middle Eastern areas and throughout Africa, and reported on propaganda, political influence and recruitment opportunities for further KGB development. While Sakharov was in Egypt, Father Kaznovetsky undertook a mission to Ethiopia which was considered highly successful. Sakharov gained no specific information on Soviet clandestine relationships with Muslim conservatives in Egypt, however. Father Kasnovestsky is unlikely to have been usable for such purposes. It is conceivable that Muslim conservatives were at this time considered only a negative target, but they are unlikely to have remained so.[47]

The post-Nasser period was a time of troubles for the Soviets in Egypt, but the usual Soviet response to setbacks is to redouble efforts and refine techniques.[48] Egypt was one of the most active theatres of Soviet forgery operations during the late 1970s. Major themes of these forgeries were all negative and destructive: US duplicity toward Egypt and Sadat in particular and US undermining and disparaging of Islam. The US was repeatedly accused of conspiring to have Sadat killed. Is this revealing, perhaps, of the Soviets' own intentions or desires in an era when strong circumstantial evidence from several other areas raised the possiblity of Soviet complicity in assassination schemes?[49]

The question of Soviet complicity in creating the climate which led to increasing polarisation in Egyptian society in the period following the signing of the Camp David agreements (March 1979) has not yet been adequately researched and extends beyond the scope of this chapter. Discussion of the scope and nature of Soviet clandestine activities in Egypt during the late 1970s and early 1980s is simply absent from Mohamed Heikal's detailed exposition of developments leading to the assassination of Sadat on 6 October 1981 in his book *Autumn of Fury*. Sadat is depicted as having brought on—and deserved—his gruesome end. It is difficult to accept this analysis in view of the fact that many aspects of the background of the group who carried out the assassination have never been completely explained.

It is equally difficult to make a case for direct Soviet encouragement or complicity that does not rely entirely on deduction, extrapolation and insinuation. During the great wave of arrests of Egyptians in early September 1981 Sadat undoubtedly struck out wildly and erratically and many people innocent of plotting against him appear to have been swept into prison. His actions during the preceding years toward both Muslim fundamentalists as well as the Coptic partriarch had generated complex resentments. On the other hand, at the time of the arrests, seven Soviet diplomats (including the ambassador) and two Russian correspondents were expelled with the accusation that they had been involved in exacerbating religious tension and encouraging strife among both Copts and Muslims. From everything we know of patterns of Soviet clandestine activities in Egypt as they developed over a period of 30 years, these were not illogical or uncharitable accusations. They fit also the pattern of

greatly expanded Soviet subversive operations of all kinds, characterised by greater intensity and a higher degree of risk-taking that
became apparent in most parts of the world in the 1970s and which
has continued, with little evidence of abatement, into the 1980s.
Given the pivotal position of Egypt in the Mediterranean, the Middle
East and the African Horn-Indian Ocean region, it would be folly
to expect the Soviets to have downgraded its high priority—even if
its ultimate purpose is primarily destructive. The subject should
receive more intensive study.

What conclusions can be drawn from the Soviet-Egyptian experience? The motivation of both partners for the rather hastily arranged
marriage was extension of their own power and influence. For Nasser
the appeal of Soviet support was short-term and there was little
expectation that a price would have to be paid. On the Soviet side
the main thrust of policy was much more long-term and basic. The
Soviet Union has, like the Russian empire before it, always exhibited
a thrust toward the Middle East. The goal is a complex one which
on its western side melds into another long-term Soviet/Russian goal:
influence in the entire Mediterranean. To the east there has been a
two-century old Russian drive for power in the Indian subcontinent
and a desire to extend naval power to the Indian Ocean. Behind
these thrusts lie more basic and older drives to gain territory, influence and wealth from the Turkish and Persian empires. Blocked from
gaining leverage in the countries lying along its southern borders, the
attractiveness of expansion of influence in the Arab Middle East was
irresistible to the optimistically aggressive Soviet Union dominated
by Nikita Khrushchev.

The welfare of an Islamic people as such was not a consideration
that moved the Soviet Union to invest in the Aswan Dam—the aim
was the much simpler one of outsmarting the West as a provider of
economic aid to serve as a basis for economic development and
modernisation. But even at a very early stage of the Soviet-Egyptian
relationship, military aid took precedence over economic aid. After
the 1956 Suez War, the prospect of using Egypt as a base for all
sorts of operations directed at the Middle East, Africa and the Third
World at large grew in attractiveness for the Russians. To maximise
this potential, steady and occasionally increasing tension was
required. Israel provided a convenient focus for generation of
tension. Thus, the Soviet Union found any development that moved
toward reduction of tension between Israel and its neighbours—let

alone achievement of peace between Israel and any or all of them—
very much to its disadvantage. War in the Middle East was not,
therefore, for the Soviet Union an unwelcome development. The
Soviets bear a major share of responsibility for the outbreak of both
the wars of 1967 and 1973. Agitation against Israel also served Soviet
domestic purposes, for the leadership was steadily moving toward
more systematically oppressive policies toward its own Jewish
minority.

The Soviets never achieved anything approaching genuine
hegemony over Egypt. Their efforts to expand their influence and
capability to manipulate Egyptian actions generated counter-currents
in the country, from the top leadership level to the 'broad masses'.
The Russians found Nasser's genuine devotion to Islam awkward,
difficult to understand and increasingly at odds with their own objectives. Their hope that the Egyptian élite could be won away from
loyalty to Islam and that a party of the Marxist-Leninist vanguard
type could be brought into being proved vain. The rise of Sadat to
occupy the position of Nasser's successor and the discrediting of the
Arab Socialist Union the more it was brought to tilt toward Soviet
positions were not accidental developments. The Soviets did not
succeed in winning any significant body of Egyptian society to a pro-
Russian position. They were able to create only a network of
agents—a miniscule portion of the population at large and even a
tiny minority of the élite—to try to use it to achieve, by essentially
clandestine and conspiratorial methods, a permanently pro-Soviet
Egyptian government. The effort failed miserably with the fall of Ali
Sabry and his group, and no substitute for this network could be
devised. In the end—by the time of the expulsion of Soviet technicians in 1972—the Russians were perceived as crassly opportunistic, ignorant and narrowly self-serving by the great majority of
Egyptians, both masses and élite.

Unable to manipulate the Egyptian situation to create circumstances where they could be perceived as even mildly beneficial to
Islam, the Soviets in Egypt found themselves face to face with the
fact that they had reached a dead end. All the major political and
social trends in Egyptian society which frustrated their long-term
objectives were deeply Islamic. Communists and allied intellectual
leftists in Egypt do not represent an alternative around which the
Soviets can hope to rebuild influence. During the heyday of the
Soviet-Egyptian marriage Egyptian communists were treated with
scorn by all parties and exposed as the ultimate mercenaries on the

Egyptian scene. Their credibility as nationalists was lost. They are deprived of the opportunity to serve as catalysts between Islamic (or Coptic) religious elements and more secular nationalists by their inability to be credible as supporters of Islam. It is true, of course, that many of the factors in Egypt which frustrate Soviet efforts also hamper Western objectives. The United States had pre-empted the task of supplying military aid and only American and other sources of economic aid and investment are credible. While the Soviets might hope to compete again at some future time in the military aid field, they are hopelessly uncompetitive in the economic area. Thus the Soviets are driven to employing essentially negative approaches to Egypt. They cannot hope to exploit fundamentalist Islamic currents for positive political purposes, but they are likely to find it very difficult to resist manipulating these currents for destructive efforts.

A mid–1970s study of the Soviet-Egyptian relationship concluded that 'The Egyptian connection has been Moscow's costliest in the Third-World—and its most valuable'.[50] The connection was valuable because it not only enabled Moscow to inject an essential increment of disruptive influence into its competive relationship with the United States and gain leverage on the world scene (consider the effects of the petroleum embargo following the 1973 war); it was also specifically useful to Moscow as a base for building influence and operational capability in the Arab world and, from time to time, the entire Third World.

7 The Russians and Arabia—Marginal Success

Soviet interest in the Arabian Peninsula naturally focuses on Saudi Arabia, the largest, most powerful and wealthiest (though not the most populous) of the eight states that are now recognised as independent political entities. It is also the home of Islam and custodian of its most sacred sites, each year the goal of millions of pilgrims who visit them. Oil was discovered in Saudi Arabia only in 1938. The Soviets were originally attracted to the Peninsula not because of oil but because it represented a relative power vacuum astride the British lifeline to the east. The British favoured the Hashemites at the end of World War II. The Soviets established diplomatic relations with the Hashemite King Hussein of the Hejaz in 1924. When Ibn Saud, leader of the Wahhabis, captured Mecca and then Jeddah, Medina and Yanbu in 1925, the Soviet Foreign Ministry feared a setback but the Comintern was more optimistic—it appreciated Ibn Saud and the Imam Yahya in nearby Yemen as independent Arab leaders opposed to British influence. The Soviet Union was the first country to recognise Ibn Saud's supremacy in Hejaz in February 1926. A Tatar, Karim Khakimov, was sent to head the Soviet legation and a delegation of Soviet Muslims was sent to attend the Congress of Mecca which Ibn Saud convened to ratify his claim to the holy cities.[1]

There was, however, no flowering of relations. Ibn Saud was deeply suspicious of Soviet Marxists, difficulties developed over Soviet dumping of trade goods, and Ibn Saud's anti-British attitudes moderated. Though Prince Faysal (who later became king) was given a warm reception when he visited Moscow in 1932 (meeting with President Kalinin), the Saudis were reluctant to agree to any treaty arrangements that would have consolidated trade or political relations. It was the Soviets who let relations lapse in 1938. Agabekov's evaluation of 1930 remained valid: 'I have to admit that Soviet activity in Arabia never acquired a really systematic character'.[2]

The Soviets had also permitted relations with North Yemen to lapse in the same year, although ten years before they had expended a good deal of effort to persuade the Imam Yahya to sign a treaty of commerce and friendship. Here, too, the initial attraction was alliance with a local ruler—no matter how religious and feudal in his outlook—who was antagonistic toward Britain. Such an attitude was almost inevitable for a Yemeni ruler, given the British position in Aden. The Soviets were able to restore diplomatic relations with Yemen in 1955, largely as the result of a mission by the same Abdurrahman Sultanov who had been active in the Soviet Embassy in Cairo during World War II.

Meanwhile, Imam Yahya had been assassinated in 1948 in a complex and initially successful coup attempt by 'Free Yemenis' based in Aden who had developed extensive contacts with disaffected elements in North Yemen, including members of the Imam's family. Civil strife resulted in the triumph of the Imam's son, Ahmad.[3] Imam Ahmad became upset at British efforts to organise the Aden Protectorate into a more cohesive and manageable political unit. It was his desire to obtain backing against Britain which made him receptive to Soviet overtures. These resulted in a new friendship pact, signed in November 1955—the beginning of a period of intense Soviet activism in the Arab World. Imam Ahmad's son, Prince Badr, toured Eastern Europe and the Soviet Union in 1956. Several assistance pacts were signed as a result of this flowering of Yemeni-Soviet friendship. Early in 1957 an arms agreement was signed with Czechoslovakia. Yemen also established diplomatic relations with Peking, a move not immediately seen (by the Yemenis) as contradictory to close relations with Moscow.

Prince Badr soon fell into conflict with his father. Badr found Nasser's Arab socialism attractive and recognised the need for reforms to bring Yemen nearer to the modern age. According to Soviet defector Vladimir Sakharov, whose first foreign assignment was in Taizz, the Soviets offered Badr enticements to orient the country completely toward the Soviet Union and break ties with the US and Saudi Arabia,[4] but Badr was caught in too many conflicting cross-currents. He succeeded his father as Imam when Ahmad, in spite of repeated plots agaist him, died in bed in September 1962, but a few days later Badr was overthrown by an army colonel, Abdallah Al-Sallal, whom he had appointed chief of staff. Al-Sallal proclaimed Yemen a republic. These events marked the beginning of the Yemeni civil war, which continued through the 1960s. The

Soviets, though deeply committed to the Imamate, were able to shift their support to the republican government with remarkable ease. *Izvestia* and *Pravda* correspondents rushed to Sana'a and wrote dispatches praising the new republic for choosing the 'non-capitalist path of development'. Although the Russians made a great deal of noise about the danger of British, Saudi and Jordanian intervention in Yemen, it was their client Nasser who intervened most energetically and on whose support the Al-Sallal regime became almost entirely dependent. The Saudis eventually provided sufficient support to the Royalists to enable them to hold large segments of territory.

Yemen became a nightmare for Nasser, but he did not follow a uniformly pro-Soviet policy there and in 1965 achieved a brief agreement with the Saudis. In return for cessation of Saudi support for the Royalists, Nasser promised to withdraw Egyptian troops. He invited President Al-Sallal to Cairo in September 1965 and held him there until August 1966 when he returned him to Sana'a where the Prime Minister, General Hassan al-Amri was trying to break free of Egyptian influence.[5] Meanwhile, the Saudi reconciliation, which even the Russians had briefly backed fell apart. Neither Nasser nor the Saudis trusted each other. In the aftermath of the 1967 June War, Nasser, embarrassingly defeated, finally withdrew the 80 000 troops he had maintained in Yemen. President Al-Sallal could not survive the departure of the Egyptians and was overthrown in November 1967 while en route to Moscow for the celebrations of the 50th anniversary of the Great October Socialist Revolution.

China had also competed in Yemen in the 1960s. There is still controversy about the importance of the Sino-Soviet rivalry:

If Peking sought its 'Albania' in the Arab World, Yemen for some years was a leading candidate. The magnitude of the Chinese threat to Soviet policies, however, should not be exaggerated. Chinese aid and technical assistance were small, compared to Russian, and trade remained negligible. Meanwhile arms, the principal commodity of interest to Sana'a during the long struggle with the Royalists, were provided by Moscow, not Peking.[6]

On the other hand, Vladimir Sakharov, who served an internship in the Soviet diplomatic establishment in Yemen at this time and who a few years later was a KGB operative in Kuwait, maintains that the Soviets were deeply concerned about the Chinese. He contends, in fact, that Al-Sallal was overthrown at Moscow's instigation because he was cozying up to the Chinese. According to him:

. . . the Soviets saw the Chinese as a more serious threat than the Americans. The Soviets wanted to get rid of Chinese competition before it upset the applecart of [their] long-term economic and political strategy for the Middle East.[7]

Sakharov arrived in Yemen in 1967 on a short-term assignment which was part of the final phase of his intensive Arabic language training at the Moscow Institute of International Relations (IIR).[8] His description of the atmosphere in Yemen when he arrived gives the impression of a good deal of Soviet self-confidence:

. . . chanting the rhetoric of anti-colonialism every step of the way the two communist superpowers were locked in a struggle to recolonise the Third World for themselves. North Yemen, in 1967, was a key battleground in the struggle. China and the USSR were pouring military and economic aid into the region and had sent in large contingents of technicians, military advisors and trouble-makers.[9]

The Soviet ambassador was a former Tajik minister of culture, Mirzo Rakhmatov. The Soviet mission had grown to enormous size and did not fit smoothly into the still traditional tribal society of Yemen:

. . . the Soviet colony . . . consisted of six or seven hundred specialists who worked on civil construction projects, road building, and agricultural development. While military advisers were no problem, the construction and agricultural workers were not easy to control. For the first time in their lives they were taken out of their Tadshik, Turkmen, Russian, Georgian and Ukrainian villages and forced into a multinational whole. Their centuries-old antagonistic animosities suddenly exploded here in Yemen, resulting in fist fights, broken ribs, bloody faces and beat-up wives. Later on the CPSU Central Committee, having considered the Yemeni experience, would more carefully select and match the groups of Soviet specialists for contracts abroad.[10]

True to the principle of using its establishment in one country for operations against others, the Soviets were active in many directions out of Yemen:

. . . first secretary of the embassy . . . had been working in Yemen for three years. His main responsibility was to organise and direct guerrilla operations in Aden and the east coast of Ethiopia, control the embryonic liberation movement in Oman and Saudi Arabia and interface with . . . the Front for the Liberation of South Yemen . . . The long-term objective [Zaitsev, the first secretary] would remind me . . . echoing views about Third World strategy I had heard at the IIR, was to establish long-term Soviet influence by whatever means necessary, be it through above-board diplomatic approaches or underground armed struggle. Moscow was interested in controlling the Arabian Peninsula and its oil, directly or indirectly, so as to have the Western capitalist nations eventually at its mercy.[11]

Both Royalists and Republicans experienced drastic changes of fortune in the civil war that continued in Yemen until 1970, when Saudi Arabia was instrumental in promoting compromises that brought the war to an end. The short-lived British-organised Federation of South Arabia had meanwhile become the independent People's Democratic Republic of Yemen on 30 November 1967. Despite a 1971 agreement to unite the two Yemens in one country, relations were uneasy and erupted into a border war in 1972. The Russians, disillusioned by the turmoil of the 1960s, appear to have down-graded North Yemen in the 1970s in favour of the more dependably radical South Yemen.

To Soviet Islamic strategists in the mid–1960s, who were increasingly frustrated by Nasser's reluctance to bend dependably to their will or to compromise on basic issue of creed, that is, Islam vs. communism, South Yemen was an alluring prospect. Here was a small country in a highly strategic location, not populous enough to represent an economic burden. Its political activists were all young and leftist. True, it was a region of enormous contrasts. On the one hand there was the polyglot port of Aden, into which the British had made a substantial investment in the early post-World War II years, with a highly politicised labour movement. In the mountainous hinterland, traditional rulers still maintained a medieval style of life; there was

. . . an incredibly complex set of principalities, sheikhdoms and other statelets of various sizes, powers and wealth, most often organised on the basis of some form of tribal affiliation (or tribal confederation).[12]

The territory (it could not then have been called a country) was rent with tensions, rivalries and contradictions that bedevilled every British attempt to weld it into a state with provision for some of the institutions that could have assured representative government with checks and balances and a modest degree of protection for individual citizens. The British eventually gave up and in the framework of the policy of withdrawal from east of Suez, abandoned the federation they had worked so hard to create and let radical forces take over. It was, to be crass, a cut-and-run operation:

> The new state in South Arabia was named the People's Republic of South Yemen only in the last days before independence on 30 November 1967, but this was of small importance beside the fact that the territories it would include were uncertain even three months earlier . . . The two militant parties—FLOSY and the NLF—stood for exactly the same thing and the British offered them everything they wanted in the end, but there was no halt to the fighting until one party emerged the victor.[13]

The political rivalries and the inherent complexity of the territory did not discourage the Russians. They were in a very assertive, optimistic phase 20 years ago, confident that energetic young Marxist devotees, amenable to their manipulation, could build the kind of state they (that is, the Soviets) envisioned as ideal for the Islamic World:

> The guiding principle of Soviet policies in Aden during the turbulent years before its independence in 1967 was to avoid a firm commitment to any of the factions struggling for power in the protectorates and to focus attention instead on the evils of British imperialism. The British-inspired projects for federation in South Arabia were regularly denounced, while the various nationalist movements were pictured as united in their search for independence . . . As independence grew closer and the internecine struggle . . . more fierce—especially between the . . . Front for the liberation of South Yemen (FLOSY) and the . . . National Liberation Front (FLN)—the Russians persisted in their neutrality.[14]

It was a very special kind of 'neutrality' that the Russians practiced, for it consisted of giving support to both major contenders and, we have good reasons for presuming, occasionally to some of the minor ones as well. The approach was almost an exact duplicate of that followed a decade later in Ethiopia after the 1974 revolution, where the Soviets supported several radical political movements at the same time they were feeling their way into a relationship with the military junta which had an uncertain hold on power.[15] Nasser had developed a direct relationship with FLOSY. This gave the Soviets a form of reinsurance, but with the benefit of hindsight, it appears that the NLF may have become their favoured group before independence. It was more effective in rural areas and it had outwitted FLOSY in Aden and took over the government on independence. The Soviets recognised the new state the day after independence was declared. But there were moderates and extremists among the NLF Marxists and a contest quickly developed between them:

> The short history of the PDRY is dominated by growingly radical internal and external policies, accompanied by an endemic financial crisis and a ruthless struggle for power within the NLF.[16]

The NLF was not originally Marxist-dominated and was opposed by the Aden communist party, the People's Democratic Union, until it absorbed it in 1975.[17] The Soviets may have encouraged this tactic, applying the lessons they drew from their less satisfactory experience with the party organisation in Egypt. By 1969, less than two years after independence, the moderate wing of the NLF had been eclipsed by the radicals, who aimed to transform the state into a model of Marxism in practice. Chinese influence grew steadily stronger. The most enthusiastic supporter of a strong Chinese orientation was President Ruba'i Ali whose rival, Secretary-General of the NLF Abdul Fattah Ismail, was pro-Soviet. The country had been divided into six provinces to eliminate tribal boundaries, but tribal feelings remained a major factor in internal political competition and were often at the root of what on the surface appeared to be ideological differences. A so-called Maoist insurrection in the Hadhramaut in 1968 was essentially a rebellion by disgruntled regional elements.

Religion proved as difficult as tribalism to relegate to the trash-heap of history. Anti-religious educational policies generated resistance among the still socially conservative population of the hinterlands. Through it all, Moscow remained compulsively optimistic about developments in South Yemen, which was declared a People's Democratic Republic in October 1970, only three years after its establishment.[18] *Pravda* observed in July 1970 that while many other Arab countries had to experience 'both religious-feudal and bourgeois-liberal stages' before the emergence of a 'socialist-oriented regime', South Yemen was already on the 'course of socialist development'.[19]

Although some researchers have devoted a great deal of effort to either-or analysis of both Soviet motives in South Yemen and the policies and attitudes of PDRY leaders, the most rational conclusion to which examination of the complex and seemingly bewildering events of the 1970s and early 1980s can lead is that Soviet motives have always been many-faceted, Soviet techniques of exercising influence multi-layered and PDRY leaders' actions affected by a great many cross currents. The Russians saw South Yemen as a unique opportunity for rapid establishment of the first Marxist-Leninist state in the Arab World; they saw it as a base for operations in neighbouring parts of the Arab Peninsula and the Horn of Africa; they were motivated by a strong compulsion to prevent the Chinese from gaining a significant foothold in the PDRY; they were also eager to exploit the country's strategic location militarily. Soviet military aid began in earnest in 1968, grew steadily through the 1970s and is estimated to have totalled at least $2 billion by 1983.[20] The most specific pay-off the Russians received from this investment came in the summer of 1977 when South Yemeni military contingents rendered crucial services in and for Ethiopia at a time when Mengistu's armed forces had almost disintegrated. Aden subsequently served as an essential transfer point for the Soviet airlift to Ethiopia during the final weeks of 1977 and first months of 1978.

During the extremely active 1970s the Soviets exploited the PDRY in combination with Kuwait as bases for supporting radical political movements targeted at all the conservative states of the Arabian Peninsula. Vladimir Sakharov's summary description of the situation at the beginning of this decade may be too sweeping in some of its generalisations and implications but it undoubtedly reflects maximal Soviet intentions in a period when Britain had for the most part withdrawn from an area where it had ensured stability for more than a century and when the United States, self-crippled by over-involvement in Vietnam, appeared to be incapable of replacing Britain with the same kind of effectiveness it had exhibited a quarter century earlier in the Eastern Mediterranean at the time of the enunciation of the Truman Doctrine toward Greece and Turkey:

> By 1971 the KGB established several insurgent movements around South Yemen that were to drive out the Chinese and clear the way for the Soviet advance on the Arabian Peninsula. The KGB

set up a base in the Dhofar region of Oman . . . There the KGB and the GRU organised, armed and trained guerrillas of the Front of Liberation of Saudi Arabia, the Popular Front for Liberation of Oman, the Front for Liberation of Dhofar, and the anti-Chinese tribesmen who belonged to the Front for the Liberation of South Yemen (FLOSY). The FLOSY insurgents and other Soviet-aided factions succeeded in pushing the Chinese out of South Yemen by 1974 and bringing that country into the Soviet camp. The takeover of South Yemen turned out to be doubly important to Moscow, because in the meantime the Saudis, recognising the threat, had moved to wrest neighboring North Yemen from the Soviet grip . . .

Sakharov goes on to draw an important lesson, still relevant, in Soviet adherence to a steady, long-term, flexible effort to attain their objectives:

> The struggle of these obscure tribes in remote Yemen may seem trivial . . . but for the Saudis it represented a real threat. Through Yemen, Moscow established itself as a power on the Saudi door-step; the Soviets could subtly intimidate the Saudis and make them think twice about their relations with the United States.[21]

The Chinese, who abandoned their support of the insurgency in Eritrea through South Yemen after their 1971 agreement with Haile Selassie and the establishment of diplomatic relations with the Imperial Ethiopian Government, faded gradually from the Arabian scene as major competitors for exerting influence as the 1970s progressed. They provided military advisors for the PDRY effort against Oman until 1975, then withdrew. Their prime supporter in PDRY, Ruba'i Ali, who could hardly have expected much from the Chinese during his final years in power, disappeared from the scene in 1978—executed and replaced by his long-time rival, Abdul Fattah Ismail, following the brief-case assassination of North Yemeni President Al-Ghashmi, which he was accused of instigating.

The PDRY established regular diplomatic relations with Qatar, Bahrain and the United Arab Emirates in 1975 and with Saudi Arabia in 1976. Moscow denounced 'rightists' for taking this latter step. The real incentive was largely economic—securing Saudi finan-cial support and remittances from South Yemeni workers in Saudi Arabia and the Gulf. The economy of South Yemen had been in disastrous condition from the first year of independence, for the closing of the Suez Canal after the Six Day War of 1967 was a final blow to the long-declining port of Aden and the British Petroleum refinery which operated well below capacity and at a loss. Nationalisations and imposition of Soviet-style controls over internal commerce during the late 1960s and early 1970s blighted the economy further.

South Yemeni internal politics were affected by the presence of large numbers of North Yemenis, including important elements in the leadership. The temptation to meddle in North Yemeni affairs was always present and may have been encouraged at times by the Russians as they became frustrated by their inability to exercise decisive influence in Sana'a. Border wars erupted in 1972 and again in 1979. The 1979 war provoked a US-Saudi emergency assistance operation. The Carter Administration, stung by Soviet advances in the Horn of Africa during the previous two years, was unwilling to tolerate even the semblance of Soviet free-wheeling on the opposite side of the Red Sea. American military support of North Yemen has continued ever since. The country is a rare example of a situation where both the US and the USSR maintain military aid programmes.

The Dhofar rebellion was a serious problem for Oman from 1965 to 1975. The Popular Front for the Liberation of the Occupied Arab Gulf (PFLOAG, its final name) was for several years heavily Chinese-supported, though it may originally have been Soviet inspired. It aimed to establish a Marxist-controlled area in the south-western part of the country, next to the PDRY border, where an unusual range of rugged, wooded mountains close to the coast catch the monsoon rains and constitute ideal terrain for insurgent operations. In the early 1970s, as Chinese interest in the Dhofar insurgency declined, the Soviets exerted themselves to take control of it. They estimated it as having high prospects for success. They were unequivocal in attacking the young Omani sultan, who was embarking on energetic efforts to modernise the country, as a British stooge, as anachronistic as the sultans and emirs in the hinterland of Aden who had long since been deposed. Iran, with US blessing, dispatched troops to Oman to aid the Sultan's forces in Dhofar in 1972. These began to have a favourable impact on the situation the next year, but the Soviets did not begin to reverse their position until 1974 and encouraged PDRY support for the Dhofar rebels throughout 1975. A cease-fire between PDRY and Oman was finally achieved in 1976. The Omani Government launched a vigorous programme of rehabilitation of the areas coupled with generous treatment of rebels who laid down their arms. Inclusion of Oman in

Western defence arrangements in 1979 left the Soviets with little hope of reviving the Dhofar insurgency even if the economically hard-pressed Aden Government had retained high enthusiasm for it. The PDRY and Oman reached an agreement to establish diplomatic relations and regulate all traffic in the border region in 1982. The Soviets were happy to establish diplomatic relations with the government of Sultan Qaboos in 1985.[22]

Although the Soviets had the satisfaction of seeing the successor to the National Liberation Front transformed into the Yemeni Socialist Party in October 1978 and signed a treaty of friendship and co-operation a year later, they could gain little permanent comfort from their Marxist Arab state on the Indian Ocean. The government which had come to power in 1978 was overthrown in April 1980 and Prime Minister Abdul Fattah Ismail had to go into exile in the Soviet Union. The internal strains in the PDRY leadership exposed during this period have persisted ever since and, in fact, worsened, as the violent civil war which erupted in Aden early in 1986 demonstrated. In its way the violence which lasted for two bloody weeks in January 1986 was as embarrassing to the Russians as the nuclear accident at Chernobyl four months later. Neither could be hidden from the outer world. Both raise fundamental questions about the viability of Soviet systems. Chernobyl has caused a far-reaching, though belated, re-assessment of Soviet nuclear power technology and methods of coping with disasters and has provoked doubts about the capacity of the Soviet political system to respond effectively to crises. We know much less about the after-effects of events in Aden. In the short-term

. . . Soviet intervention in the South Yemen crisis, sloppy and belated as it was, enabled Moscow to emerge quickly with its interests in Aden more or less intact, and its relations with neighboring countries only slightly strained.[23]

But the longer-term effects are bound to be greater, perhaps primarily in Moscow itself. What have more than two decades of high adventure in both Yemens accomplished for Moscow? The Russians are no closer to success in the prime target—Saudi Arabia—than they were 25 years ago. Encouraging young radicals in the belief that they can be turned into docile Marxist-Leninist bureaucrats, free of tribal and religious prejudices, has brought no dividends. Instead it has brought failure, waste of resources and embarrassment.

Neither of the two Yemens' experience with the Soviets—or with trying to play off the Soviets against the Chinese, an option no longer open—has produced results other countries would willingly emulate.

Among Marxist-oriented leaders in the Yemens, in fact, one of the most attractive features of the Soviet model has failed to work: the justification it provides for leaders to rule in the name of the 'broad masses' without consulting them and nevertheless retaining their hold on power. No Yemeni leader has been able to feel comfortable in power for long. Marxism appears, if anything, to have intensified rather than mitigated tribal and personal rivalries.

Soviet strategy for gaining a foothold in the Arabian Peninsula, the very heartland of Islam, has entailed a large outlay of effort and resources but has brought no permanent gains. It has not significantly weakened the pro-Western, pro-capitalist, profoundly anti-socialist orientation of the dominant elements of the economically most important countries of the Peninsula. These depressing conclusions may well be recognised and acknowledged in the course of whatever reviews of Arab policy may be taking place in the early years of the Gorbachev era. Of only one thing we can be quite certain: Moscow will not abandon efforts to expand its influence in the Arab heartland.

During World War II and its immediate aftermath, the Soviets did not exert themselves in respect to Saudi Arabia. It was denounced as a feudal monarchy which had sold itself to American capitalists for oil concessions. The American air base at Dharan was the object of special Soviet rancour.[24] Khrushchev ushered in a more positive era and was encouraged by Saudi refusal to participate in the Baghdad Pact. The Buraimi oasis imbroglio, which alienated the Saudis from the British, was a major factor in this rejection. The Russians saw an opportunity to fish in troubled waters and hoped to sell the Saudis arms, as they had Egypt, through Czechoslovakia. King Saud even accepted Egyptian military advisers and Soviet writers praised Wahhabism—the puritanical form of Islam practiced by the Saudis—as progressive. For a year or two Soviet hopes rose for a closer relationship, paralleling the blossoming Egyptian one, but the deeply conservative Saudis were not to be easily manipulated—nor did they cherish pan-Arab territorial ambitions. In fact, the Saudis became rapidly more sceptical of the effect of Nasser's ambitions on their country following the 1956 Suez War and in 1957 renewed the US lease on Dharan.

During the 1960s the close support Moscow gave Nasser (in spite of periodic strains in the relationship), Soviet adventures with radical regimes in Iraq and North Yemen and the general activism of Soviet policy toward the Third World disillusioned those elements in the Saudi leadership who had been inclined to bargain with the Russians. The Soviets did nothing to counter this trend:

> . . . the Soviet attitude toward Saudi Arabia in these years became increasingly churlish . . . Modern Wahhabism was accused of having discarded its 'positive' (i.e. egalitarian) attributes, and of having forsaken its original mission to restore the pristine simplicity of Islam. Instead [Moscow maintained], it had become a mere tool of the 'feudalists' for the exploitation of the Saudi people, part of the wider conspiracy to substitute religion for the growth of class feelings among the Arab masses.[25]

Just before the coup in Yemen in September 1962 there was a brief burst of friendly contacts which illustrates the Soviet practice of flexible opportunism. The Saudi decision not to renew the Dharan agreement with the US in 1962 heartened Moscow and the Mayor of Riyadh was invited to Soviet Central Asia (and accepted) while the Saudi UN ambassador visited Moscow and was warmly received by Khrushchev. There were conversations about Soviet arms sales again, but the overthrow of the Imamate in Yemen changed everything. The Soviets made a new effort at friendship when they welcomed the accession of Prince Faysal to the throne in late 1964— but during the remainder of the decade the situation in Yemen, with the Soviets providing support to the Republicans while the Saudis aided the Royalists, bolstered Saudi doubts that the Soviets could wish them well in any respect. After 1967, Soviet support for radicals in Aden added an additional element of strain while the Saudis became actively engaged in supporting South Yemeni emigres against the Soviet and Chinese backed Aden regime. Soviet support for the Dhofar rebellion confirmed Saudi doubts about Moscow's real desires and intentions in the Arabian Peninsula.

Moscow continued periodically, in spite of Saudi hostility, to propose establishment of diplomatic relations and regularly sent Saudi National Day congratulations. In 1973, following the Yom-Kippur War and proclamation of the Arab oil embargo, King Faysal reciprocated and sent congratulations for the first time to the Soviet head of state (Podgorny) on the anniversary of the October revolution, but no other actions leading to a warming of contacts followed. There was another brief period of verbal *rapprochement* after the accession of King Fahd in 1975, but Moscow's activism in Africa, and especially in the neighbouring Horn, alarmed the Saudis, as did events in the Yemens.

When Camp David negotiations leading to a successful agreement again strained the US-Saudi ties (which had become steadily closer during the 1970s) Moscow once more tried to capitalise on the situation and Crown Prince Fahd even predicted establishment of diplomatic relations. The Soviet invasion of Afghanistan shattered what slight chance there might have been of such a development. Since that time Soviet-Saudi attitudes toward each other have remained cool. The Saudis have repeatedly stated four conditions for improvement: (1) withdrawal of Soviet forces from Afghanistan; (2) reduction of the Soviet presence in South Yemen and Ethiopia; (3) cessation of hostile Soviet propaganda against Saudi Arabia; and (4) greater religious freedom for Soviet Muslims. Moscow has never abandoned the position that it would like to have formal diplomatic relations with Riyadh, but the only condition of the four listed above which it could even pretend to meet would be the third. Prospects for formal relations of any kind, let alone warm ones, between the Soviet Union and Saudi Arabia must be judged today no better than they were 30 years ago.

The most interesting question for the future is whether Moscow is likely to increase its subversive efforts against Saudi Arabia. Restive intellectuals, dissidents in the armed forces, Shia populations in the Eastern Province are all targets Moscow appears to have encouraged in the past at arm's length through various Arab front groups. Nasser had organised a Saudi Arabian National Liberation Front (SANLF) in 1962 and supported several other radical groups such as the Union of the Peoples of the Arabian Peninsula (UPAP), but none of these developed any independent momentum. In 1975 the SANLF announced that it had become the Saudi Arabian Communist Party, but it has shown little evidence of significant membership or activity inside Saudi Arabia.[26]

The Soviets condemned the seizure of the Grand Mosque in Mecca in November 1979 and the Saudis did not publicly allege a Soviet role. The speed with which the incident led to violent anti-American actions in many Muslim countries—notably Pakistan where a mob burned the American embassy—aroused suspicion that the KGB was, at a minimum, ready to exploit the episode to the disadvantage of the United States. Such actions appear in keeping with other efforts by the Soviets to divert Islamic rancour over Afghanistan and related issue from themselves by directing fundamentalist rancour against the United States and encouraging actions that heighten American—and general Western—fear of Islamic extremists. Such actions are entirely in keeping with the basic Soviet readiness to exploit Islamic feelings to advance its own purposes that has been apparent since the early 1920s. The subtle exploitation of conservative religious and political forces to destabilise societies in states the Soviets consider obstacles to their goals, as well as to generate tensions with the United States and other Western countries, was both intensified and refined during the 1970s. What the Soviets themselves have been doing was well described theoretically in the fake US Army field manual FM 30–31B which was originally publicised in a small leftist Turkish newspaper in 1975 and has since appeared in more than 20 countries. In the manual, of course, the techniques are attributed to the United States.[27]

Surveying Soviet efforts to gain influence in the Arabian Peninsula, we have examined several techniques: (1) support of traditional rulers and conservative governments when they are actually or potentially hostile to the West; (2) manipulation of revolutionary republican governments through military and (mostly promises of) economic aid; (3) subversion at many levels, from propaganda and overt methods of gaining attention and influence at the relatively benign end of the spectrum to participation in active political plotting and plans for overthrowing groups considered less favourable to Soviet purposes than those by whom they can be replaced; (4) cultivation of Marxist radicals, military or civilian, with active assistance in building Marxist-Leninist or other kinds of 'socialist' parties; (5) support of political conspiracy and guerrilla movements with the aim of violent overthrow of traditional regimes; (6) destructive subversion—encouragement and manipulation of negative forces—conservative traditionalists or religious fundamentalists without any immediately constructive purpose. The aim can be to weaken or destablilise societies and cause Western powers difficulties or, in the case of religious extremists, to discredit and undermine them, and indirectly to discredit Islam in the USSR itself.

Let us turn now to Kuwait to examine an example of a Soviet approach that differs in most respects from others in the Arabian Peninsula and which appears, to date at least, to have been uniquely beneficial to both the Kuwaitis and the Soviets. Small in area and population, Kuwait has a long history of playing off hostile forces against each other to preserve its political freedom. It avoided falling under Ottoman domination while also playing off the Saudis and Persians and eventually became a British protectorate at the very end of the 19th century. It became apparent that Kuwait was rich in petroleum deposits during the 1930s but production did not begin until after World War II. For its size and population, Kuwait possesses the most valuable oil reserves in the world and during the last two dacades has become so rich that military or economic aid could not be an enticement to closer relations with a major power.

Kuwait became formally independent in 1961 but remained under British military protection for another decade, an arrangment attractive to Kuwait because of the radical regime that had come to power in Iraq in 1958. Qassem in fact laid claim to Kuwait. The Soviets stayed in the background—probably because another Moscow ally, Nasser, opposed Qassem's policy. Nevertheless, both before and after independence Moscow was hostile to the Kuwaiti ruling family, condemning them as toadies of both the oil companies and of British and American imperialists. The USSR vetoed Kuwait's application for UN membership in 1961. When Qassem was over-thrown in 1963 the Soviets repudiated his claim to Kuwait and estab-lished diplomatic relations. UN membership with enthusiastic Soviet support soon followed, but after a new pro-Soviet government came to power in Baghdad Khrushchev again had unkind words for Kuwait in Cairo in May 1964:

> There is such a state as Kuwait . . . There is some little ruler sitting there, an Arab, of course, a Moslem. He is given bribes. He lives the life of the rich, but he is trading in the riches of his people. He never had any conscience and he won't ever have any. [To the Eygptians:] Will you come to terms with him on unifi-cation? It is easier to eat three puds of salt than to reach agreement with him, though you are both Arabs and Moslems.[28]

As soon as Khrushchev had been ousted his successors began to make amends—and overtures—to Kuwait. The Kuwaiti Prime Minister, who later became the Amir (that is, the ruler), was invited to Moscow in November 1964 and the following February a Soviet delegation flew to Kuwait to sign a technical assistance agreement. No one ate three puds of salt. Relations warmed through the remainder of the 1960s and from that time onward [in Kuwait] the practice of appeasement as the guiding principle of state policy was developed to the level of a higher art form.[29]

The Soviets saw Kuwait as not only of some importance in itself, but valuable as a diplomatic base from where all sorts of semi-overt and covert activities could be conducted throughout the eastern Arab World. The Kuwaitis saw an open relationship with the Soviets as a form of insurance against a hostile policy or subversive actions, especially in view of the warming trends in Soviet-Iraqi relations that always set in again after each period of strain. Defector Vladimir Sakharov pays tribute to Kuwaiti alertness to Soviet subversive habits:

> Kuwait was no Egypt—the Kuwaiti government kept the Soviets strictly limited. The Soviet colony never numbered more than fifty, including clerks and dependents, while I was there. The Soviet Embassy in Kuwait was smaller than the Soviet Consulate General in Alexandria. More importantly, Kuwait's efficient and tough-minded, British-trained security police kept sharp watch on the Soviets and had a free hand to crack down on any mischief.[30]

During the 1970s the Kuwaiti policy of maintaining close enough relations with Moscow to prevent Soviet support for an Iraqi attempt to take over the oil-rich little sheikhdom reached the point of exploring a military relationship. A 1974 attempt to purchase arms from the Russians failed, but negotiations continued intermittently through 1975 and 1976. When the US denied a Kuwaiti arms request, the Soviet's appetite for a deal was whetted. What was rumoured to be a $400 million deal at the end of 1976 materialised into a mere $50 million arrangment for Kuwaiti purchase of SAM–7s and artillery in March 1977. In 1980 the Soviets sold Kuwait $200 million-worth of arms, but Kuwait refused to permit a Soviet military mission. Kuwait diversified its arms purchases by arrangements with Britain, France and the US, engaged Western military instructors, but continued to discuss new arms purchases with Moscow throughout the mid–1980s. In January 1985 some Kuwaiti military personnel were finally sent to the USSR for training.

Moscow has consistently offered more exchanges of students, cultural groups and technical assistance specialists than the Kuwaitis have accepted. So rich that it is able to purchase any goods or services it needs from the highest quality sources in the West or Japan, Kuwaitis have to strain to find trade with the Soviets

attractive. Kuwait has been useful for Moscow as a transfer point
for Aeroflot and a base for *TASS* and other propaganda operations.
Its relatively open society provides opportunities for Soviet operatives to move around with relative ease and, as long as they stay
within the bounds of propriety in Kuwait's domestic affairs, to use
Kuwait as a base of operations for other parts of the Arab world.
As far as can be learned, the Soviets have resisted the temptation
to dabble subversively in Kuwaiti politics. While dissidents from
Saudi Arabia and the Gulf states are from time to time utilised in
Soviet propaganda operations, the Soviets have meticulously avoided
any evidence of support for Kuwaiti leftists or Marxists.

In the realm of foreign policy . . . the Soviets particularly value
friendship with Kuwait, for even though Kuwait is ruled by an
amir instead of a 'vanguard party,' the two governments have
similar foreign policy views on many issues. Foremost among these
is the Arab-Israeli dispute. The Kuwaiti government and media
have frequently endorsed the Soviet call for . . . a Middle East
peace conference . . . Kuwait has also vilified the US for
supporting Israel, criticised . . . the Camp David accords and
praised Soviet support to the Arabs.[31]

But Kuwaiti 'appeasement' has not extended to approval of Soviet
actions in Ethiopia or Afghanistan. The Kuwaiti delegation to the
January 1980 Islamic Conference comdemned the Afghan invasion
but did not threaten to break diplomatic relations or participate in
the Olympic boycott. The Kuwaitis distinguish with greater refine-
ment than most Arabs between (1) hard-core domestic and closer
regional issues where they make no concessions to the Soviets; (2)
propaganda issues where they are strong on principle but weak in
practice; and (3) issues where they take a soft or pro-Soviet stand.
In this latter category falls the question of Muslims of the USSR.
Kuwaiti officials praise freedom of religion in the USSR.

Thus we see in the case of Kuwait an example of pragmatic opportunism on both sides. Kuwaiti 'appeasement' of the Soviets may go
on paying off for a long time. Were the conservative regime to be
overthrown in Kuwait by either Islamic fundamentalists or leftist
radicals, however, it is difficult to see Moscow having any trouble
adjusting to new circumstances. And if there were clear gains to be
made from a shift to a hostile policy toward Kuwait, Moscow would
not hesitate to engage in active subversion. It is difficult to believe
that the small number of highly skilled KGB operatives regularly

assigned there have not succeeded in establishing stand-by agents who would be useful in just such an eventuality. It is even more likely that the KGB *rezidentura* in Kuwait has succeeded in developing assets in the other Gulf sheikhdoms where Moscow has so far been unable to establish a presence.

8 The Strategic Long View: The Nile Valley and the Horn of Africa

In chapter 6 I have analysed in some detail the Soviet-Egyptian initial infatuation that began in the mid–1950s and lasted for nearly two decades, because it provides so many insights into Soviet strategy toward the Arab World. Khrushchev, an adventurous, optimistic expansionist, believed he could exploit Gamal Abdal Nasser's ambitions for leadership of the Arab World to lock the Arabs into a permanent 'socialist' embrace. Khrushchev underestimated both the religious and nationalistic components of Nasser's appeal. Nevertheless, both Khrushchev's successors and Nasser himself found the relationship indispensable and it continued until Nasser's successor. Anwar Sadat, who had a different vision for Egypt and much more scepticism about ultimate Soviet intentions, expelled the unpopular Soviet advisers and technicians and reorientated Egypt toward the west. The Soviet-Egyptian experience was only one aspect of a larger Soviet strategy, aimed at gaining hegemony over the Nile Valley and the Horn of Africa as well as predominant influence over the Arab World. This strategy was—and is—not merely a communist strategy. It rests on well established Russian imperial ambitions. Soviet leaders have always been conscious of history. We can ignore the historical background of Soviet expansionist efforts only at the expense of being needlessly surprised, misled, and willfully self-deceived, which is in fact, the most unfortunate kind of deception.[1]

Examination of the manner in which the Soviets have pursued their goals in the Nile Valley and the Horn of Africa—with considerable success—sheds light on several important aspects of Soviet strategy: the deep historical foundations of Kremlin policy; the exploitation of religion; the utilisation of varied devices to gain access and influence—modest and seemingly benign when other avenues are closed, dynamic and with high-risk potential when opportunities present themselves; the capacity for quick tactical shifts; the use of varied approaches at varying tempos simultaneously. Whatever the tactical twists and turns or the contortions that the principle of flexible opportunism dictates, the long-term goal always remains the same: the expansion and consolidation of Soviet influence and, ultimately, control.

Russian awareness of the peoples of northeast Africa can be traced back to the 17th century, but until the mid–19th century the Tsars were busy driving the Ottoman Turks out of the Black Sea Steppes, the Crimea and the Caucasus and pushing the Persian empire into retreat from the Caucasus and Central Asia. Nevertheless, always one step ahead in plans, by the 1840s they were already looking beyond to broader horizons: the Horn of Africa, the Red Sea and the Indian Ocean. The Imperial Russian Geographical Society sent a mining engineer (who also happened to be a military man), Lt. Col. E. P. Kovalevsky, to explore the sources of the Nile in 1847. When he returned the next year, he was decorated by Nicholas I and published a two-volume account of his travels.[2] During the 1850s the Reverend Porfirii Uspensky, a priest who headed the Russian Orthodox Mission in Jerusalem, became fascinated with Ethiopia and formulated a programme for Russian rejuvenation of what we would now call the Third World by helping the Ethiopians modernise themselves and serve as the spearhead for a Russian-dominated effort to gain control over Africa and orient it toward Moscow.[3]

Although Russia's actual accomplishments in this early stage amounted to little, leaders in this part of the world became aware of Russian ambitions and tried to exploit them. Ethiopian Emperor Tewodros sent the Tsar a letter in 1855 proposing that as an Orthodox ruler he join him in a campaign to liberate Jerusalem from the Turks. It was an unpropitious moment—for Russia had just been defeated in the Crimean War by a combination of British, French and Turkish forces and had to accept severe limitations on its Black Sea fleet to secure peace. Jerusalem was as unrealistic a goal for the Tsar as it was for Tewodros. But less than two decades later Russia was marching southward again. The Russians were quick to realise the advantages of the Suez Canal. Four years after it was opened in 1869, Russia ranked eighth among users. During the 1880s the Russians became directly involved in efforts to gain a foothold on the Red Sea and influence in Ethiopia. Senior members of the Orthodox Church establishment always accompanied Russian delegations.

A Cossack freebooter was encouraged by ardent nationalists to set up a colony—New Moscow—on the coast north of Djibouti in 1888. He could hardly have picked a geographically less hospitable spot and, furthermore, the venture challenged the already established French presence in the Gulf of Tajura. The undertaking became an embarrassing disaster and was officially disavowed.[4]

The next phase of Russian activity was much more successful, both for the Russians' imperial ambitions and for Ethiopian Emperor Menelik II, their main beneficiary. Several thinly disguised 'scientific' expeditions laid the basis for military aid to Ethiopia as it was preparing for the confrontation with Italy, which culminated in the great victory at Adowa in March 1896. In the following years Tsarist officers helped Menelik consolidate control over the southwestern parts of the country and supported French efforts to gain a foothold on the upper Nile.[5]

Competition with Britain gave the Russians strong incentive to expand their influence in the Nile/Horn region—just as less than half a century later it spurred the Soviets to establish relations with Saudi Arabia and Yemen. The Soviet Russians, like their tsarist predecessors, are always tempted to encourage any movement that promises to cause trouble for rival powers. The habit of exploiting religion for political purposes is deeply established in Russian foreign policy tradition. The same factors were a spur to Russian efforts to make contact with the Sudanese Mahdists—messianic religious militants—in the 1890s. An army officer, Major A. V. Eliseev, disguised as an Arab, embarked in 1893 on a journey from Egypt into northern Sudan but was forced to turn back before reaching Omdurman. In an article which he published the following year in the *Journal of the Imperial Russian Geographical Society* he concluded that the Mahdists' chances of setting up a successful state were not good. But he also noted that there was interest among the Russian empire's own Muslim citizens in Mahdism. Tsarist Russia was prepared to exploit Islamic links to further its political purposes but found Orthodox ties more comfortable.[6]

No longer under Arab disguise, Eliseev was sent next to Ethiopia in charge of a 'scientific' expedition in 1895. He was accompanied by two other military officers and an Orthodox priest, Father Efrem. This expedition was welcomed at Harar by Ras Makonnen (father of the future Haile Selassie) and told of Menelik's urgent need of help against the Italians. Eliseev returned to Russia to lay the groundwork for a visit by an Ethiopian mission. It included several Ethiopian military officers as well as a bishop. The Ethiopians played the Russian game and emphasised the religious character of the undertaking but the real purpose was to secure arms and military advisers. Eliseev meanwhile died, but his place was taken by Captain

N. S. Leontiev who became prominent in Ethiopia in the years that followed, serving as a member of a council which Menelik formed to develop plans for resisting the Italian military threat.

The standard interpretation of the Ethiopian victory at Adowa has been that the Italians seriously underestimated both the strength of Ethiopian nationalism and Menelik's capacity to lead and manoeuvre. The advice of Captain Leontiev and his Russian associates may have been equally important. He urged the Ethiopians to employ classic Russian tactics, luring the Italians deep into the country where the terrain was against them, getting them over-extended, cutting their supply lines and then decimating them. These are the same tactics Kutuzov employed against Napoleon in 1812. They were not , of course, unknown in Ethiopian traditional warfare. Captain Leontiev was given the Ethiopian title *Dejazmach* after the Adowa victory, and Menelik sent a message of appreciation to the Tsar. The Russians sent a Red Cross mission headed by a Lt. General to Addis Ababa and a party of 60 technicians to set up a hospital which was officially opened in 1898. But it was always politically controversial. A contemporary observer characterised it as 'essentially a diplomatic institution' rather than a reliable medical establishment.[7]

After their defeat by the Japanese in 1905, the Russians lost interest in Ethiopia, and after 1912 Ethiopia itself fell into a period of internal crisis. The Horn of Africa and Nile valley had low priority in Moscow during the early Soviet period and attracted major attention again only as a result of the Italian invasion of Ethiopia and the international commotion it generated. The Soviets tried to play all sides—and did so rather successfully—during this crisis. They did not wish to alienate Mussolini because they feared Hitler but they also wished to appear as champions of Ethiopia's fight to defend its independence. They sold oil and grain to Italy but they refused to recognise the Italian conquest. This gave them a basis for establishing a presence in Ethiopia after its liberation in 1941. By this time the Stalin-Hitler alliance was failing and when the Soviet Union was invaded by German armies, it was welcomed as an ally of the Western powers. Stalin established diplomatic relations with Ethiopia in 1943 (there had heretofore been no diplomatic relations during the Soviet period) and announced plans to 'reopen' the Russian hospital which had been set up half a century before. The new Soviet legation opened a 'Permanent Exhibition' in Addis Ababa to publicise the Soviet way of life. During the Italian occupation of

Ethiopia, Russian academics had been mobilised to produce research and a great many books recounting previous Russian involvements with the area were published. At the end of World War II, Russian academics were systematically assigned the task of gathering information on Ethiopia and other parts of Africa as well. Even when resources were severely limited and other regions held higher priority, Moscow was preparing for the long haul in Africa.[8]

Ethiopia's high standing as the first victim of fascism and a charter member of the United Nations as well as its close wartime association with Britain and the United States made consolidation of a special relationship with Britain and, after 1950, the United States, a logical development. There was little opportunity for Soviet gains in this kind of situation, but poor prospects did not deter the Russians from trying. They sought a say in the disposition of Italy's colonies, seeking trusteeships over both Libya and Eritrea. They were rebuffed but participation in the various United Nations commissions which eventually arranged for the disposition of these territories, as well as Somalia, gave Soviet officials first-hand knowledge of the political complexities of the region. The common denominator of Soviet behaviour in this period was their own advantage, sometimes seen in very tactical terms. In a manner reminiscent of some of the Soviet manoeuvres during the Italo-Ethiopian War, the Russians tilted toward residual Italian interests in the former colonies during the period when it appeared that the Communist Party of Italy had a chance to gain predominant influence through the ballot box.

When Eritrea was federated with Ethiopia in 1952 and Somalia returned to Italy in trusteeship with the obligation to prepare it for independence by the end of the decade, the Soviets no longer had a basis for direct involvement there. Libya became an independent monarchy in 1951. Relations were established with the USSR in 1955, but by that time Libya had already become an important link in the American network of strategic bases in the Mediterranean. If Soviet behaviour at the end of World War II had been more co-operative—or more skilfully deceptive—chances are good that the Soviets might well have gained some degree of foothold in one or more of the former Italian colonies. Patience and persistence in the end paid off, nevertheless, for a generation later the Soviets had gained predominance in Libya and Somalia and had underwritten a major insurgency in Eritrea which eventually became a factor in the downfall of the imperial regime in Ethiopia.[9]

Despite diplomatic recognition, Soviet-Libyan relations remained cool until Qadhafi deposed the king and took power in 1969. By this time Libya had become the fourth largest oil exporter in the world and was thus an economic prize of real consequence. The Russians immediately recognised Qadhafi and praised his programme, began negotiations on expansion of trade and offered to explore new oil-fields. Soviet enthusiasm for Qadhafi took a long time to be recipro-cated, though many of his actions—expelling US and British bases, support of Palestinians and other terrorists, extreme anti-Zionism—were pleasing to Moscow. But he also refused to legalise the small Libyan communist party and condemned the USSR itself for its policy of *détente* with the West, terming it 'a betrayal of the anti-imperialist cause'.[10] Qadhafi fell to quarrelling with most other Arab leaders, spent oil profits lavishly, and proclaimed an Islamic Cultural Revolution in 1973.

It was Qadhafi's need for arms and the Russians' eagerness to supply them that finally cemented a relationship. A Libyan delegation visited Moscow in May 1974, Kosygin came to Libya in May 1975 and Qadhafi paid his first visit to Moscow in December 1976. The result of all this visiting was a heavy Soviet flow of arms, estimated to total $1 billion by the end of 1976. Deliveries grew rapidly in the years that followed. Qadhafi showed great skill in playing off other countries, especially France and China, against the Russians, exploiting requests for nuclear power-plants and advanced weaponry. The Soviets found Qadhafi much more difficult to handle than Nasser had been—but the close relationship with Libya helped compensate for the loss of Egypt.

The Soviets would clearly have preferred a less flamboyant, less demonstratively Islamic, more controllable leader in Libya and there was speculation that the KGB may even have had a hand in some of the coup and assassination attempts against Qadhafi that kept recurring.[11] But Qadhafi had two overwhelming advantages for Moscow: (1) rich with oil money, he paid for his arms, thus providing Moscow with a source of foreign exchange; and (2) as Soviet policy placed more stress on terrorism and subversion, Qadhafi as a brazen self-starter who could be disavowed as subject to Moscow's control, served Moscow's purpose without any need for expenditure of Moscow's funds or resources, except perhaps for occasional KGB training and advice. He continues to do so in the 1980s.

It is not difficult to imagine that Qadhafi's antics may sometimes have caused hand-wringing in Moscow. He sometimes conspired against regimes Moscow favoured. His refusal to have any truck with Soviet-style party organisation must have been distasteful to communist ideologues. His strong Islamic orientation must also have caused discomfort, for there was always some danger of feedback to Soviet Muslims. (Not surprisingly, his late 1970's request to Brezhnev to open a Libyan consulate in Tashkent was abruptly refused). But there were also compensatory considerations: his extremism, often exercised in the name of Islam, tended to discredit Islam and reawakened residual anti-Muslim fears and prejudices among Europeans and Americans. From the view-point of those Russians who have become increasingly interested in playing on and magnifying fears of Islamic fanaticism in the West, Qadhafi's extremism, on balance, was a gain for Soviet purposes. The image of Qadhafi as a fanatic Muslim pay-master for terrorists, now so widespread in the West, complicates Western dealings with the Islamic world more than it does Moscow's. In all respects, the Soviet relationship with Libya is a striking example of the principle of flexible opportunism in operation. And when the time comes for abandoning Qadhafi, Moscow will be able to do so with little real loss, for the actual investment in him has been minimal. He has more than paid his own way.

So we see in this example of Soviet Islamic strategy the principles which underline it in their crassest form: eagerness to welcome a fanatic, erratic military strongman; use of arms to develop a relationship; willingness to ignore a strong Islamic orientation; eagerness to profit monetarily; the attractiveness of a surrogate operating on a major scale in the most odious and vicious aspect of international operations which the Soviet Union countenances: terrorism and subversion. If Libya had had a serious communist movement, the Soviet ability to exploit Qadhafi would have been greatly complicated. I will examine in a separate section below another important country in this region where exactly this occurred: Sudan. Before turning to it let me survey briefly a third situation in the Nile Valley/Horn region where a military leader seized power in 1969: Somalia. The possibility cannot be excluded that the Soviets may have had a clandestine hand in supporting all three of these 1969 military coups—of Qadhafi, Nimeiry and Siad Barre—that undermined the stability of the region and disadvantaged the West at a time when Nasser was still powerful in Egypt and the Soviets appeared to be in the ascendancy in most parts of the Arab World.

In Somalia the Soviets had sought influence immediately after independence—when former British Somaliland was combined with the Italian trust territory to form the Somali Republic—was granted in 1960. But it was not until 1964 that they were able to move onto the Somali scene as generous arms suppliers. Alone of the countries of the region, Somalia was threatened neither by its neighbours nor by internal insurgency, but it had major territorial claims against three of them: Kenya, Ethiopia and Djibouti (then called French Somaliland, later renamed the Territory of the Afars and Issas). Unlike other newly independent African countries, Somalia was unwilling to ascribe to the principle embodied in the charter of the Organisation of African Unity that colonial-era boundaries, irrational as they might be, would be recognised as valid unless revised by the mutual consent of both states involved. To contain Somali irredentist ambitions, the US and its European allies agreed to provide only sufficient military aid to arm a small military force to be used for internal security purposes. The Russians were willing to cater to Somali nationalism for the sake of getting a foothold in a region where they had long coveted a basis for influence. They made massive deliveries of arms to Somalia in 1964 and 1965. These enabled Somalia to build an army and generate a major insurgency in the Ethiopian Ogaden and parts of Bale and Sidamo provinces from 1965 onwards, as well as to support subversion in Kenya.[12]

Somalia, aside from the military relationship, was not an easy country for the Soviets to manipulate. Somali society is fundamentally egalitarian but extremely class-oriented and Somali nationalism is deeply bound up with Islam. Moreover, Somalia was launched into independence with a parliamentary democratic system and managed to maintain it, with a multiplicity of parties but no communist movement, until Siad Barre's coup in October 1969. Siad Barre did not disavow Islam but he favoured modernisation of Somali society—emancipation of women, settlement of nomads, spread of literacy and education. These attitudes plus his active interest in socialism—state domination of the economy—and a desire to orient Somalia toward the Arab World more than compensated for his Islamic orientation in Soviet eyes. After Siad had successfully established his hold on power, the Soviets greatly increased their presence in the country and expanded military deliveries. Somalia, with its long Indian Ocean coastline and ports that could be developed for military support purposes, appeared an ideal acquisition—a major outpost of the Soviet Russian Empire and a realisation of the Tsars' wilder dreams. The Soviets signed a Friendship and Mutual Assist-

ance Treaty with Somalia in 1974, just after the Ethiopian revolution
was gaining momentum, and in the following years greatly stepped
up the flow of military aid to Somalia.[13] Analysis of concrete Soviet
actions during the next three years leads to the conclusion that at
least two potential Horn policies competed during this period, but
the advocates of Somalia as the centre-piece of Soviet efforts to
expand influence in the area consistently won out until the late
summer of 1977. Ethiopia was obviously the greater prize but there
were many reasons for the Soviets to regard it as risky—there was
the danger of Western reaction to too rapid Soviet moves to consolidate power there; there was uncertainty about the ability of the Derg
to maintain control; there was uncertainty about Mengistu himself.

So the Soviets played a complex, several-track game in the Horn
during the 1970s, maintaining support for the insurgency in Eritrea
until 1977 and encouraging several radical political movements in
Ethiopia to compete. This brings us ahead of the story, however.
The whole dramatic sequence of events in the Horn during this
period cannot be retold here and has already been well chronicled,[14]
but I will return to examine certain issues that have bearing on the
central topic of this study: Islam in Soviet Strategy. Directly relevant
to this issue is Soviet activity in respect to the Sudan.

The Sudan was unique in Africa in having an indigenous communist
party with as genuine 'grass roots' as any in the Islamic world—more
so, in fact, than the Egyptian communist movement. The earliest
beginnings of communism in the Sudan can be traced to the anti-
British, Egyptian-oriented 'White Flag Movement' that grew up
among Sudanese students and officials in the 1920s. Until it was
banned by the British administration in Khartoum, this movement
attracted a modest degree of Comintern attention. We see a familiar
pattern here: a Soviet Tatar named Lumitoff and a Soviet Jew,
Belkin, operating out of the Soviet legation in Jeddah, served as
contacts through Sudanese railway workers, but little came of their
efforts.[15] The Comintern terminated its Nile Valley activities in 1930
and paid no attention to the region until World War II, concentrating
on West and South Africa.

Developments which led to the formal establishment of the Sudan
Communist Party (SCP), the first and for a long time the only such
party in Black Africa, involved two merging currents. Sudanese
students in Cairo, influenced by Egyptian communists, founded a
Sudanese Movement for National Liberation in 1946. Meanwhile a

group of British officers in Sudan who were members of the British Communist Party had influenced students and intellectuals around Khartoum to study communism and organise themselves. They set up the first communist cell at Khartoum University in 1946. The emerging party was handicapped by controversy over orientation: toward unity of the Nile Valley (that is a pro-Egyptian stance)or nationalism within Sudanese territory? Those who favoured the Egyptians were labelled 'Royal Communists' by their opponents[16] and were eventually purged. The party henceforth concentrated on building a following among trade unionists and agricultural workers in new development projects, but its real strength remained among intellectuals, professionals and journalists. Championing the cause of independence and opposed to all imperialism—including Egyptian—the Sudanese communists found themselves facing a succession of dilemmas as Nasser came to power in Egypt and gradually oriented his Arab socialist revolution toward the Soviet Union. Soviet advice to the party seems often to have been contradictory, and undoubtedly accounts for some of the strains which the SCP experienced during the period immediately before and after independence in 1956. SCP leader Abdal Khaliq Mahjub explained in 1954 that the only enemy of communism was imperialism while believers, whether Muslim or Christian, who were willing to fight against imperialism,

. . . were the communists' natural allies. Furthermore, communism sought to harness human knowledge and scientific achievements and to exploit them for the benefit of society. Here again, Mahjub asserts, communism and Islam were striving to achieve identical aims.[17]

Nevertheless, the SCP had difficulty overcoming Muslim opposition. Both before and in the years immediately after independence (1956) the SCP operated through the Anti-Imperialist Front, a device which drew several other organisations, including trade unions, into association with it and gave it a greater claim to legitimacy. Although rent by factionalism it gained strength as the party of the 'educated', in contrast to the larger parties that occupied the centre of the political spectrum and the Muslim Brotherhood, which appealed to intellectuals disillusioned with Western secularism as well as traditionalists. From 1958 to 1964 Sudan was under military rule which the SCP claimed had come about as a result of collusion between the military and traditional politicians. Politics did not cease during this period, for the military had promised to restore parliamentary government. This proved to be difficult. By opposing the military and accusing General Ibrahim Abbud of collusion with foreign interests and mismanaging the economy, the SCP was able to gain considerable credibility, present itself as a champion of national interests and at the same time serve basic Soviet purposes by condemning Sudan's orientation toward the United States.

By 1963 rebellion had become a serious problem in the south. The SCP avoided too close an identification with the Christian southerners. The situation in the south contributed to the unrest, culminating in a general strike, which forced General Abbud to surrender power to a civilian 'National Front' coalition in October 1964. 'It was generally acknowledged, even by critics . . . that the SCP played an important role, far exceeding its actual strength, during the October upheaval.'[18]

Recognising their inability to create a true revolutionary situation, the SCP's leaders decided to participate in general elections called in May 1965. They won 11 of the 15 seats designated for 'graduates' (that is the educated) in parliament—but no seats in any ordinary constituency. This demonstrated that in spite of efforts to win support among workers and peasants the SCP had gained no dependable mass following. Sadiq al-Mahdi, descendant of the famous Mahdi, leader of the Umma party and the Ansar religious sect, attacked the SCP for its efforts to politicise society, its foreign policy and its stance toward Islam. The Muslim Brothers also organised demonstrations against the SCP. In November 1965 the constitution was amended to outlaw communist or atheist propaganda. Sadiq al-Mahdi declared communism antithetical to the Sudanese spirit because of

> its contradiction of the belief in the existence of God, its binding of Sudanese sovereignty with an international creed and tie and its dependence on class dictatorship would undoubtedly supply the need for the establishment of other political movements and groupings (that is, allied and surrogate groups).[19]

Thus what appeared to be a solid success for a party that had followed classic Soviet advice for building a following in a developing country turned into a serious setback. The SCP eventually obtained a Supreme Court decision declaring the ban illegal. Meanwhile the government accused the SCP of involvement in an abortive coup and then had the Constituent Assembly overrule the Supreme Court. It would be tedious to follow all the twists and turns of the political, legal and constitutional infighting that continued for the next three years. Most interesting for purposes of this analysis is the SCP's response—the establishment of a legal socialist party. Elections in 1968 nevertheless gave the traditional parties who were Islamic-oriented over three-quarters of the seats in parliament. The lesson for the SCP was that it stood very little chance of increasing its influence through the democratic process.

The democratic process was not producing effective government in the country, nor could it develop consensus for dealing with the spreading southern rebellion. In May 1969 Col. Gaafar Nimeiry seized control of the government. His movement was revolutionary and anti-sectarian, unlike the previous Abbud regime. He suspended all political parties and took measures against those based on loyalty to religious sects: the Ansar and the Khatmiyya. His attitude toward the SCP was much more tolerant. The Sudanese communists had taken a public stand against military intervention only two months before Nimeiry seized power. It is nevertheless possible that individual communists had been aware of and abetted the coup. The SCP made it clear that it was prepared to support Nimeiry ideologically and to co-operate on practical isues. Each needed the other. Nimeiry appointed four communists to his Cabinet as individuals and he had three pro-communist officers in his Revolutionary Command Council. The SCP had been active in many directions in the preceding years and expansion of its influence in the armed forces had been a major goal. Nimeiry was impressed by the extent of communist penetration in the army and felt it was better to have communists and sympathisers participating in his government openly rather than operating from the shadows. He was naive in this expectation—for subsequent developments were to prove that they were operating on both levels, as communists always do. He was naive in another respect as well: he assumed he could have a relationship with Moscow on his own terms. He flew to Moscow to seek economic and military aid. The Soviets were delighted to respond. Within less than a year 1800 Soviet military advisers had arrived, putting tanks, aircraft, vehicles and arms of all kinds into operation for the Sudanese army which, as almost always occurs with a close Soviet military relationship of this kind, quickly doubled in size. Soviet pilots flew missions against the southern rebels. Economic aid was meagre amd much slower in coming.

Sudan, occupying the heart of the Nile Valley, the largest country in area in Africa, bordering on eight other countries and with a long Red Sea coast, appeared to Mosocw to be a major prize all but securely in hand. Nimeiry proved amenable to permitting Moscow to step up the flow of arms to the insurgents in Eritrea and permitted the Eritreans to make more open use of Sudanese territory. The KGB and the Central Committee had high hopes that the SCP could soon gain predominance in Nimeiry's still loosely consolidated government. They miscalculated on Nimeiry himself. He was a believing Muslim and a nationalist, though also a convinced moderniser and a genuine opponent of what he considered narrow Islamic sectarianism. Islamic sects and Sufi brotherhoods have been unusually strong in Sudan since medieval times,[20] explainable in part at least by the country's location on the boundary between Black and North Africa and the nature of its population, which ranges from Nilotic and animist Blacks through every gradation of colour to Arabs who trace direct descent from the Prophet. The Ansars, both sect and a political movement based on the Mahdi tradition, rose in rebellion in March 1970 and succeeded in gaining control of Aba Island, a stronghold in the Nile near Khartoum where their movement originated. The fight against the Ansars became an embarrassing bloodbath and did not work to Soviet advantage in the Islamic world, although the Soviets tried to avoid direct participation in suppressing the rebellion.

The SCP, in all likelihood encouraged by the Russians, attempted to capitalise on the Ansar defeat which it believed made Nimeiry more directly dependent on it. He saw the situation in contrary light and became increasingly apprehensive of communist efforts to gain advantage and extended influence by setting up front organisations. In February 1971 he abandoned his tactical alliance with the SCP. He ordered dissolution of the party in May, but stressed that his action did not mean abandonment of the close relationship with Moscow. It was a high-risk approach, but outwardly the Soviets seemed to accept it. It is impossible to believe however, that they were unaware of the SCP's plans to strike back if, indeed, they did not help develop them. On the second anniversary of his taking power, Nimeiry announced establishment of the Sudan Socialist Union as the country's sole political party. Five days later the SCP published a declaration of war, branding Nimeiry as anti-revolutionary and called upon the population to unseat his military dictatorship. Communist leader Abdal Khaliq Mahjub escaped from prison on 29 June. Warned that communists in the army were preparing a coup, Nimeiry began a series of mass arrests. Communists and their supporters were prompted to act sooner than they had planned. On 19 July a leftist major, Hashim al-Ata, mounted a coup to avoid his own arrest. Two other coup leaders who were abroad were arrested by Qadhafi as they were flying back to Khartoum. Qadhafi felt a close affinity to Nimeiry at this time. Nimeiry and his immediate entourage were held in the Presidential palace but not killed. Sadat sent emissaries to negotiate with al-Ata and at the same time ordered Egyptian troops to advance on Khartoum. By 22 July the coup attempt had been defeated and Nimeiry reinstalled in power.

Most revealing is the behaviour of the Soviets during this hectic episode. TASS and the Soviet press greeted the new Sudanese leadership the day after the coup occurred and the Soviet ambassador in Khartoum called on al-Ata on 21 July to congratualte him. Then Moscow fell silent but a few days later began condemning Nimeiry for oppressive measure taken against communists. *Izvestia* in an authoritative 'Observer' article on 30 July declared ominously that 'the Soviet people are not indifferent to the destinies of the fighters against imperialism'. Meanwhile, the Soviet leadership, following a separate track, sent Nimeiry a message on 26 July assuring him that they had no intention of interfering in what they regarded as an internal Sudanese problem and asked that unfriendly acts against Soviet advisers be stopped.[21]

From this time onward, Soviet fortunes in Sudan went downhill, but the process of disengagement from the Soviet military and economic relationship was not easy. The Soviets maintained some advisers and provided further military aid, though on a much reduced scale. Before the end of 1971 Nimeiry sought Haille Selassie's aid in reaching an agreement with the leaders of the southern rebellion, in return for which he sharply cut aid to the Eritrean insurgents. The reorientation of Sudan toward the conservative Arab states and the West gained momentum from the mid–1970s onward. The SCP has never recovered from the collapse of the 1971 rebellion and the strong measures that were taken to suppress it in the wake of its failure. But neither has Sudan itself recovered from the effects of the political misfortunes of the 1970s. Overemphasis on the military blighted an already far from healthy economy. A strong reorientation toward the United States, in the aftermath of the Ethiopian revolution and the crises which gripped the Horn from 1976 onward, was not sufficient, in the final outcome, either to enable Nimeiry to establish a stable government or gain mastery of the economy. During the mid–1980s the Sudan again fell into a downward spiral of political and economic deterioration. Compensating perhaps for his past flirtation with socialism and revolutionary ideology, Nimeiry reverted to extreme Islamic obscurantism before he was deposed in 1985.

What lessons have the Soviets drawn from their Sudan experience? Forced into a minor role, they have nevertheless consistently striven to maintain some presence and to offer the prospect of support to any Sudanese regime that might wish for a warmer relationship. They have undoubtedly also worked to maintain an underground communist infrastructure. But, given their approach to other Islamic countries, it seems unlikely that they would again bid for hegemony in Sudan through the SCP. They have totally reversed their earlier position in respect to the rebellious southerners. Having supplied Nimeiry with pilots and aircraft to try to bomb them into submission in the early 1970s, they have in recent years given substantial support to the re-ignited southern rebellion through Ethiopia. They have also encouraged Qadhafi to meddle in Sudanese politics.

As of 1988, leadership in Sudan has come full circle. For lack of any better alternative, the country again turned to the leader of the Ansar sect, Sadiq al-Mahdi, to attempt to rescue it from the economic decay and political confusion in which it found itself after the fall of Nimeiry. The prospect of taking responsibility for the country may now seem daunting to a Moscow leadership which is hard pressed to maintain the gains of the 1970s in African countries such as Ethiopia and Angola and which may of necessity be giving up on Mozambique. Sudan now ranks with Mozambique as having one of the most helplessly deteriorated economies in Africa.[23] As an alternative to drawing these countries away from Western orientation, the leadership in the Kremlin may prefer simply to make them a greater burden on the West. Not much would need to be done in Sudan to achieve this end, but one tempting way of ensuring continuing deterioration and decline would be to encourage sectarianism and Islamic extremism.

As we have already observed, Somalia was a greater success for the Russians in the 1970s than Sudan. Soviet support of Somalia was the most overt and most expensive aspect of the three-pronged programme for destabilising Ethiopia and eventually gaining hegemony there. It was a very long-range programme, accelerated at the end of the 1960s, but an effort for which even the more optimistic enthusiasts in the Kremlin seem to have had little expectation of rapid success. If at this time there was a 'time-table' for gaining Soviet predominance in the entire Horn, it is likely that it did not envision attainment of most Soviet basic aims before the end of the 20th century.

The two other programmes directed toward destabilising Ethiopia were (1) development of insurgency in Eritrea and (2) radicalisation of students and intellectuals in Ethiopia. Insurgency in Eritrea might have developed on a very modest scale without Soviet support and, with sustained and substantial Arab backing, it might have reached proportions where it would have been a chronic nuisance to the imperial regime. Without the input of the Soviets—mostly through a considerable range of surrogate (Cuba, Syria, Iraq, East European countries, Egypt and Somalia) and, in competition with the Chinese (who were major supporters of Eritrean insurgency for a brief period, essentially 1967–1971—both the Chinese and Soviets made use of the PDRY), the Eritrean situation would never have become a major embarrassment to the Ethiopian armed forces.

The closing of the Suez Canal in 1967 had a profoundly depressing effect on the Eritrean economy just as the region was beginning accelerated economic development. Recruitment of unemployed young men thus became much easier. Nevertheless, at its most serious, the insurgency required no more than half the strength of the then quite small Ethiopian armed forces (total manpower on the eve of the revolution: 45 000 men) to contain it. Cessation of Chinese support and Nimeiry's reduction of support after 1971 reduced it to the level where it was containable, though a serious irritation to Ethiopian.

From the time they developed momentum in the mid–1960s until the early 1970s, the dominant elements among the always highly factionalised Eritrean insurgents were conservative Muslims. The Soviets preferred a movement more radical in ideology and worked steadily to build up groups—often more Christian than Muslim in origin—who were inclined toward more radical orientation. In the wake of the setbacks which the Eritreans suffered in 1971–72, the Soviets gave strong encouragement and support to the most Marxist faction—the Eritrean People's Liberation Front.[23] The EPLF during subsequent years asserted itself at the expense of co-operation with the predominantly Muslim factions—and at the expense of slowing the momentum of the rebellion which the Russians, at least until the mid–1970s, appear to have evaluated as not having high chances of early success.

As the political tensions and confusion which followed the 1973
Yom-Kippur War combined in Ethiopia with economic strain caused
by the oil price hike, stalemate in Eritrea became a factor in precipi-
tating the crisis of the Ethiopian imperial system which made the
1974 revolution possible. The degree to which the Russians may
have had a hand in supporting and encouraging the military officers
who seized control in Addis Ababa to move toward radicalism is still
shrouded in mystery. The Eritrean situation—amenable to settlement by a strong government but a source of vicious and murderous
disagreements among a still ill-consolidated revolutionary junta—
precipitated a series of events that turned the Ethiopian revolution
bloody and propelled it into a declarative pro-Soviet stance by the
end of 1974. But the Ethiopian revolutionaries who vied for power
in the Derg were—at least some of them—much more eager for a
Soviet embrace than the Soviets were to embrace them. The Soviets
continued support for the Eritrean Marxist insurgents throughout
1976 and have never completely cut political links to them.

By far the cheapest component of the Soviet destabilisation
programme in Ethiopia was the effort to radicalise students and
intellectuals. It was also the most successful in a negative sense.
During the period of intense revolutionary ferment which continued
in Ethiopia from late 1974 to 1978 and brought on the Somali
invasion in 1977, Marxist students and intellectuals fought each other
and generated so much confusion that it was often difficult to deter-
mine who would emerge on top. Best evidence is that the Soviets,
unsure of Mengistu and, furthermore, unsure of the desirability of
attempting to take direct, positive control of the Ethiopian revolutionary process, preferred that the situation develop this way. They
could test contenders for leadership and back those who best meas-
ured up to their criteria.

During this period religion played a minor but interesting role.
The revolutionary leadership in Ethiopia had a serious problem
developing a basis for legitimacy. This may explain why the Derg
initially tilted strongly toward Islam. Muslims had not been particularly disadvantaged in Ethiopia and relations between the dominant
Orthodox Christians and the large Muslim minority had seldom been
a source of political or social strain. Anticipating strong conservative
Christian opposition to much of its radical reform programme,
however, the Derg needed supporters wherever it could find or
create them and thus made an early and ostentatious effort to
'equalise' Muslims, giving Muslim holidays the same status as Chris-

tian ones, seeking Muslim participation in revolutionary activities and favouring Muslim peasants in distribution of land taken from Christian landlords in some parts of the country. Both some prominent Muslims and some prominent Oromo (Galla) officials of the imperial regime were treated with greater leniency than comparable Christian and Amhara/Tigrean officials and dignitaries. The Derg itself, as far as is known, had only one Muslim member, Major Ali Musa. He was never prominent, fell into disgrace in 1983, but later reappeared as an official in Gondar, one of Ethiopia's most conservatively Christian provinces.[24] After an early period of the Revolution the Ethiopian leadership showed no inclination to favour Muslims. Muslims were never in the forefront of the radical student/intellectual organisations that laid the groundwork for the Derg's political radicalism.

The Russians have ended up following a relatively anti-Islamic policy in the Horn, although our best evidence indicates that this has been more a by-product of improvised tactics than a conscious strategy. Nevertheless, it represents a degree of logical continuity with Russian imperial policies in the Horn at the end of the 19th century.

The Soviet leadership did not shift readily to support of Ethiopia during the summer of 1977. In March of that year Fidel Castro was engaged to travel to both Addis Ababa and Mogadishu as well as to Aden to try to sell a grand federation plan in the framework of which the Russians would not only be able to contain the rapidly rising tensions between Ethiopia and Somalia, but would end up establishing hegemony over the entire Horn regions. The plan was basically far more favourable to Somali (and Muslim) interests than Ethiopian, for it envisioned making both the Ogaden and Eritrea separate components of a Horn federation which would also include South Yemen. Not surprisingly, Mengistu found the scheme unacceptable. As late as August 1977, after the Somalis had penetrated deep into Ethiopian territory, Moscow was still trying to persuade the Ethiopians to accept this scheme. The Russians argued with an Ethiopian delegation that went to Moscow in August 1977 to plead for rapid supplies of arms that sacrifices had to be made for the sake of socialism—and cited their own 'sacrifices' in respect to Finland and Poland—countries to which they had made concessions for the sake of ultimate longer-term gains. The Ethiopians were unpersuaded.[15] Until this time the Soviets kept up the flow of arms to Somalia and 3–4 000 Soviet advisers supported the Somali military and security forces who were both guiding the guerrilla liberation fronts and participating directly in the offensive against Ethiopia.

The shift in Soviet policy toward military aid for Ethiopia had taken place the previous year, following the US presidential election of 1976. But the condition set for a full military support relationship was that Ethiopia must sever all military ties with the United States. This the Ethiopians did in April 1977, when they unilaterally abrogated the US-Ethiopian military assistance and co-operation agreements of 1953. At this time, it seems clear, the Soviets did not anticipate the extraordinary demands the rapidly escalating Horn crisis would place upon them. They appear not to have faced up to the need to abandon their Somalia/Eritrea-based strategy for the Horn until sometime in late September 1977. When they did, they rapidly ceased supplying the Somalis and the Eritrean insurgents (who had made dramatic gains during 1976 and early 1977) and organised the unprecedented air- and sea-lift which brought $2 billion worth of weapons and 18 000 Cubans to Ethiopia during the next few months. To bolster the beleaguered Ethiopian forces resisting the Somalis, armour and infantry were also airlifted from South Yemen. South Yemenis fought beside the Ethiopians in both the Harar-Diredawa area and in Eritrea. Mengistu's appreciation of the help the radical Marxists of the PDRY supplied at this crucial juncture was shown in early 1986, when he gave Ali Nasser Mohammed refuge after he lost out in the bloody civil war that broke out among contenders for power in Aden.

Many of the Russian advisers working in Somalia were shifted directly to Ethiopia. It was not the Soviets, however, who broke off the relationship with General Siad Barre. He expelled them in early November but permitted diplomatic relations to continue. True to the principles of flexible opportunism, the Soviets have maintained a modest diplomatic establishment in Mogadishu ever since. The predicament into which Mengistu's rash and risky policies plunged Ethiopia—civil war, Somali invasion, intensified Eritrean activity which brought 90 per cent of the province under insurgent control by the end of 1977—forced the Soviets to opt for Mengistu and for Ethiopia. Soviet-Cuban efforts to move Mengistu toward establishment of a Marxist-Leninist 'vanguard party' in the summer of 1978 precipitated a crisis which strained the relationship severely. Both the Soviet and Cuban ambassadors were expelled along with several of their staff members and members of the PDRY embassy as well, which was also involved in a scheme to force the pace of 'political development' toward a 'people's republic'. Mengistu won Soviet acquiescence to his desire to pursue their objective on his own schedule and a Treaty of Friendship and Mutual Co-operation was signed at the end of 1978. Since that time no serious strains are known to have arisen in the Soviet-PMGSE relationship.

Two decades of intense Russian activity in the Nile Valley/Horn region have brought Ethiopia into a close Soviet relationship but have achieved no permanent Soviet gains in Sudan or Somalia. The Ethiopian situation is still far from consolidated. Several insurgencies, especially those in Eritrea and Tigre, challenge the central government's control of half the country. The great famine which developed in 1984 and continued into 1985 was in part the result of deliberate neglect of rebellious regions by the government, which has since pressed its aim of gaining a stranglehold on the peasantry and crippling the insurgents by collectivising agriculture—using resettlement and villagisation programmes as devices for undermining existing rural society. The Nile Valley/Horn region has proved to be far from a zero-sum game between the Soviets and the West, for not only in Sudan and Somalia, but also in Egypt, economic and political deterioration threaten to keep the whole region in a state of ferment indefinitely. If we count deliveries to Libya as well as Egypt and add the rest of the Nile Valley/Horn area, we can conclude that the Russians have poured a minimum of $25 billion worth of arms into the region during the past third of a century. The result is less security for all the people who live there—and for the governments themselves—than they had before; as well as severely truncated economic developments and vast loss of life, not to mention hordes of refugees who move from one country to another and live off Western charity.

Costly as Soviet aggressive opportunism has been for the Russians in this part of the world, the highest price, both absolutely and relatively, has been paid by the inhabitants of these countries themselves. The Russians have little to offer them in the future—but Russian failures have never been sufficient in themselves to deter other hopeful contenders for power from temptation to accept renewed offers of Russian support.

Qadhafi has been a valuable auxiliary for the Soviets in their undertakings in the Nile Valley and the Horn. Soon after he took power in Libya, he began supporting the Eritreans, although his original preference was for the Muslim insurgents who were less favoured by the Soviets. His approach was thus complementary rather than contradictory to that of the Soviets in Eritrea. Qadhafi developed a warm relationship with Somalia during the mid–1970s and, as Nimeiry moved toward the West, became involved in efforts to topple him and encourage anti-Western elements in Sudan. Since Qadhafi had taken a hostile position toward the imperial government in Ethiopia, he was naturally inclined to favour the radical revolutionaries who seized power in 1974. Here, however, he faced a dilemma, for support of the Derg meant abandonment of the Eritrean cause. Qadhafi had little difficulty making the shift in 1977, although for a period afterwards he may have continued support for both in keeping with the Soviet policy of trying to get the good Marxists of the Eritrean Popular Liberation Front to compose their differences with the Marxists of the Derg.

In August 1981 a tripartite alliance was concluded between Qadhafi, Marxist Ethiopia and the PDRY. It proved to be neither as politically disruptive as many Western observers feared nor as economically advantageous as many Ethiopians and South Yemenis hoped. Still flush with oil earnings, Qadhafi at that time could have helped ease the increasingly severe financial problems of the Addis Ababa and Aden regimes, as well as relieve the Russians of the embarrassing pressure for help from those two ultra-loyal Marxist clients. There is no evidence, however, that either of the two poor partners in this radical alliance ever received more than a few million dollars in Libyan aid.

In June 1983 Mengistu and Qadhafi came close to a public falling-out in the course of a tense meeting of the organisation of African Unity in Addis Ababa that took up the problems of the Polisario movement and Chad.[26] Qadhafi left Addis Ababa in a huff when Mengistu was elected OAU chairman for 1983–84, and the tripartite alliance was, in effect reduced to not much more than a propaganda episode. Since that time there has been Ethiopian-Libyan collusion against Sudan and both governments have supported Soviet initiatives in the Third World. In return, Moscow—through all the leadership changes of the first half of the 1980s—has backed both Libya and Ethiopia internationally in spite of the increasingly poor reputation both have acquired. Libya has become notorious as a backer of international terrorism and the Ethiopian regime disreputable for its brutal internal practices. Neither Qadhafi nor Mengistu enhances the Soviet image on the international scene, but according to any calculus of net advantage Moscow is likely to make in the foreseeable future, Kremlin leaders will probably continue maintaining close ties with both. The much abused and long-suffering 'broad masses' of both countries in whose name Qadhafi and Mengistu rule meanwhile show growing disillusionment and dissatisfaction with them, but change is unlikely until opposition elements in the military forces (from which both leaders themselves emerged) are ready to bid for power.

More then 30 years of Soviet engagement in the Nile Valley/Horn region have left the USSR a status-quo power in Libya and Ethiopia, where any change in the existing regimes is likely to be to Soviet disadvantage. Enormous investments in arms for Egypt, Sudan and Somalia have produced no return. They have, in effect, been lost. Resumption of a close Soviet relationship may have some tactical appeal to small and frustrated opposition groups in all three countries, but no credible strategic concept for the future political, economic and social development of any of these countries could be based on the notion of close alliance with Moscow. Lacking credibility as an advocate of positive formulae for the future of all the countries of the region, the Russians have no alternative for the immediate future but to bide their time and/or attempt to undermine the chances of the West—as well as moderate domestic forces—to set this sad and problem-ridden part of the world on a more hopeful course of economic and political development.[27]

Appendices

APPENDIX A

Foreign Muslim Delgations Visiting the USSR, 1973–79

1973 (five delegations)
—Iraqi delegation, led by Nafi Qasim, Chairman of the Department of *Waqfs*, to Tashkent, Samarkand, Bukhara and Leningrad.
—Singapore delegation, led by Mohammed Khan ibn Khan Mohammed, Chief *Qadi*, to Moscow, Ufa, Tashkent, Samarkand and Bukhara.[1]
—Young Muslim Society of Egypt delegation, led by Ibrahim al-Tahavi and Yajya Ramazan, at the invitation of Ziauddin Babakhanov, to Tashkent, Moscow, Baku, and Ufa.[2]
—Iranian *ulema* delegation, led by Senator Alam-i Vahidi, at the invitation of Ziauddin Babakhanov, to Tashkent and other cities in Uzbekistan.
—Pakistani *ulema* delegation, led by the sheikh Al-Kasemi, Deputy Chairman of the World Association of Readers of the Koran and Chairman of the Jama'at-i Ulema-yi Islam of Pakistan, at the invitation of Ziauddin Babakhanov, to Tashkent and Moscow (reception by Barmenkov, Deputy-Chairman of the Council for Religious Affairs. The last reception was an occasion for the guest to denounce Zionism and US imperialism.[3]

1974 (five delegations)
—Malayan delegation, led by Sharif Ahmad, Vice-Minister of Information.
—Kuwaiti historian, Faruh Omer, personally invited by Ziauddin Babakhanov.
—Hamza Boubaker, rector of the Paris Muslim Theological Institute and imam-khatib of the Paris mosque.
—Mukti Ali Abdallah, Indonesian Minister of Religious Affairs, to Moscow, Tashkent, Baku and Ufa.
—Abdullah Salih, Grand Mufti of Sudan, at the invitation of the Sheikh ul-Islami of Transcaucasia, to Baku.

1975 (two delegations)
—Abdul Razak Muhammad, Deputy Prime Minister and leader of the Muslim community of Mauritius, at the invitation of Ziauddin Babakhanov, to Tashkent, Bukhara, Samarkand and Leningrad. The guest was received in Moscow by Viukto Titov, Deputy-Chairman of the Council for Religious Affairs.
—Somali *ulema* delegation, led by the Sheikh Ali al-Sufi, to Tashkent and Baku.

1976 (six delegations)
—Afghan delegation, led by the Sheikh Inayatollah Iblaghi, to Tashkent, Samarkand, Leningrad and Moscow. In Moscow the delegation was received by A. A. Nurallaev. The Afghans expressed great enthusiasm for what they saw.[4]

—Jordanian delegation, led by Dr Abdul Aziz al-Hayat, Minister of *Waqfs* and of Religious Affairs and of Holy Shrines; by Sheikh Mohammed Abdul Hashim, Grand Mufti of Jordan; and by Sheikh Asad Bayud al-Tamimi, imam-khatib of the al-Aqsa mosque in Jerusalem; to Moscow (reception by A. A. Nurullaev), Leningrad, Baku, Tashkent, Bukhara and Samarkand. Dr al-Hayat's comments on completing the tour: 'Soviet Muslims enjoy full civil rights and freedoms.[5] Dr al-Hayat later told a friend known to the authors that he had nothing but contempt for the Soviets.[6]

—Egyptian journalist, Abdurrahman Ali Shakir, Chief Editor of the journal *Rose al-Yousef* of Cairo, at the invitation of Ziauddin Babakhanov, to Tashkent and Moscow.

—North Yemeni delegation, led by Sheikh Mohammed Ahmad Zabara, Grand Mufti of Yemen (who had already visited the USSR four times previously), accompanied by his entire family. Visits to Moscow, Ufa and Tashkkent. Speaking to Radio Moscow, Sheikh Zabara insisted on the 'total freedom of religion of every citizen of the USSR'.[7] The same Sheikh Zabara later told a foreign visitor in Sana'a known to the authors that 'if you want to know the truth about Muslims in the USSR, read the book by A. Bennigsen.[8]

—Lebanese delegation, two weeks in Central Asia.

—Afghan delegation, members of the Ministry of Justice, at the invitation of Ziauddin Babakhanov, to Tashkent, Samarkand, Moscow and Leningrad.

1977 (three delegations)
—Chad delegation, headed by Imam Ibrahim Musa, to Tashkent, Samarkand and, exceptionally, Kazan.

—Jordanian delegation, to Tashkent.

—Turkish delegation, led by Dr Lutfi Dogan, Minister of State for Justice and Religious Affairs, to Moscow (reception by Kuroedov), Baku (reception by the Government of the Azerbaijan SSR), Tashkent (reception by the Government of the Uzbek SSR and by Ziauddin Babakhanov), Samarkand and Bukhara.[9]

1979 (three delegations)
—South Yemeni delegation, headed by Mufti Abdullah Mohammed Hatem, Chairman of the Department of Religious Affairs, Member of Parliament and imam-khatib of the Mosque of Aden, to Tashkent, Dushanbe, Moscow and Ufa. Hatem promptly denounced 'the imperialist calumnies' about the absence of religious freedom in the USSR.[10]

—Pakistani *ulema* delegation, led by the Minister of Religious Affairs, Mahmud Haroon, to Tashkent and Moscow.

—Afghan *ulema* delegation, led by Abdal-Aziz Sadeq, Chairman of the council of the Ulema of Afghanistan, two weeks in Tashkent, Samarkand, Bukhara, Dushanbe, Moscow, and Leningrad.[11]

Other

This list is not exhaustive; it should include mention of delegations and individuals visiting the USSR for whom we have only incomplete information, usually the specific time frame, during the period under examination. For example:

—*Muslims of the Soviet East* (no. 3, 1975) noted in passing that several delegations of foreign Muslims had visited Ufa. Among them are Kemal Tarzi, Chairman of the Department of Religious Affairs of Tunisia; Rashid Abdallah ibn Farhan, Minister of *Waqfs* of Kuwait; Date Haji Ismail Panjang, Secretary-General of the Department of Islamic Affairs of Malaysia; Mohammed Ketani Hasani, Professor at the University of Qarawiyin (Fez, Morocco); Mohammed ibn Gali, Professor at the University of Tripoli (Libya). It is probable that many other foreign delegations of religious figures visited Tashkent and Baku but were not recorded by Soviet media.

APPENDIX B

Foreign Muslim Students in the USSR and Soviet Teachers Abroad

The receiving of foreign Muslim students in the USSR and the sending of Soviet teachers abroad to teach foreign Muslims in their countries constitute supplementary channels through which Soviet policies are intended to influence the Muslim world. How successful these programmes are has yet to be determined. In fact, we have interviewed a number of former Muslim students to the USSR who seem to have taken away from their exposure to Soviet reality precisely the impressions other Soviet propaganda, especially regarding the condition of Islam in the USSR, attempts to disguise.

Data on the range of contacts in this regard are difficult to find. The following incomplete sample, however, illustrates the scope of the Soviet effort.

—Cameroon: 40 students are sent to the USSR for training[1] departure for the USSR of a large group of Cameroonese students to be trained as doctors, engineers and agronomists.[2]

—Ghana: 42 scholarships for Ghanian students in 1977, 56 scholarships in 1978.[3]

—Iran: 'Iranian students had attended courses at Moscow University, Astrakhan Fisheries School, Baku Institute of Hydro-electric Engineering, Leningrad Technicum of Engineering. In 1972, 1100 Iranian specialists in metallurgy, engineering and hydro-electric and gas completed their training in the USSR'.[4]

—Sudan: 200 Sudanese students in 1973 in the USSR. Over 400 have already graduated from Soviet institutes.[5]

—Nigeria: 700 Nigerian students have graduated from Soviet colleges, and in 1975 there were about 800 Nigerians in Soviet universities and colleges[6]; 42 Nigerians received medical diplomas in the USSR in 1975.[7]

—Algeria: 2500 Soviet specialists, including 1000 teachers, are working in Algeria.[8]

—Bangladesh: 270 Bangladeshi students sent to the USSR in 1975[9]; and 140 in 1976.[10]

—Pakistan: USSR grants 45 scholarships to Pakistani students in Soviet educational establishments and ten scholarships for post-graduate research.[11]

—Somalia: 1000 Somali students are studying at Soviet schools; 1500 have graduated from colleges and universities[12] large number of Somalis at Lumumba University (Moscow).[13]

—Jordan: USSR grants 120 scholarships in Soviet universities to Jordanian students[14]; 1000 Jordanian students studying medicine and engineering in the USSR.[15]

—Kenya: USSR granted scholarships to 70 Kenyan students and postgraduates.[16]

—Benin: 300 Benin students in Soviet schools and universities; 100 have already graduated, another 55 scholarships will be granted in 1979.[17]

—Ethiopia: 700 Ethiopians have received scholarships in the USSR[18]; 430 Ethiopians have left to study in the USSR.[19]

—North Yemen: 74 North Yemeni students in various Soviet universities in 1973; in 1974 there are 150.[20]

—Africa (general): Students from 29 African countries are studying in Azerbaijan alone.[21]

APPENDIX C

Agreements Signed between the USSR and Muslim States, 1973–1979

1973

—*Iraq*: Agreement for Scientific co-operation between Basra University and Baku University.

1974

—*Mali*: Twinning of the cities of Ashkhabad and Bamako.

—*Afghanistan*: Agreement for cultural and scientific co-operation for 1974–75.[1]

—*Syria*: Agreement for cultural and scientific co-operation for 1974–75.[2]

—*Syria*: Agreement for cultural and scientific co-operation for 1974–75.[2]

—*Mali*: Cultural exchanges protocol (health, education, sport, information, culture).[3]

—*Sudan*: Bi-lateral co-operation agreement (education, art, information, sport).[4]

—*Lebanon*: Scientific co-operation agreement.[5]

1975
—*Iran*: Cultural exchanges protocol (art, films, education, science).[6]
—*South Yemen*: Agreement for scientific and cultural co-operation.[7]
—*Pakistan*: Agreement on broadcast co-operation.[8]
—*Libya*: Agreement for cultural co-operation.[9]
—*Guinea-Bissau*: Cultural co-operation protocol.[10]
—*Algeria*: Cultural and technical co-operation protocol.[11]
—*Guinea*: Cultural co-operation protocol.[12]
—*Ghana*: Co-operation agreement with Ghana-Soviet Friendship Society.[13]
—*Sudan*: Cultural co-operation agreements with Sudan-USSR Friendship Society and with the Sudanese National Council for Peace, Solidarity and Friendship.[14]
—*Algeria*: Protocol on radio and television exchange.[15]
—*Bangladesh*: Cultural exchange agreement.[16]
—*Egypt*: Protocol for cultural co-operation and exchange of scholarships.[17]

1976
—*Libya*: Establishment of Libyan-Soviet Friendship Society.[18]
—*Benin*: Protocol for cultural and educational co-operation.[19]
—*Jordan*: Co-operation on television exchanges agreement.[20]

1977
—*Egypt*: Cultural co-operation agreement.[21]
—*Bangladesh*: Establishment of Tajikistan branch of Bangladesh-Soviet Friendship Society.[22]
—*Iran*: Agreement for cultural and educational exchanges.[23]
—*Morocco*: Cultural co-operation agreement (education, cinema, sports, art).[24]
—*Ethiopia*: Agreement on television and radio co-operation.[25]
—*Sudan*: Suspends activities of Soviet Cultural Centre in Khartoum.[26]
—*Ethiopia*: Constituent meeting of the Ethiopian-USSR Friendship Society (Addis Ababa).[27]
—*Benin*: Radio and television co-operation agreement.[28]
—*Senegal*: Protocol on cultural exchanges.[29]
—*Ghana*: Cultural-scientific co-operation for 1977–78.[30]
—*Iran*: Cultural co-operation agreement.[31]
—*Afghanistan*: Protocol for sports co-operation32

1978
—*South Yemen*: Radio and television co-operation agreement.[33]
—*Morocco*: Agreement on scientific and technical co-operation.[34]
—*Jordan*: Sports co-operation agreement.[35]
—*Iraq*: Co-operation agreement between Iraqi and Soviet Friendship Societies.[36]
—*Bangladesh*: Cultural and scientific exchange agreement.[37]
—*Afghanistan*: Protocol on training Afghan students in the USSR.[38]
—*Syria*: Agreement between the Syrian Baath Party and the CPSU.[39]

—*Kuwait*: Cultural and scientific exchange agreement.[40]
—*Central African Empire*: Television and radio exchange agreement.[41]
—*Burundi*: Broadcast co-operation agreement.[42]
—*Pakistan*: Cultural exchange agreement (teachers, students, cinema, broadcasters, writers).[43]

1979
—*PLO*: Exchange of delegations and of children between Soviet and Palestinian Friendship Societies.
—*Gambia*: Sports co-operation agreement.
—*Jordan*: Co-operation on tourism agreement
—*Morocco*: Sports co-operation agreement.
—*Kuwait*: Broadcast co-operation agreement.
—*Afghanistan*: Protocol establishing Soviet Cultural Centre in Kabul.

APPENDIX D

List of Delegates for use by those attending the Tashkent Conference September1980

Algeria
Al-Moukhtar al-Loumi, Counsellor, Ministry for Religious Affairs

Afghanistan
Mowlawi Muhammad Kasem
Mowlawi Abdul Karim
Mowlawi Abdul Shekur
Mowlawi Abdul Rahim
Seyid Muhammad Amin Sader
Seyid Iskander Shah

Austria
Dr Ismail Balic, Chancellor, Austrian National Library

Benin
Youssoufou al-Haj Moibi, Imam-khatib, Cotonou mosque

Bulgaria
Toopchiev, Mehmet, Chief Mufti
Ivanov, Ilya, Head of the Department for Muslim Religious Affairs, Bulgarian Foreign Ministry.
Iliyev, Chavdar, Mufti of Smolin region
Osmanov, Osman, Imam of the Sofia Mosque
Yakubov, Tahsin, Mufti of Plovdiv region

German Democratic Republic
Bassarak, Gerhard, professor

Ghana
Ben Omar Ahmad Tijani, Secretary-General, National Committee for
    Islamic Festivals

Jordan
Sheikh Ibrahim al-Kattan, Supreme *Qadi* of Jordan
Sheikh Abd al-Hamid al-Saikh, Chairman of the Committee for the
    Salvation of Jerusalem
Ali Hassan Udah, Dean of the Faculty, Amman University, former minister
    Hassan Muhammad Zubyan, Editor-in-Chief of the journal *Al-Shariya*,
    Secretary of the association of Islamic Studies
Rajab al-Tamimi, *Qadi* (Palestinian)
Daud Muhammad Salah al-Abadi, Minister of *Waqfs*, Inspector of Islamic
    Education

Yemen Arab Republic (North Yemen)
Ahmad B. Muhammad Zabarra, Grand Mufti of Yemen

Cyprus
Erkin Sayid Ahmad, Counsellor, Department of *Waqfs* and Religious Affairs
Yunsal Rauf, Chairman, Executive Committee for *Waqfs* and Religious
    Affairs

Kuwait
Yusuf al-Sayid Hashem al Rifal, Dean of the Theological faculty, former
    minister
Abdurrahman Rashid al-Walayiti, Editor-in-Chief of *Al-Balagh* (weekly)
Salah Muhhammad Abd-al-Latif Abu Hamza, Editor, *Al-Balagh*
Abd al-Wahhab Abd al-Khaliq Salah al-Khashan, correspondent, Kuwaiti
    Press Agency, Moscow Office

Lebanon
Sheikh Hasan Tamim, *gadi*, Head of Religious Section of the journal *Al-
    Quds*
Wajih Sayid al-Ajkuz, journalist

Libya
Dr Muhammad Ahmad al-Sharif, Secretary-General of the Islamic Call
    Society
Rajab Abu Bakr Sasi, Secretary of Islamic Affairs of the Libyan Government
    (Qadhafi's advisor on islamic matters)
Dr Al-Hadi Abdallah Hanij, Director of the General Board for Islamic
    Affairs

Mauritius
Piru Abdul-Razak Muhammad Amin, Minister of Labour
Kassen Ali Ahmad Saulay, Deputy Rector of the University of Mauritius,
    Deputy of the National Assembly
Edu Hosein Jie, teacher and writer

Mali
Haj Muhammad Fudi Keita, Secretary-General, Union of Islamic Progress
    Umar Saaf Toure, Director, Centre for the Promotion of the Arabic
    Language, Inspector-General for Arabic Education

Mongolian Peoples Republic
Maam Dugerjavyn, scientific worker, Institute of Oriental Studies, Academy
    of Science

People's Democratic Republic of Yemen (South Yemen)
Khalid Fazl Mansur, Minister of Justice and Waqfs
Abdallah Muhammad al-Madawi, Minister of Justice, Inspector of Religious
    Affairs
Salem Omar Baharmaz, secondary teacher of Arabic and religion
Mahdi Salem Hunaish, Secretary in Department of Justice

Senegal
Al-Jaj Mustafa Nyang, Chairman of Union of Islamic Progress
Saeed Diope, General-Secretary of Union of Islamic Progress, Inspector for
    Arabic Education
Dr Issa Tchao, Inspector for Arabic Education
Doudou Kei, Inspector for Arabic Education, primary schools

Syria
Muhammad B. Muhammad al-Khativ, Minister of Waqfs and Religious
    Affairs
Sheikh Ahmad Quftaru, Grand Mufti of Syria
Rajab Muhammad al-Khatib, Islamic preacher
Faiz al-Saigh, Press attaché of the Syrian Embassy in Moscow, Director of
    Syrian Press Agency, Moscow
Sheikh Mahmud Qurgaru, Director of Shariyat Institute, Damascus
Salah al-Din Reihan, Cabinet director, Ministry of Religious Affairs

Sudan
Sadiq Abd al-Rahman Al-Mahdi, Minister of Economy, Chairman of Al-
    Ansar Religious sect, ex-Prime Minister (PM again in 1985)
Abd al-Rasul al-Nur Ismail, Secretary of Al-Ansar sect
Abdallah Muhammad Ahmad Hassan, Head of Foreign Department of Al-
    Ansar sect

Tanzania
Sheikh Mdidi Musa Abdu-Rahman Sayidi, Official of the Ministry of Finance
Sheikh Simba Issa Shaban

Togo
Coubaja Idrissou Toure, General Director of Islamic Schools
Arimiyao Imam Bawa, Chairman, Muslim Federation in Lamakara

Turkey
Cubukcu Ibrahim Aga, Head of the Chair of Islamic Philosophy, Faculty of
Theology, Ankara

Uganda
Sheikh Mbugu Ali, Head of Department of Education, Supreme Council
for Islamic Affairs
Sebukhin Thabit, Public relations officer, Supreme Council for Islamic
Affairs

Finland
Ali Abdullah, Vice-President of the Islamic community
Dakher Oqano, General-Secretary of the Islamic community

Sri Lanka
Dr Badiuddin Mahmud, Minister of Education

Ethiopia
Haj Ibrahim Abd al-Salam, Vice-President of the Supreme Islamic Council
Muhammad Awal Ahmad, General-Secretary of the Supreme Islamic
Council, member of the Ministry of Transportation and Communication

Japan
Abu-Bakr Morimoto, President of the Islamic community
Fujimitsu Tamasutu, President of the Peace Fund Shotokan Taeki
Hisham Toshio Kuroda, teacher, Director of the Islamic Centre

Bangladesh
Abu-Jaffar Shamsuddin, journalist

Guinea
Bouba Kamara, journalist, Guinean Information Agency

Pakistan
M. Assadullah, journalist, *Viewpoint* magazine

France
Georges Martin, Editor-in-Chief *France-URSS* magazine, member of the
French Communist Party

Switzerland
Pierre Grunter, journalist

The following foreign delegates were elected members of the Presidium of
the Conference: Piru Abdul-Razak (Mauritius), Khalid Fazl Mansur (S.
Yemen), Muhammad al-Khatib (Syria), Muhammad Ahmad Zabara (N.
Yemen), Ahmad Quftaru (Syria), Topchiev (Bulgaria), Sadiq al-Mahdi
(Sudan), Mustafa Nyang (Senegal), Yusuf al-Rifai (Kuwait), and Ibrahim
Abd al-Salam (Ethopia).

APPENDIX E

Chronology of Soviet Muftis' Travels Abroad, 1982–85

1982 (five delegations)
—The *hajj* to *Saudi Arabia*, led by the Mufti of Ufa, Talgat Tajeddin; reception by King Khaled and Muhammad Ali Harakan, Secretary-General of the Muslim World League; visit to Syria on the return voyage.[1]
—*Bulgaria*, delegation led by Ziauddin Babakhanov and Talgat Tajeddin, 26 Janury–3 February.[2]
—*USA*, an inter-confessional delegation (Muslim, Christian, Jewish), including Sheikh Abdulgani Abdullaev, to Ohio and California.[3]
—*Ghana, Benin, Upper Volta, Mali*, led by Mahmud Gekkiev.[4]
—*Delhi*, Sheikh Y. Shakirov, Deputy-Mufti of Tashkent took part in a conference on the 'Transformation of the Indian Ocean into a Zone of Peace', organised by the World Council of Peace and the Organisation of Afro-Asian Solidarity.[5]
—*Afghanistan*, many delegations, too numerous to mention.

1983 (14 delegations)
—*Saudi Arabia*, 15–21 January; Shamsuddin Babakhanov is invited by the Muslim World League to participate at the Eighth Session of the World Council of Mosques Mission in Mecca. Returning home, he stopped in Cairo, where he was met by Sheikh Ibrahim al-Dasuki, Minister of *Waqfs*, Dr Jemaleddin Mahmud, Secretary-General of the Council of Islamic Affairs; and Abdul-Latif Hamza, Grand Mufti of Egypt.[6]
—*Ethiopa*, *qadi* Abdullah Kalan, representative of the Muslim Spiritual Directorate in Tashkent for Tajikistan, on the occasion of the 'Tajik SSR Days' in Ethiopa.[7]
—*Ghana*, visit by Mohammed Sadyq Mamaysup(ov), Deputy-Rector of the Institute ismail al-Bukhari of Tashkent.[8]
—*Tunisia*, Sheikh Usmanjan Rahimjan(ov), imam-khatib of the Imam al-Bukhari mosque, led a delegation of Uzbek *ulema* to Kairwan.[9]
—*Mozambique*, a delegation of Uzbek *ulema* led by Sheikh Abdulgani Abdullaev, Abdul Axix Mansur, chief of the *fetwa* section of the Muslim Spiritual Directorate of Tashkent, and Sheikh Arifjan Yuldashev, imam-khatib of the Yangi-Yul mosque. The invitation was issued by Abu Bakr al-Haj Musa Ismail, Secretary-General of the Islamic Council of Mozambique. Reception by President Samora Machel and Ocher Montero, Minister of Justice.[10]
—*Finland*, 4–7 May, delegation led by Mufti Tolgat Tajeddin of Ufa and Sheikh Mirmahmudov, Secretary of the Muslim Spiritual Directorate of Tashkent; reception by Abdullah Ali, President of the Islamic Association of Finland. This particular piece of 'courting' is aimed at the substantial Volga Tatar community in Finland.[11]
—*Morocco*, 28 April–15 May, a group of Soviet *ulema* presented a special exhibition devoted to the religious life of the Muslims of the USSR at the Soviet exhibition at the International and Commercial Fair in Casablanca.

Books published by the Muslim spiritual directorate of Tashkent were present; the Soviet exhibit was visited by Prince Mawlawi Rashid, the Minister of Commerce and Industry, and the Governor of Casablanca.[12]

—*Algeria*, July, Sheikh Abdulgani Abdulaev participated at the conference 'The Islamic Concept' in Constantine; invitation issued by Mohammad Abdurrahman al-Shiban, Algerian Minister of *Waqfs*.[13]

—*India*, a delegation of Uzbek *ulema* led by Sheikh A. Abdullaev, visited Delhi, Trivandrum, Madras, Calcutta, at the invitation of the Society for Indian-Soviet Friendship; lavish reception by leaders of the Muslim League of India.[14]

—*Jordan*, August, large delegation led by Mufti Shamsuddin Babakhanov; delegation included Abdullah Kalan, *qadi* of Tajikistan, Timur Urunbaev, *qadi* of Kirghizia, Osman Iskhaq, Secretary of the Ufa Muslim Board. Invitation issued by Sheikh Ibrahim al-Qattan, Supreme *qadi* of Jordon. Sumptuous reception by the Crown Prince Hasan, the Prime Minister, Muzar Badran, Dr Kemal al-Sharif, Minister of *Waqfs*, Dr Abdu-Salam al-Majali, Rector of Amman University, Muhammad Mohilian, Chairman of the Shariyat Court of Appeal, the Sheikh Abd-al-Hamid al-Saikh, Chairman of the committee for the Salvation of Jerusalem, Dr Abdal-Aziz al-Hayat, Dean of the Shariyat Faculty of the Amman University. On the return journey, the delegation stopped in Syria, at the invitation of the Muhammad al-Khatib, Minister of *Waqfs*; the delegation was received by Abdurrahman al-Kasim, the Prime Minister. Substantial coverage in the Syrian press.[15]

—*Kuwait*, October, delegation led by Mufti Mahmud Gekkiev of Makhach-Qala including Sadyq Kamal, imam-khatib of the mosqe of Osh (Kirghizia), Zahid Abdul-Kadir, professor at the Ismail al-Bukhari Institute of Tashkent. Reception by Crown Prince Saad Abdullah al-Sabah; another unusual reception by the Soviet ambassador, P. Akopov. Widespread coverage on Kuwaiti television.[16]

—*Canada*, July, Sheikh Y. Shakirov leads a delegation to the Conference of the World Council of Churches in Vancouver.[17]

—*Czechoslovakia*, June, Shamsuddin Babakhanov leads a Soviet delegation to the conference 'For Peace and Life Against Nuclear War'.[18]

1984

—*North Yemen*, Mahmud Gekkiev received by the Minister of *Waqfs*, the Prime Minister, the Minister of Justice, the Governors of Sanaa and Hodeida, the Rector of the University of Sanaa and Ahmed Zabara, Grand Mufti of Yemen.[19]

—*Afghanistan*, 20 March, Shamsuddin Babakhanov and Y. Shakirov participate at a conference of Afghan *ulema* in Kabul.[20]

—*Jordan*, 24 April–1 May, Shamsuddin Babakhanov invited by the Royal Jordanian Academy and elected a member; received by the Crown Prince.[21]

—*Saudi Arabia*, 27 August–18 September, *hajj* led by Shamsuddin Babakhanov; received by the King of Saudi Arabia. On return journey, the delegation stop in Damascus, where they are received by Ahmad Quftaru, Grand Mufti of Syria, and Dr Muhammad al-Khatib, Minister of *Waqfs*.[22]

—*Turkey*, summer, Mufti Gekkiev accompanied by his deputy, Pulatjan Babamuhammedov, Ataullah Mavlankul of the Tashkent Directorate, and

Sabir Huseinoglu of the Islamic Directorate of Baku; received by Dr Tayyar Kulac, Chairman of the Department of Religious Affairs, and by Dr Ekmeleddin Ihsanoglu, Director of Research Centre for Islamic History, Art and Culture of Istanbul.[23]

—*Saudi Arabia*, 23–28 December, Shamsuddin Babakhanov attended the Tenth session of the World Council of Mosqes in Mecca, where he delivered a long report denouncing Israeli 'genocide' in Lebanon.[24]

1985

To our knowledge, only a few Soviet Muslim delegations were sent abroad in 1985. It is still too early to be able to understand this apparent reduction of Soviet mufti activity abroad. It is possible that Soviet leaders had come to appreciate the potential danger of a backlash to their Islamic strategy among foreign Muslims; it is also possible that the new Soviet muftis have proved to be less popular abroad because of their heavy 'Soviet' veneer, despite excellent academic credentials. In 1985 and 1986, for example, we interviewed a number of high-ranking Arab Islamic leaders, who passed rather severe judgements in particular on Shamsuddin Babakhanov. He is thought of by many as too much of a creature of the Soviet political establishment, lacking the subtle ambiguities of his predecessor. The slowdown of official Soviet Islamic activity abroad may also reflect the increased efficiency of other propaganda channels. We have been able to identify the following outreach activities, however:

—*Jordan*, Spring, Shamsuddin Babakhanov and Sheikh ul-Islam Pasha Zade took part in the Fourth Conference of the Jordanian Royal Academy in Amman.[25]

—*Afghanistan*, May, Y. Shakirov led a delegation of the Tashkent Spiritual Directorate to Kabul.[26]

—*Morocco*, Sheikh A. Abdullaev represented Soviet Muslim clerics in a delegation led by Pulat Habibullaev, President of the Uzbek SSR Supreme Soviet and Chairman of the Uzbek Academy of Sciences, on the occasion of 'The Days of Soviet Culture'.[27]

—*Algeria*, September, Abdullaev and Ratbek Nisanbaiev, *qadi* of the Kazakh SSR, participated in the 19th International Congress of Islamic Thought in Bija. Ironically, the general theme of the conference was 'the cultural aggression of the Western powers against Muslims and Islam'. From all appearances, the Soviet representatives were treated as Muslims, and not as representatives of a Western imperial power.[28]

—*USA*, September, a group of Uzbeks, headed by the mayor of Tashkent Shukurullah Mirsaidov, including Y. Shakirov, toured Seattle, a city twinned with Tashkent since 1971, and Los Angeles. Public prayers were conducted by Shakirov in both cities.[29]

—*Saudi Arabia, hajj*, conducted by the Mufti of Ufa, Talgat Tajeddin En route home, the muftis stopped in Damascus, where they were received by Dr Muhammad al-Khatib, Minister of *waqfs*, and Ahmad Quftaru, Grand Mufti of Syria.[30]

APPENDIX F

Foreign Muslim and Non-Muslim Delegations to the USSR as Guests of the Soviet Islamic Establishment, 1982–85 (excluding Afghan delegations)

1982
—*Tunisia*, delegation to Tashkent to celebrate the decade of 'friendly ties' between the cities of Tashkent and Tunis. Headed by the Dean of the University of Tunis, Ben Mami, and by the Mayor of Tunis, Zakaria ben Mustafa; reception by the Tashkent *gorkom*, the University of Tashkent and the mufti.[1]
—*Nigeria*, delgation headed by Yusuf Dan Soho, Vice-President of the Nigerian-USSR Friendship Society and including at least one Muslim cleric, *qadi* Umah Ibrahim; visits to Ufa, reception by the Mufti Talgat Tajeddin, and to Tashkent, reception by Ziauddin Babakhanov.[2]
—*Benin*, delegation of religious leaders (their first visit to the USSR), at the invitation of Ziauddin Babakhanov.[3]

1983
—*India*, Dr Muhammad Azizullah, Director of the Islamic Cultural Centre of Hyderabad was the guest of the Mufti of Tashkent.[4] Also K. K. Mohieddin, Secretary-General of the Islamic Society of India, who visited Uzbekistan and Tajikistan.[5]
—*Bangladesh*, August, delegation of *ulema* at the invitation of Shamsuddin Babakhanov; group included Nurul-Islam, Secretary-General of the Council of Islamic Societies of Bangladesh, Abu Fazl Muhammed Seyfullah, member of the Executive Committee of the Islamic Mission of the Qoran and of the Sunna, and Mawlana Amin-ul-Islam, imam of the Lambagh mosque of Dacca; visited Uzbekistan.[6]
—*Algeria*, delegation of the Islamic Council of Algeria, invited by Shamsuddin Babakhanov; also including university professors and journalists.[7]
—*Jordan*, April, group of high-ranking religious leaders visited Tashkent, Samarkand, Baku and Moscow. Reception by the Presidium of the Uzbek Supreme Soviet, the *gorkom* of Tashkent, the University of Tashkent, the *obkom* of Samarkand, the University and Academy of Sciences of Azerbaijan. Delegation headed by Abdusalam al-Majali, Rector of the University of Amman; also including, Dr Aziz al-Hayat, Dr Muhammad Amin Salman Kuzat, Mahmud Ahmad Abdullah Abuleyl, and Faiz Muhammad al-Rabi al-Falah.[8]
—*UNESCO*, September, delegation led by Amadu Muhtar M'Bo, Director General, and including Abdurrazak Kaduri, Deputy Director-General; received in Tashkent by Sheikh Abdulgani Abdullaev.[9]

1984 (excluding numerous Afghan delegations)
—*Kuwait*, delegation of Kuwaiti journalists, led by Mustafa Nabil Abdul-Halik Mustafa, editor of *Al-Arabi* magazine, to Uzbekistan at the invitation

156   *Appendices*

of Shamsuddin Babakhanov; reception at the Institute Ismail al-Bukhari, prayers at the Shah-i Zenda Islamic shrine in Samarkand.[10]

—*Libya*, Spring, delegation led by Muhammad Abu Setta of the Libyan-Soviet Friendship Society; reception in Tashkent by Yusufkhan Shakirov.[11]

—*North Yemen*, June-July, delegation led by Ali ben Ali al-Saman, Minister of *Waqfs*, to Moscow, Makhach-Qala, Tashkent, Samarkand, and the Ferghana Valley. Red carpet reception by three muftis in Tashkent, by Munavar Tursunov, Vice-President of the Council of Ministers of the Uzbek SSR. For the first time since World War II, the delegation was allowed to visit the city of Gudermes in the Checheno-Ingush ASSR. The invitation was issued by three muftis.[12]

—*South Yemen*, delegation led by Khalid Fazl Mansur, Minister of Justice and of *Waqfs*, with several executives of his ministries and the imam-khatibs of the mosques of Aden and Abyan; to Leningrad, Moscow, Baku, Tashkent, and the Ferghana Valley. Red carpet treatment by religious and Party authorities: in Moscow by Boris Kravtsov, Minister of Justice of the USSR, and by Mahmud Rahmankulov, Vice-Presidnet of the Council of Religious Affairs of the USSR.[13]

—*Tunisia*, Spring, delegation of the city of Tunis, led by its mayor, Zakariya ben Mustafa, to Tashkent; reception by the *gorkom* of Tashkent and Shamsuddin Babakhanov.[14]

—*Syria*, delegation of Syrian peasants (!), led by Abdul-Qadir Khalil, to Tashkent. Reception by the Muslim Spiritual Directorate.[15]

—*Jordan*, October, important delegation led by Abdul-Khalaf Daudiya, former Minister of *Waqfs*, including Sheikh Muhammad Shakra, Chairman of the Department of the Al-Aqsa mosque (Jerusalem), and Nasir Abu Rajab, Chief of Cabient of the Minister of *Waqfs*; to Leningrad, Moscow, Baku, Tashkent and Samarkand. Red carpet treatment at all levels of Party, Government and religious organisations, and wide Soviet media coverage.[16]

—*Lebanon*, 26 September–6 October, delegation headed by Sheikh hasan Khalid, Grand Mufti of Lebanon, including Sheikh Nasir al-Salih of Tripoli and Sheikh Khalil Mais, President of the Da'wa Faculty of Lebanon; to Daghestan (Derbent, Hasav-Yurt), Gudermes, Tashkent, Ferghana Valley and Margelan. Invitation issued by the muftis of Tashkent and Makhach-Qala.[17]

—*Sudan*, Autumn, delegation led by Dr Yusuf al-Khalifa Abu Bakr, Chairman of the Supreme Council for Religious Affairs and *Waqfs*, including Ahmad Muhammad Shibrin, Chairman of the National Council of Culture, and Professor Ismail Muhammad of Khartoum.[18]

—*Tanzania*, Summer, delegation of *ulema*, led by Sheikh Hamid ben Juma Hamadi, to Tashkent, Samarkand, Margelan, Ferghana and Andijan; invitation issued by Shamsuddin Babakhanov.[19]

—*Algeria*, Winter 1983–84, important delegation headed by Muhammad Salih Ait Siddik, member of the Supreme Islamic Council of Algeria, including Khalid Huwaitri, Deputy-Secretary-General of the Supreme Islamic Council and professor at Baba Zuwar University, Abdal-Qadir Shiad, Inspector-General of the Ministry of Religious Affairs for the province of Constantine, and Muhammad Farah, Chief Editor of the journal *Ayu Asr*; to Tashkent, Samarkand, Ferghana Valley.[20]

—*Turkey*, delegation led by Taiyar Altinkilic, Chairman of the Sama Board, and Haidar Hatipoglu, Mufti of Izmir; to Tashkent, Makhach-Qala, Samarkand and Moscow; red carpet treatment, invitations issued by the muftis of Tashkent and Makhach-Qala.[21]

—*Mozambique*, Autumn, Muslim delegation led by Abu Bakr Haji Musa Ismail, Secretary-General of the Islamic Council of Mozambique; to Moscow, Tashkent, Dushanbe, Samarkand and Bukhara; invitation issued by Shamsuddin Babakhanov.[22]

—*Finland*, Spring, Muslim delegation led by Abdullah Ali, Chairman of the Islamic Association of Finland; invitation issued by Talgat Tajeddin, Mufti of Ufa. (The Muslims of Finland are mostly Tatars who have emigrated from Kazan). To Ufa, Moscow, Kazan and Tashkent.[23]

—*India*, several delegations; Autumn, delegation led by Dr Sayed Asrar ul-Haq, member of Parliament of India and Chairman of the Committee for National Unity of India; invited by Shamsuddin Babakhanov, to Moscow, Leningrad, Baku, Samarkand, Tashkent.[24] Spring, Siradjul-Haq, editor of the newspaper *Bataha*, invitation issued by Shamsuddin Babakhanov.[25]

—*Lebanon*, Autumn, 1985, Shamsuddin Babakhanov received Salam Saleh, Editor-in-Chief of the newspaper *Al-Liwa* of Beirut and a member of the Consultative Council of the Muftiat of Lebanon, in Tashkent.[26]

1984–85. Non-religious delegations invited by the Soviet muftis (excluding Afghan delegations)

—*Indonesia*, April 1984, group of journalists.[27]

—*Vatican personalities*, to Tashkent and Samarkand.[28]

—*Belgium*, Muhammad Abdu-Jalil, Director of the magazine *Dialogue* of Brussels.[29]

—*India*, group of Indian politicians, members of the Congress Party, led by Rafiq Zakariya.[30]

—*India*, second delegation of Congress Party officials, to participate in a symposium in Moscow, visited the Mufti of Tashkent.[31]

—*Bangladesh*, delegation of Peace Partisans of Bangladesh, led by Abu-Zafar Shamsuddin, President of the Peace Council of Bangladesh.[32]

—*Kuwait*, delegation led by Salim al-Sabah, Minister of Defense.[33]

—*Morocco*, visit by Abdul Gharbi, member of the Central Committee of the Progress Party.[34]

—*Switzerland*, visit by Faradj Musa, President of the World Organisation for the Protection of Intellectual Property.[35]

—*USA*, group of Congressmen and several Muslims, including Saifullah (Chicago?); received in Tashkent by Yusufkhan Shakirov.[36]

—*Indonesia*, members of the Council of People's Representatives, led by the Council's Chairman, Horjanto Sumodisastro; received in Tashkent by Y. Shakirov.[37]

—*Angola*, Domingoush Koel'o da Koush, President of the Angolan Solidarity League, welcomed in Tashkent by Shamsuddin Babakhanov.[38]

APPENDIX G

Cultural Agreements and Student Exchanges, 1980–83

1980
—*Ethiopa*, 18 February 1980; protocol signed in Addis Ababa on students and professorial training of Ethiopians in USSR.[1]
—*Algeria*, 18 March; agreement on the expanding co-operation between Soviet and Algerian trade unions.[2]
—*Morocco*, 22–23 April; exchange of news and commentaries between Moscow (*TASS* and Novosti) and Rabat.[3]
—*South Yemen*, 2 June; agreement on cultural co-operation and broadcasting.[4]
—*Jordon*, 8 July; agreement on cultural co-operation. In 1981–82 the USSR offers 150 univserity scholarships and 15 post-graduate studies scholarships to Jordanian students.[5]
—*Gabon*, 22 August; agreement on Gabon students in the USSR, and on Soviet teachers in Gabon.[6]
—*Afghanistan*, 17 October; agreement of Soviet Komsomol and Afghan youth exchange programme.[7]
—*Third World (general)*; N. Sofinskii, Deputy Minister of Higher Education announced that in 1979–80, the number of Third World students in the USSR reach 35 000.[8]

Muslims of the Soviet East, no. 1, 1980, lists the following Soviet religious students in Arab universities:
—*Libya*; Mohammed Sadyq Mohammed Yusupov, at the Islamiya Institute.
—*Syria*; Hudayberdyh Egamberdiev and Sharaffuddin Mirmahmudov, at the Islamiya University.
—*Egypt*; Iliyas Iliyasov and Nasrullah Ibadullaev, at Al-Azhar.
—*Jordan*; Muslihiddin Mukaramov and Shukrullah Mejanov.

1981
—*Algeria*, 10 January; protocol for 1981 on co-operation between the Algerian Youth Union and the Soviet Komsomol.[9]
—*Ethiopa*; 30 January; a three-year protocol agreement on cultural and scientific co-operation.[10] In 1980–81, 2000 young Ethiopians were studying in the USSR.[11] 30 scholarships were provided for Ethiopians at Lamumba University (Moscow) alone.[12]
—*Uganda*, 6 February; agreement on cultural-educational co-operation.[13]
—*Mozambique*, 20 May; long-term economic and trade agreement.[14]
—*Mozambique*, 9 July; agreement to train professional and educational personnel in the USSR.[15]
—*Guinea*, 14 July; cultural-scientific co-operation.[16]
—*Jordan*, 14 December; agreement on co-operation between Yarmuk University and Kalinin Institute of Technology in Leningrad.[17]

1982

—*Kuwait*, 16 March; agreement on 1982–83 cultural and scientific exchange.[18]

—*Mozambique*, 6 April; agreement on economic and technical co-operation (geology, mining, cotton).[19]

—*Congo*, 13 May; agreement on a plan for development between CPSU and the Congolese Labor Party.[20]

—*Tunisia*, 18 May; co-operation agreement between *TASS* and the Tunis-Afrique Presse.[21]

—*Tanzania*, 8 June; plan for party links between CPSU and Tanzanian Party (Chama Cha Mapindujziu).[22]

—*Algeria*, 17 December; protocol on relations between Friendship Societies in the USSR and Algeria.[23]

1983

—*Algeria*, 24 March; medical co-operation agreement.[24]

—*Iraq*, 26 April; Radio and TV co-operation agreement.[25]

—*Iraq*, 2 June; cultural and scientific co-operation agreement.[26]

—*Pakistan*, 18 July; two-year cultural-scientific co-operation agreement.[27]

—*Iran*, 20 July; sports co-operation agreement.[28]

—*Nigeria*, 13 August; announcement that in 1983–84, 130 Nigerian students and 45 post-graduates will be trained in the USSR.[29]

1984

—*Asia/Africa general*; announcement that 1500 African and Asian stuents were studying in Kiev University alone.[30]

Notes

Part I
1 The Forging of the Soviet Islamic Weapon

1. A brilliant commentary on this frequently debated topic is Leszek Kolakowski's 'Permanent vs. Transitory Aspects of Marxism', in *Marxism and Beyond* (London: Pall Mall Press, 1968), pp. 193–207.
2. Karl Marx, 'The Future Results of the British Rule in India'. *op. cit.*, August 1853, in Ian Cummins, *Marx, Engels and National Movements* (New York: St. Martin's Press, 1980), p. 70.
3. For a summary of this confrontation and a substantial bibliography, see Paul B. Henze, 'Fire and Sword in the Caucasus: The 19th Century Resistance of the North Caucasian Mountaineers'. *Central Asian Survey*, vol. 2, (1983), no. 1. pp. 5–44.
4. Marx to Engels (in Ramsgate), London, 18 July 1877, in Saul K. Padover, (ed.), *The Letters of Karl Marx* (New York: Prentice-Hall, 1979), pp. 316–17.
5. Karl Marx, 'The Real Issue in Turkey', *op. cit.*, in Cummins, p. 131.
6. For an excellent essay on Russian historical perceptions of Asia and Islamic societies, see Nicholas V. Riasanovsky, 'Asia Through Russian Eyes', in Wayne S. Vucinich, (ed.), *Russia and Asia* (Stanford: Hoover Institution Press, 1972), esp. pp. 8–9. See also Serge A. Zenkovsky, *Panturkism and Islam in Russia, 1905–20* (Cambridge, Mass: Harvard University Press, 1960) and Alexandre Bennigsen and Chantal Lemercier-Quelquejay, *Islam in the Soviet Union* (London: Pall Mall Press, 1967, esp. Part I.
7. Cf. Paul Dumont, 'L'Axe Moscou-Ankara—Les relations turco-sovietiques de 1919 a 1922'. *Cahiers du Monde Russe et Sovietique*, XVIII, 3 (1977), pp. 165–93.
8. Roy's *Memoirs*, p. 195, as cited in Dan N. Jacobs, *Borodin, Stalin's Man in China* (Cambridge Mass: Harvard University Press, 1981), p. 69.
9. As cited in Peter Hopkirk, *Setting the East Ablaze* (London: John Murray, 1984), p. 157. Hopkirk's highly readable book contains the best account of the adventures of M. N. Roy and a host of other characters who figured in early Soviet efforts to revolutionise the East, as well as some of the men who worked against them.
10. Şevket Süreyya Aydemir, *Enver Paşa*, Istanbul, Remzi Kitabevi, 1978, vol. III, p. 513.
11. Col. Frederick Bailey, *Mission to Tashkent* (London: 1927); and P. T. Etherton, *In the Heart of Asia* (London; 1925).
12. Hopkirk, pp. 161–4.
13. Vartan Gregorian, *The Emergence of Modern Afghanistan* (Stanford: 1969) p. 214.

14. Sir Percy M. Sykes, *History of Afghanistan* (London: 1940). vol. II, p. 265.
15. Gregorian, p. 231.
16. Ibid., p. 232.
17. Ibid., p. 266.
18. Louis Duprée, *Afghanistan* (Princeton: Princeton University Press, 1973) p. 457.
19. Mustafa Chokaev, 'The Situation in Afghanistan', *Asiatic Review*, April 1980, as cited in Gregorian, p. 274.
20. See S. Enders Wimbush, 'The Politics of Identity Change in Soviet Central Asia', *Central Asian Survey*, vol. 3, (1984) no. 3, pp. 69–78.
21. Aleksandr M. Nekrich, in *The Punished Peoples* (New York: Norton, 1978), provides perhaps the most vivid and comprehensive account of this operation. The book was originally in *samizdat*.
22. Chantal Lemercier-Quelquejay, 'Muslim National Minorities in Revolution and Civil War,' in S. Enders Wimbush (ed.) *Soviet Nationalities in Strategic Perspective* (London and New York: Croom Helm and St. Martin's Press, 1985), p. 54.
23. Chantal Lemercier-Quelquejay, 'Le Vaisisme a Kazan. Contribution a l'histoire des Confréries musulmanes chez les Tatars de la Volga'. *Die Welt des Islams*, vi, no. 1–2 (1959), pp. 99–112.
24. One of the best expressions of this *jadid* position is Ismail bey Gasprinskii, *Russko-Musulmanskoe Soglashenie* (1897).
25. Alexandre A. Bennigsen and S. Enders Wimbush, *Muslim National Communism in the Soviet Union* (Chicago: University of Chicago Press, 1979), *passim*.
26. Quoted in Zbigniew Brzezinski, *Game Plan*, (Boston: The Atlantic Monthly Press, 1986), p. 34.
27. Ibid., pp. 79–81; Edith Ybert-Chabrier, 'Gilan, 1917–1920: The Jengelist Movement According to the Memoirs of Ihsan Allah Khan'. *Central Asian Survey*, vol. 2, (November 1983), no. 3 pp. 36–61; Cosroe Chaqueri, 'The Jangali Movement and Soviet Historiography: A Critique', ibid., vol. 5, (1986), no. 1, pp. 57–64.
28. Bennigsen and Wimbush, *Muslim National Communism in the Soviet Union*, esp. chap. 4.
29. See, among others, Xenia Eudin and Robert North, *Russia and the East, 1920/1927: A Documentary Survey* (Palo Alto: Stanford University Press, 1964); Demetrio Boersner, *The Bolsheviks and the National and Colonial Question (1917–1928)* (Geneva-Droz-Paris: Minard, 1957); Jane Degras, (ed.), *The Communist International, 1919–1943* (Oxford: Royal Institute of International Affairs-Oxford University Press, 1956); C. L. R. James, *World Revolution, 1917–1936: The Rise and Fall of the Communist International* (London: 1937); Enrica Colotti-Pischel and Chiara Robertazzi, *L'Internationale Communiste et les Problemes Coloniaux, 1919–1935* (Paris-La Haye: Mouton, 1968).
30. One exception to this general rule of using non-Muslims was the Soviets' sending of the Bashkir Sherif Manatov to Turkey to bring some centralised order to the various Turkish communist organisations. Even this exception, however, should not be seen as a break with

162 *Notes*

larger Soviet policy of encouraging the establishment of stable national governments on the USSR's southern periphery. Soviet complicity has been suggested in the eventual (January 1921) liquidation of the Turkish Communist Party leadership by Turkish police. Bennigsen and Wimbush, *Muslim National Communism in the Soviet Union*, pp. 78–79.

31. Cf. the special issue of *Central Asian Survey*, vol. 2. (July 1983), no. 1. devoted to Russian and Soviet experience with Muslim guerilla warfare, especially Alexandre Bennigsen, 'Muslim Guerilla Warfare in the Caucasus (1918–1928)', pp. 45–56, and Marie Broxup, 'The Basmachi', pp. 57–81. The latter work contains an extensive bibliography on the Basmachi experience. A two part article on the Basmachi provides substantial analysis and documentation: Glenda Frasure, 'The Basmachi', in *Central Asian Survey*, vol. 6, nos. 1 and 2 (1987). On the importance of Sufi participation in North Caucasian resistance movements, see Bennigsen and S. Enders Wimbush, *Mystics and Commissars: Sufism in the Soviet Union* (London: C. Hurst, 1985).

32. Cf. Alexandre Bennigsen and Marie Broxup, *The Islamic Threat to the Soviet State* (London: Croom Helm, 1983), pp. 44–50.

33. Adam B. Ulam, *Expansion & Coexistence* (New York: Praegar, 1968), p. 227.

34. *In and Out of Stalin's GRU: A Tatar's Escape from Red Army Intelligence* (Frederick, MD: University Press of America, 1984).

35. Akhmedov, op.cit, p. 160.

36. *Nauka i Zhizn'*, December 1950, pp. 44–5; as cited by Harry J. Psomiades, 'Soviet Russia and the Orthodox Church in the Middle East'. *Middle East Journal*, Autumn 1957, pp. 371–81.

37. Cf. Alexander R. Alexiev, *Soviet Nationalities in German Wartime Strategy, 1941–1945*, the Rand Corporation, R–2772-NA, Santa Monica, California, August 1982, pp. 23–5, 31–3. This work contains an extensive bibliography dealing with the extent and nature of Soviet Muslim collaboration with the Germans (pp. 35–9).

38. Joachim Hoffmann, *Die Ostlegionen 1941–1943* (Freiburg: Verlag Rombach, 1976).

39. Susan L. Curran and Dmitry Ponomareff, *Managing the Ethnic Factor in the Russian and Soviet Armed Forces: An Historical Overview*, The Rand Corporation, R–2640/1, Santa Monica, California, July 1982, pp. 31–3.

40. Cf. Robert Conquest, *The Soviet Deportation of Nationalities* (London: Macmillan, 1960); and Aleksandr M. Nekrich, *The Punished Peoples* (New York: W. W. Norton, 1978).

41. In Cairo, Babakhanov (who later would become Mufti of Tashkent himself and then pass the honour on to his son, the current holder, Shamsuddin Babakhanov) was interviewed in *Al-Ahram* (28 July 1947). He declared in the interview that the USSR at that time had 3000 'working mosques'. This conspicuous lie could be seen as the hallmark of the Soviet Islamic weapon which would soon emerge.

42. *Al-Ahram*, 19 September 1947.

43. Radio Moscow, 19 October 1947.

44. Article on 'Islam' in *Bol'shaia Sovetskaia Entsiklopedia*, vol. 28, 2nd ed, pp. 516–19.
45. *Al-Misri*, 9 April 1950.
46. *Izvestia*, 27 February 1954.
47. For example, this was the Soviet position at the International Muslim Conference in Jerusalem (then controlled by Jordan), January 1960.
48. Yaacov Ro'i, 'The Role of Islam and the Soviet Muslims in Soviet Arab Policy', *Asian and African Studies*, vol 10 (1974) no. 2, pp. 166–7; this article was concluded in ibid., vol. 10 (1975) no. 3, pp. 259–80. See also N. A. Smirnov, *Ocherki istorii izucheniia islama v SSSR* (Moscow, 1954) esp. chap. 5.
49. Soviet muftis appear for the first time in front organisation activities in October 1966 at the first Soviet Afro-Asian Solidarity Conference in Dushanbe, which was attended by many Arab delegates. The Mufti of Tashkent played a major role. Radio Tashkent (in English, for Pakistan and India) 9 October 1966.
50. Ro'i, *Asian and African Studies*, vol. 10 (1975) no. 3, p. 266.
51. Radio Moscow, 3 December 1953.
52. Radio Moscow, in Arabic, 20 May 1955.
53. Radio Moscow, in Arabic, 24 June 1955.
54. Radio Moscow, in Arabic, 19 July 1955.
55. Radio Moscow, in Arabic, 2, 3 and 20 May 1958.
56. See TASS, in Russian, 23 May 1954; and Radio Moscow, in Arabic, 16 March 1956.
57. Radio Moscow, in Arabic, 22 September 1958.
58. Radio Moscow, in Arabic, 17 June 1960.
59. Radio Moscow, in English, 3 March 1963.
60. In 1959, for example several books and articles appeared in Egypt, a main target for Soviet influence, denouncing the Soviet treatment of Islam, suggesting that the efforts of Soviet clerics to show the USSR as a benevolent homeland to millions of Muslims had been less than effective. See Ro'i, *Asian and African Studies*, vol. 10 (1975) no. 3, pp. 261–2.
61. Radio Moscow, in Arabic, 30 April 1957.

2 The Brezhnev Era Prior to the Soviet Invasion of Afghaniston, 1964–80

1. 'Parallel' Islam is often associated with the Sufi brotherhoods in the USSR. Bennigsen and Wimbush, *Mystics and Commissars, passim*.
2. G. M. Kerimov, 'Islamskii anti-Kommunizma na sovremennom etape', *Religiia v planakh Anti-Kommunizma* (Moscow: 1970) esp. pp. 170–96.
3. Radio Moscow, 9 June 1973.
4. *Izvestiia*, 30 June 1973.
5. Ibid.
6. Radio Moscow, 30 November 1968 (in Arabic).
7. For example, Mufti Babakhanov's strident speech in Cairo appeared in *Anba Musku*, 24 April 1971.

8. *Anba Musku*, 13 February 1971, for example, published the sermons on the imam-khatibs of the Leningrad and Moscow mosques.
9. For example, the important group of Moroccan *ulema* of Qarawyin University (Fez) led by sheikh Mohammed al-Kattani, who visited Tashkent, Samarkand and Bukhara in August-September 1971. *Muslims of the Soviet East*, no. 2, 1974.
10. Texts and analysis of the conference appear in *Muslims of the Soviet East*, no. 2, 1974; no. 3, 1975; and no. 4, 1976.
11. Commentaries on this journey were made by Radio Moscow, 16 April 1974, in Arabic.
12. See *Muslims of the Soviet East*, no. 3, 1978, pp. 3–5.
13. *Muslims of the Soviet East*, nos. 2–3, 1975.
14. *Muslims of the Soviet East*, no. 3, 1977, pp. 22–3.
15. Ibid., 24.
16. *Muslims of the Soviet East*, no. 4, 1978, p. 21.
17. Ibid., pp. 5–6. During this conference, Babakhanov confided in private to a Pakistani known to the authors that the condition of Islam in the USSR is very difficult. Private communication to the authors.
18. *Muslims of the Soviet East*, no. 1, 1979, p. 24.
19. Ibid., pp. 4–5.
20. *Muslims of the Soviet East*, no. 1, 1974, pp. 23–6.
21. *Muslims of the Soviet East*, no. 2, 1974, pp. 25–9.
22. *Muslims of the Soviet East*, no. 1, 1975, pp. 8–13.
23. *Muslims of the Soviet East*, no. 3, 1977, pp. 18–20.
24. *Muslims of the Soviet East*, no. 3, 1978, pp. 8–11.
25. *Muslims of the Soviet East*, no. 4, 1978, pp. 15–19.
26. *Muslims of the Soviet East*, no. 2, 1974, p. 7; no. 4, 1976, p. 3; Radio Moscow, 13–15 November 1973 (in Arabic).
27. *Muslims of the Soviet East*, no. 4, 1974.
28. *Muslims of the Soviet East*, no. 1, 1977, pp. 2–7.
29. *Muslims of the Soviet East*, no. 2, 1979.
30. *Muslims of the Soviet East*, no. 4, 1979, pp. 1–2; and Radio Moscow, 12, 15 and 17 September (in English to Southeast Asia).
31. To these activities one must add the increase in the numbers of Muslim students invited to study in the USSR and the substantial increase in the number of Soviet teachers sent to work in Muslim countries abroad. The results of these programmes are ambiguous, however. See Appendix B.
32. See Appendix C.

3 The Soviet Islamic Strategy After the Invasion of Afghanistan, 1980–86

1. Radio Tehran, 10 August 1980 (in Arabic).
2. For example, Ziauddin Babakhanov on Radio Moscow, 14 January 1980 (in Arabic), to the Arab world.
3. Ibid.; Radio Moscow, 14 January 1980 (in Arabic).
4. TASS, 31 January 1980.

5. Radio Moscow, 31 January 1980 (in Arabic).
6. Radio Moscow, 11 May 1980 (in English); and *Muslims of the Soviet East*, no. 2, 1980, pp. 9–10. All Muslim ambassadors to Moscow were invited to the opening of the exhibition, but only those from Syria, Libya, Algeria and South Yemen attended.
7. See, for example, A. Vasil'ev, 'Islam and the political struggle', *Pravda*, 14 January 1980.
8. *Muslims of the Soviet East*, no. 2, 1980, p. 9. See Appendix D for a list of representatives from an internal document distributed to delegates at the conference.
9. Personal communication to the authors from a member of an African delegation.
10. Reports by delegates from Syria, Kuwait and Cyprus in *op. cit.*, no. 4, 1980, pp. 13–15; by delegates from Jordan, South Yemen, Ethiopia and Lebanon in *op cit*, no. 1, 1981, pp. 4–7.
11. *Muslims of the Soviet East*, no. 2, 1981, pp. 19–20.
12. *Muslims of the Soviet East*, no. 1, 1984, p. 16.
13. *Muslims of the Soviet East*, no. 2, 1985, p. 13.
14. See, for example, *Muslims of the Soviet East*, no. 1, 1981, pp. 13–14; no. 4, 1983, pp. 12, 19; no. 4, 1984, pp. 17–18; no. 1, 1985, p. 5; and no. 2, 1985, p. 13.
15. See, for example, *Muslims of the Soviet East*, no. 3, 1983, pp. 5–7, about a modest Islamic-Christian dialogue chaired by Shamsuddin Babakhanov.
16. *Muslims of the Soviet East*, no. 3, 1982, pp. 3–11.
17. In part, this may have been due to a reassessment by Soviet authorities of the inter-relationship of Islam and politics, with a view toward re-arming their Islamic strategy for the post-invasion period. One indication of this new awareness was the declaration by academician Evgenii Primakov at the All Union Conference of Orientalists, held in Baku on 25–27 May 1983, that Soviet orientalists must develop a more sophisticated and sensitive approach to the study of 'the Islamic factor in the countries bordering the USSR in the south'. It was decided that the Institute of Peoples of the Near and Middle East in Azerbaijan would serve as the centre for new investigations in this regard. See *Bakinskii Rabochi*, 27 May 1983.
18. See, for example, the report in *Muslims of the Soviet East*, no. 1, 1980, p. 22, which describes the Soviet delegation's reception in Saudi Arabia—the King did not receive them as was customary—for the *hajj* in Winter 1980.
19. See, for example, ibid., which describes the same delegation's reception in Syria, and *Muslims of the Soviet East*, no. 1, 1981, about a delegation to North Yemen, and no. 2, 1980, pp. 15–16, about another delegation's reception in Jordan. Of particular interest concerning the latter delegation, is the presence of a certain Anvar Makhamov as one of the leaders. Makhamov is described as 'a member of the Council for Religious Affairs of the Council of Ministers of the Uzbek SSR', a position usually held by a KGB officer rather than a spiritual figure. We can find no immediate explanation—other than the obvious one

166   *Notes*

of the delegation requiring a proper 'chaperone'—for this unusual procedure. Several individuals attended religious conferences abroad, for example, *Muslims of the Soviet East*, no. 1, 1981, pp. 13–14; and another delegation went to Mali. Ibid., p. 14.

20. *TASS*, 17 November 1981.
21. See Appendix E for a chronology of Soviet muftis' travel abroad from 1982 to 1985.
22. For example, see *Muslims of the Soviet East*, no. 3, 1980, p. 14, for an account of the visit of a South Yemeni Muslim delegation; and no. 1, 1982, for coverage of Ahmad Zabara's visit. Perhaps the most dramatic use of its Islamic profile during this period occurred during the visit of Colonel Qadhafi to the USSR in April 1981. During his visit, Qadhafi prayed at the Moscow mosque, and for this occasion the call to prayer was broadcast on loudspeakers, an exceptional event. The Soviet media commented on the visit with great enthusiasm, as did the Libyan media. Already in 1980, the former Libyan ambassador to Moscow, Abdul-Wahhab Muhammad Zintani had published a book entitled *Myths about the Iron Curtain and the Land of the Soviets— Impressions of a Libyan About the Soviet Union* (Beyrut, 1980), in which he described with gusto the prosperity, freedom and happiness of Islam in the USSR. The book was given a warm welcome by Soviet media during Qadhafi's visit.
23. Tehran Radio, 16 February 1981.
24. Radio Moscow, 20 March 1981 (in Persian).
25. However, it appears from these and other contacts that the Iranians are not easily persuaded that the Soviets are real friends of Islam. Unlike many Muslim countries, Iran is prepared to base its relations with the USSR largely or in part on the Soviet occupation of Afghanistan, which shows the Iranians' understanding of the important geopolitical and military issues involved. Moscow has come to appreciate more the importance of Islam in the Iranian struggle and frequently accuses the Iranians of intending to establish an Islamic regime in Afghanistan. For example, see *Jane's Defence Weekly*, 14 June 1986. For a wider discussion of Soviet perceptions of revolutionary politics in Iran since 1978 and their understanding of the Islamic factor, see Aryeh Y. Yodfat, *The Soviet Union and Revolutionary Iran* (London: Croom Helm, 1984), and Muriel Atkin, 'Rethinking the Iranian Revolution', *Problems of Communism*, March-April 1986, pp. 86–92.
26. See Appendices F and G for a list of foreign Muslim and non-Muslim delegations hosted by the Soviet Islamic establishment; cultural agreements and student exchanges with Muslim countries; and Party, front organisation and Soviet Government exchanges.

4 Conclusions

1. *Inquiry* (London), December 1986, p. 64.
2. Ann Sheehy, 'International Islamic Conference Meets in Baku', *Radio Liberty Research* RL 372/86, 6 October 1986.

Part II

6 The Russians in Egypt: Key to the Arab World

1. See Jaan Pennar, *The USSR and the Arabs, the Ideological Dimension 1917–1972* (London: Hurst, 1973) pp. 28 ff.
2. Cited in Pennar, *op. cit.*, p. 35.
3. As cited in Mohamed Heikal, *The Sphinx and the Commissar, The Rise and Fall of Soviet Influence in the Middle East* (New York: Harper & Row, 1978) p. 40.
4. Georgi Agabekov, a Soviet Armenian OGPU agent who defected from Turkey in 1930 and was subsequently murdered in Belgium in 1938, relates in his memoirs (*OGPU—The Russian Secret Terror*, New York: Brentano's, 1931) that Egyptian Communists were supported out of the OGPU *Rezidentura* in Berlin. An OGPU agent named Axelrod was sent to Egypt in 1930: 'He was to study the political groupings and especially the Wafd party; it was hoped to create a rift in that party, resulting from which its left wing should collaborate with the Egyptian Communist Party. Axelrod was also to familiarise himself with various other questions—as that of the fellaheen . . . and the Nubians. He was not to concern himself with the correspondence of the British High Commissioner in Egypt, as the OGPU was already obtaining copies thereof through other channels . . . [He] was, however, to keep a close eye on the Egyptian merchant class and (still more important) on the Armenians established in that country . . . through [whom] it was hoped to establish liaison with India'. (Op. cit., pp. 236–7). Agabekov's account demonstrates that OGPU operations in Egypt were at this period far-reaching in concept but not very highly developed.
5. Heikal, *op. cit.*, p. 46.
6. See 'The Strange Career of Henri Curiel', in Claire Sterling, *The Terror Network* (New York: Holt, Rinehart & Winston, 1981) pp. 49–69.
7. 'Instruments in Soviet Policy', in Karen Dawisha, *Soviet Foreign Policy Towards Egypt* (London, Macmillan, 1979).
8. Heikal, *op. cit.*, p. 50.
9. Haggai Erlich, *Students and University in Egyptian Politics* (London: Frank Cass, 1988) ch. IV.
10. A. J. M. Craig, 'Egyptian Students', *Middle East Journal*, Summer 1953, pp. 293–9.
11. See Paul B. Henze, 'Getting a Grip on the Horn', in Walter Z. Laqueur (ed.), *The Pattern of Soviet Conduct in the Third World* (New York: Praeger, 1983) pp. 150–86.
12. Heikal, *op. cit.*, p. 49.
13. Mohamed Heikal, *Autumn of Fury, the Assassination of Sadat* (New York: Random House, 1983) p. 78.
14. John Waterbury, *The Egypt of Nasser and Sadat, The Political Economy of Two Regimes* (Princeton: Princeton University Press, 1983) p. 397. The most thorough study of the military relationship is contained in Jon D. Glassman, *Arms for the Arabs, the Soviet Union*

and War in the Middle East (Baltimore: John Hopkins University Press, 1975).

15. Cited in Dawisha, *op. cit.*, p. 22.
16. A more formal statement of Ulianovsky's advice appeared in a signed article 'Some Problems of the Non-Capitalist Development of Liberated Countries', in *Kommunist*, January 1966. Steps to be taken to consolidate socialism, he stressed, included: special attention to the armed forces; mobilising the labouring masses; and creating an avant-garde political party to manage and control the state. Communists must fight against religion, he reminded his readers, but must do so tactfully.
17. Heikal, *Sphinx*, pp. 134–5.
18. Roy Medvedev, *Khrushchev* (New York: Anchor Doubleday, 1983) pp. 231–2.
19. Medvedev, *op. cit*, pp. 239–45.
20. Heikal, *Sphinx*, p. 154–5.
21. *Ibid.*, p. 162.
22. *Ibid.*, p. 166.
23. *Ibid.*, p. 166. Again, the observation seems rather naive, especially for such an astute and experienced a participant in the Soviet relationship as Heikal. It is a measure of the naïveté of the Egyptians about the relationship during its entire first phase. Why, after all, should the Egyptians ever have expected the Soviets to be so seiflessly interested in helping Nasser become a Pan-Arab leader? The Egyptians were certainly not the first, nor have they been the last developing world leaders to fail to take into account the basic ideological nature of the Soviet system.
24. Jillian Becker, *The PLO* (New York: St. Martin's Press, 1984) p. 4.
25. *Ibid.*, p. 7.
26. Heikal, *Autumn of Fury*, p. 45.
27. Heikal, *Sphinx*, p. 254.
28. Heikal, *Ibid.*, p. 256.
29. Heikal, *Ibid.*, p. 275. Dawisha, *op. cit.*, p. 20, presents a comparable judgement: 'By the spring of 1978 Soviet influence in Egypt was at its lowest point since 1955'.
30. Hugh Seton-Watson, *The Imperialist Revolutionaries* (Stanford, CA: Hoover Institution, 1978) p. 72. Vladimir Sakharov in his *High Treason* (New York: Ballantine, 1981) p. 251), provides a similar conclusion: 'The Soviet goal is to keep the conflict boiling on low fire and to drag the Palestinians along. If everything was settled, how would the Soviets manipulate the Arabs? And how would they get to the Saudis? They would, I decided, but it would take longer'.
31. Soviet communists of Islamic origin (Azeris, Tatars, Uzbeks) who participated in the Soviet-Egyptian relationship should, presumably, have been able to guide their Russian elder brothers in understanding Arab attachment to Islam. There are several possible reasons why they appear not to have played this role. Some had perhaps become so secularised that they had lost their ability to understand their own cultural heritage. Others may have been fearful of giving an interpretation of Islamic attitudes which could have jeopardised their own

credentials as communists liberated from religious belief. It is, of course, possible that some may have voiced cautions which were ignored by Russian Communists, including Khrushchev himself.

32. A study of the Egyptian élite from 1952 to 1969 revealed that of 131 cabinet members holding BA degrees or higher 'not a single one . . . received a degree from a Soviet institution or even stayed there for prolonged specialised training'. Dawisha, *op. cit.*, p. 197.
33. This and subsequent citations are from the account of the episode in Dawisha, *op.cit.*, pp. 26–7.
34. See Heikal, *Sphinx*, p. 89.
35. Dawisha, *op. cit.*, p. 188.
36. In 1972, when the Soviet scholarhip programme was at its peak, only 1351 Egyptians were studying in the USSR compared to 1148 in the US and 362 in the UK—these compared to a total of 272, 259 enrolled in Egypt's own universities. Dawisha, *op. cit.*, p. 196.
37. *Ibid.*, pp. 198–9.
38. The United States had direct intelligence liaison with Nasser's government even after relations were severed in the wake of the 1967 war. In addition, an American interests section housed in the Spanish Embassy in Cairo maintained a wide range of discreet diplomatic relationships with Egyptian officials. See Heikal, *Autumn of Fury*, p. 64.
39. *KGB, the Secret Work of Soviet Secret Agents*, (New York: Reader's Digest/Dutton, 1974).
40. Sakharov, *op. cit.*
41. Barron,*op. cit.*, pp. 46–7.
42. *Ibid.*, pp. 59–61.
43. *Ibid.*, p. 58. The pro-Soviet group in Egypt had actually been arrested six days earlier. See Heikal, *Sphinx*, pp. 226–8.
44. Sakharov, *op. cit.*, pp. 214–5.
45. *Ibid.*, p. 197.
46. *Ibid.*, p. 198.
47. In a revealing footnote, Sakharov comments on KGB operations in Iran directed toward religious elements, of which he had only second-hand knowledge: 'KGB operatives from the Soviet Republics of Azerbaijan and Turkmenistan were working with Muslim religious oposition to the Shah'.
48. Yuri S. Kapralov, who was expelled from Egypt in 1974, turned up in the United States, assigned to Washington, where he was active in exploiting the 'Peace Movement' and encouraging nuclear-freeze advocates. John Barron, *KGB Today, The Hidden Hand*, (New York: Reader's Digest Press, 1983) pp. 280–1.
49. *Ibid.*, pp. 256–60.
50. Alvin Z. Rubinstein, *Red Star on the Nile*. (Princeton: Princeton University Press, 1977) p. 330.

170 *Notes*

7 The Russians and Arabia—Marginal Success

1. John B. Kelly, *Arabia, the Gulf and the West* (New York: Basic Books, 1980) pp. 232–40; Mark N. Katz, *Russia and Arabia* (Baltimore: Johns Hopkins University Press, 1986) pp. 131–3. According to OGPU defector Georgi Agabekov (*OGPU—the Russian Secret Terror*, New York: 1931), Khakimov was an OGPU officer, as was his deputy Axelrod, who eventually succeeded him. They were assisted by a commercial attaché, Belkin (op. cit., pp. 204–05).
2. Agabekov, op, cit., p. 206.
3. Manfred W. Wenner, *Modern Yemen, 1918–1966* (Baltimore: Johns Hopkins 1967) pp. 91–106.
4. Sakharov, op. cit., p. 148.
5. Katz, op. cit., p. 20.
6. Charles B. McLane, *Soviet Middle East Ralations* (London: Central Asian Research Centre, 1973) p. 112.
7. Sakharov, op, cit., p. 296
8. Soviet leaders gave impetus to Arabic studies only after 1956, according to Sakharov: 'It was [1959] before the IIR offered Arab studies as a formal speciality. There were plenty of Soviet minorities who spoke Arabic and had varying degrees of Middle East expertise, but in 1968 I belonged to only the third group of Soviet Arabist to graduate from the IIR. Now with 30 from the two previous years there were 45 of us. The large percentage of Middle Eastern specialists—15 in a graduating class of 60—showed the emphasis the Soviet leadership was placing on the Middle East. There were at least 5 jobs for each IIR graduate . . .', op. cit., pp. 177–8.
9. Sakharov, op. cit., p. 150.
10. Ibid., p. 155.
11. Ibid., p. 168
12. Manfred Wenner, 'South Yemen since Independence: An Arab Political Maverick', in B. R. Pridham, *Contemporary Yemen: Politics and Historical Background* (London: Croom Helm) p. 127.
13. Tom Little, *South Arabia, Arena of Conflict* (New York: Praeger, 1968) p. vii.
14. McLane, op. cit., p. 87.
15. Paul B. Henze, 'Communism and Ethiopia', *Problems of Communism*, May-June 1981, pp. 55–74.
16. Mordechai Abir, *Oil, Power and Politics: Conflict in Arabia, the Red Sea and the Gulf* (London: Cass, 1974) p. 81. Chapter II of this book, 'Crisis in South Arabia', is one of the best summaries available of the immediate pre-and post-independence period in South Yemen.
17. Katz, op, cit., p. 61.
18. The Soviets still attach an almost mystic significance to this 'transition'. Nevertheless, they have grown more conservative about urging client regimes to declare it. Ethiopia, for example, has taken 12 years to reach it, though its internal situation remains, like that of the PDRY, essentially unstable.

19. A. Vasil'yev, *Pravda*, 13 July 1970, as cited in McLane, op, cit., p. 89.
20. Katz's estimate (op. cit., p. 84) of $1 billion seems much too low. Norman Cigar, 'South Yemen and the USSR: Prospects for the Relationship', *Middle East Journal*, Autumn 1985, p. 777, estimates deliveries as 'more than 2.2 billion since 1967'. ACDA's *World Military Expenditures and Arms Transfers* (1985, p. 128) gives total arms imports for the PDRY for the 11 years 1973–83 as $1940 million in current-year dollars and $2345 million in 1982 dollars.
21. Sakharov, op. cit., pp. 295–6.
22. The Omani rationale for entering into relations with the USSR—that formal diplomatic relations impose on the Russians an obligation of proper behaviour—may well prove mistaken. Invariably, as the memoirs of Agabekov in the 1920s and those of Sakharov in the 1970s demonstrate, any Soviet diplomatic, aid, trade or religious relationship automatically serves as a base for developing subversive penetration of the local society.
23. David Pollock, 'Coping with the Coup', *Problems of Communism*, May-June 1986, p. 70.
24. Katz, op. cit., p. 133.
25. Kelly, op. cit., pp. 467–8.
26. Katz, op. cit., pp. 140–4.
27. See *Soviet Covert Action (The Forgery Offensive)*, Hearings of the Committee on Oversight of the Permanent Select Committee on Intelligence, House of Representatives, 96th Congress, 2d Session, 6 and 9 February 1980, Washington DC (USGPO) 1980, pp. 66–7.
28. As cited in Katz, op. cit., p. 162.
29. Kely, op. cit., p. 171.
30. Sakharov, op. cit., p. 278.
31. Katz, op. cit., p. 168.

8 The Strategic Long View: The Nile Valley and the Horn of Africa

1. Cf. Zbigniew Brzezinski, *Game Plan* (Boston/New York: Atlantic Monthly Press, 1986) chapter I ('The Imperial Collision').
2. *Puteshestvive vo vnutrennyuyu Afriku*, (St. Petersburg: 1849).
3. Edward T. Wilson, *Russia and Black Africa before World War II* (New York/London: Holmes & Meir, 1974) provides a good summary of Uspensky's thought.
4. Carlo Zaghi, *I Russi in Etiopia* (Naples: Guida, 1972) vol. I. pp. 55–104.
5. The basis for Franco-Russian co-operation was commonly rivalry with Britain. There are many accounts of this Russian experience, none complete; the best overall treatment of the period is by Sven Rubenson, *The Survival of Ethiopian Independence* (London: Heineman, 1976). British confrontation with the French, in which both Ethiopian and Russian officials played a part, culminated in the famous Fashoda incident of 1898.
6. This tendency was still evident in the Eastern Mediterranean during

and immediately after World War II. See, for instance, Harry J. Psomiades, 'Soviet Russia and the Orthodox Church in the Middle East',
Middle East Journal, Autumn, 1957.

7. Zaghi, op. cit., II, pp. 247 – 56.
8. Milene Charles, *The Soviet Union and Africa* (Washington DC: University Press of America, 1980) pp. 48–51.
9. Paul B. Henze, *Russians and the Horn: Opportunism and the Long
View* (Marina del Rey, CA: European American Institute for Security
Research, 1983).
10. Edgar O'Ballance, *Tracks of the Bear* (Novato, CA: Presidio Press,
1982) p. 85.
11. Ibid., pp. 85–8.
12. Paul B. Henze, *Rebels and Separatists in Ethiopia* (Santa Monica, CA:
The Rand Corporation, R–3347-USDP, 1985) pp. 26–33.
13. Paul B. Henze. 'Arming the Horn, 1960–1980', in *Proceedings of the
VIIth International Ethiopian Studies Conference*, Lund, Sweden, 1984,
pp. 637–56; also published in draft as 'Working Paper 43,' International
Security Series, Woodrow Wilson Center for Scholars, Smithsonian
Institution, Washington DC., 1982.
14. See, for instance, Paul B. Henze, 'Getting a Grip on the Horn', in
Walter Laqueur, (ed.) *The Pattern of Soviet Conduct in the Third World*
(New York: Praeger, 1983) pp. 150–86; also David Korn, *Ethiopia, the
United States and the Soviet Union* (London: Croom Helm, 1986).
15. Gabriel Warburg, *Islam, Nationalism and Communism in Traditional
Society: the Case of Sudan* (London: Cass, 1978) pp. 94, 231. For
background on the Soviet mission in Jeddah, an outpost of the OGPU,
see Agabekov, op.cit., pp. 199–206.
16. Warburg, op.cit., p. 95.
17. Ibid., p. 148.
18. Ibid., p. 115.
19. Ibid., p. 117.
20. J. Spencer Trimingham, *Islam in the Sudan* (London: Cass, 1965.
21. Warburg, op.cit., p. 135. In 1976 Sadat stated in an interview that he
had known about the intended coup prior to its execution and
considered it evidence that the Soviets were trying to regain ground
they had just lost in Egypt. Sadat said he tried to warn Nimeiry but
his message reached him too late.
22. 'Black Africa's Future', *The Economist*, 28 June 1986.
23. Haggai Erlich, *The Struggle Over Eritrea, 1962–1978* (Stanford, CA:
Hoover Institution, 1983).
24. 'The Lives and Times of the Dergue', *Journal of Northeast African
Studies*, 5/3 (1983/84), pp. 14–15, listed him as probably dead.
25. This information comes from recent defector sources.
26. See Korn, op.cit., for a description of this sequence of events.
27. For a more extensive view of the current impasse in the Horn of Africa,
see Paul B. Henze, *Is There Hope for the Horn of Africa?* (Santa
Monica, CA: RAND, N–2738-USDP, June 1988).

Notes to Appendices

Appendix A

1. *Muslims of the Soviet East*, no. 1, 1974, p. 22.
2. *Ibid.*, pp. 20–1; *TASS*, 13 July 1973.
3. *Muslims of the Soviet East*, no. 1, 1974, pp. 18–20.
4. *Muslims of the Soviet East*, no. 4, 1976, p. 20.
5. *Muslims of the Soviet East*, no. 3, 1979, p. 8.
6. Private communication to the authors.
7. Radio Moscow, 30 July 1976 (in Arabic); also *Muslims of the Soviet East*, no. 4, 1976, p. 20.
8. Private communication to the authors.
9. *Muslims of the Soviet East*, no. 4, 1978, pp. 2–5.
10. Radio Moscow, 15 May 1979 (in Arabic); and *Muslims of the Soviet East*, no. 3, 1979, p. 23.
11. *Muslims of the Soviet East*, no. 4, 1979, p. 27.

Appendix B

1. Radio Moscow, 10 February 1973.
2. *TASS*, 28 August 1973.
3. GNA, 29 September 1977.
4. Radio Moscow, 5 March 1973.
5. Radio Moscow, 29 July 1973.
6. Radio Moscow, 10 February 1975.
7. *TASS*, 4 July 1975.
8. *Pravda*, 5 July 1975.
9. *TASS*, 24 July 1975.
10. *TASS*, 16 August 1975.
11. Radio Karachi, 21 March 1975.
12. Radio Moscow, 16 January 1975.
13. *TASS*, 5 September 1977.
14. Syrian Arab News Agency, 18 August 1976.
15. Radio Moscow, 19 August 1978.
16. Radio Moscow, 20 August 1978.
17. Radio Moscow, 2 April 1979.
18. Addis Ababa Radio, 2 August 1978.
19. Addis Ababa Radio, 3 December 1979.
20. Radio Moscow, 21 May 1974.
21. Radio Moscow, 25 May 1975.

Appendix C

1. Radio Moscow, 20 March 1974.
2. Radio Moscow, 13 April 1974.
3. Radio Moscow, 21 April 1974.

4. *TASS*, 20 April 1974.
5. Radio Moscow, 19 June 1974.
6. *TASS*, 14 February 1975.
7. Radio Aden, 20 April 1975.
8. Radio Moscow, 9 April 1975.
9. *TASS*, 15 May 1975.
10. Radio Moscow, 18 May 1975.
11. *Pravda*, 3 May 1975.
12. Radio Moscow, 21 June 1975.
13. Radio Moscow, 5 September 1975.
14. *TASS*, 21 November, 1975.
15. Radio Moscow, December 1975.
16. Radio Moscow, 25 June 1975.
17. Cairo Radio, 3 February 1975.
18. *Pravda*, 29 October 1976.
19. Radio Moscow, 11 November 1976.
20. *TASS*, 21 December 1976.
21. *Pravda*, 13 May 1977.
22. Dushanbe Radio, 19 May 1977.
23. Radio Tehran, 21 May 1977.
24. Radio Moscow, 31 May 1977.
25. Radio Moscow, 10 June 1977.
26. MENA, 19 June 1977.
27. Radio Moscow, 6 July 1977.
28. Radio Moscow, 3 August 1977.
29. Radio Moscow, 23 August 1977.
30. GNA, 29 September 1977.
31. *TASS*, 24 November, 1977.
32. Kabul Radio, 8 December, 1977.
33. *TASS*, 3 January 1978.
34. Radio Rabat, 27 January 1978.
35. *TASS*, 21 March 1978.
36. *Ibid*.
37. *Pravda*, 21 May 1978.
38. *TASS*, 22 May 1978.
39. *Pravda*, 30 June 1978.
40. Kuwait Radio, 10 September 1978.
41. Radio Moscow, 3 October 1978.
42. Radio Moscow, 16 December 1978.
43. *TASS*, 30 December 1978.

Appendix E

1. *Muslims of the Soviet East*, no. 1, 1982, pp. 5–6.
2. *Ibid*.
3. *Muslims of the Soviet East*, no. 2, 1984, pp. 14–15.
4. *Ibid*.
5. *Muslims of the Soviet East*, no. 4, 1984, pp. 12–13.

6. *TASS*, 29 January 1983.
7. *Muslims of the Soviet East*, no. 1, 1983, p. 18.
8. *Ibid.*
9. *Ibid.*
10. *Muslims of the Soviet East*, no. 1, 1984, pp. 7–8.
11. *Muslims of the Soviet East*, no. 3, 1983, p. 19.
12. *Muslims of the Soviet East*, no. 4, 1983, pp. 14–15.
13. *Ibid.*, p. 18.
14. *Ibid.*
15. *Muslims of the Soviet East*, no. 1, 1984, pp. 5–6.
16. *Ibid.*
17. *Muslims of the Soviet East*, no. 4, 1983, p. 18.
18. *Ibid.*, pp. 4–5. Also no. 3, 1983, p. 19.
19. *Muslims of the Soviet East*, no. 3, 1984, pp. 12–13.
20. *Ibid.*
21. *Muslims of the Soviet East*, no. 4, 1984, p. 10.
22. *Muslims of the Soviet East*, no. 1, 1985, pp. 10–11.
23. In a private conversation with a Western visitor in 1985, Dr Ihsanoglu indicated that he was less than impressed by the Soviet *ulema*. Private communication to the authors.
24. *Muslims of the Soviet East*, no. 2, 1985, pp. 5–6.
25. *Muslims of the Soviet East*, no. 2, 1985, pp. 18–19.
26. *Muslims of the Soviet East*, no. 3, 1985, p. 17.
27. *Muslims of the Soviet East*, no. 4, 1984, p. 18.
28. *Muslims of the Soviet East*, no. 1, 1986, pp. 6–7.
29. *Ibid.*, p. 8.
30. *Ibid.*, pp. 5–6.

Appendix F

1. *Muslims of the Soviet East*, no. 3, 1982, pp. 18–19.
2. *Muslims of the Soviet East*, no. 1, 1982, p. 18.
3. *Ibid*, p. 19.
4. *Muslims of the Soviet East*, no. 4, 1983, pp. 17–18.
5. *Muslims of the Soviet East*, no. 1, 1984, p. 17.
6. *Muslims of the Soviet East*, no. 4, 1983, p. 19; and *TASS*, 14 August 1983.
7. *Muslims of the Soviet East*, no. 1, 1985, p. 17.
8. *Muslims of the Soviet East*, no. 3, 1983, pp. 11–12; *TASS*, 18 April 1983; *Kommunist* (Baku), 24 April 1983.
9. *Muslims of the Soviet East*, no. 1, 1984, pp. 9–10.
10. *Muslims of the Soviet East*, no. 2, 1984, pp. 10–11.
11. *Ibid.*, p. 16.
12. *Muslims of the Soviet East*, no. 1, 1985, p. 17.
13. *Muslims of the Soviet East*, no. 1, 1985, p. 18.
14. *Ibid.*, p. 7.
15. *Muslims of the Soviet East*, no. 2, 1984, p. 16.
16. *Muslims of the Soviet East*, no. 2, 1985, pp. 18–19.

17. *Muslims of the Soviet East*, no. 1, 1985, p. 20.
18. *Muslims of the Soviet East*, no. 2, 1985, p. 19.
19. *Muslims of the Soviet East*, no. 4, 1984, p. 18.
20. *Muslims of the Soviet East*, no. 1, 1984, pp. 10–11.
21. *Muslims of the Soviet East*, no. 1, 1986, p. 18; and no. 2, 1986.
22. *Muslims of the Soviet East*, no. 1, 1985, pp. 19–20.
23. *Muslims of the Soviet East*, no. 4, 1984, p. 19.
24. *Muslims of the Soviet East*, no. 1, 1985, pp. 18–19.
25. *Muslims of the Soviet East*, no. 2, 1984, pp. 14–15.
26. *Muslims of the Soviet East*, no. 1, 1986, p. 18.
27. *Muslims of the Soviet East*, no. 4, 1984, p. 15.
28. *Muslims of the Soviet East*, no. 3, 1984, p. 20.
29. *Muslims of the Soviet East*, no. 3, 1984, p. 27.
30. *Muslims of the Soviet East*, no. 1, 1985, p. 5.
31. *Muslims of the Soviet East*, no. 1, 1986, p. 18.
32. *Ibid.*
33. *Muslims of the Soviet East*, no. 1, 1985, p. 5.
34. *Ibid.*
35. *Ibid.*
36. *Muslims of the Soviet East*, no. 1, 1986, p. 19.
37. *Ibid.*
38. *Ibid.*

Appendix G

1. Radio Kiev, 26 May 1980.
2. Radio Moscow, 19 March 1980.
3. Rabat Radio, 23 April 1980.
4. Radio Moscow, 23 June 1980.
5. *Pravda* , 22 August 1980.
6. *Pravda*, 24 August 1980.
7. Kabul Radio, 20 October 1980.
8. *Pravda*, 21 October 1980.
9. *TASS*, 10 January 1981.
10. Addis Ababa Radio, 30 January 1981.
11. *TASS*, 30 October 1981.
12. Addis Ababa Radio, 16 February 1981.
13. Kampala Radio, 6/18 February 1981.
14. *Pravda*, 21 May 1981.
15. Radio Moscow, 10 June 1981.
16. Conakry Radio, 14 July 1981.
17. *Jordanian News Agency*, 14 December 1981.
18. Radio Moscow, 16 March 1982.
19. Radio Moscow, 6 April 1982.
20. Radio Moscow and *Pravda*, 14 May 1982.
21. *TASS*, 18 May 1982.
22. *Pravda*, 9 June 1982.
23. Radio Moscow, 17 December 1982.

24. Radio Moscow, 24 March 1983.
25. Radio Moscow, 26 April 1983.
26. Radio Moscow, 2 June 1983.
27. Radio Moscow, 18 July 1983.
28. Radio Moscow, 21 July 1982.
29. Radio Moscow, 13 August 1983.
30. *Agitator* (Moscow), 16 August 1984, pp. 31–3.

Index